"A Free Ballot and a Fair Count"

Reconstructing America Series
Paul A. Cimbala, series editor

1. Hans L. Trefousse, *Impeachment of a President: Andrew Johnson, the Blacks, and Reconstruction.*
2. Richard Paul Fuke, *Imperfect Equality: African Americans and the Confines of White Ideology in Post-Emancipation Maryland.*
3. Ruth Currie-McDaniel, *Carpetbagger of Conscience: A Biography of John Emory Bryant.*
4. Paul A. Cimbala and Randall M. Miller, eds., *The Freedmen's Bureau and Reconstruction: Reconsiderations.*
5. Herman Belz, *A New Birth of Freedom: The Republican Party and Freedmen's Rights, 1861 to 1866.*

"A Free Ballot and a Fair Count"

THE DEPARTMENT OF JUSTICE
AND THE ENFORCEMENT OF
VOTING RIGHTS
IN THE SOUTH, 1877–1893

ROBERT M. GOLDMAN

Fordham University Press
New York
2001

Copyright © 2001 by Fordham University Press

All rights reserved. No part of this publication may be reproduced, stored in a retrieval system, or transmitted in any form or by any means—electronic, mechanical, photocopy, recording, or any other—except for brief quotations in printed reviews, without the prior permission of the publisher.

Reconstructing America, No. 6
ISSN 1523–4606

An edition of this book was first published in 1990 by Garland Publishing, Inc., New York and London.

Library of Congress Cataloging-in-Publication Data

Goldman, Robert Michael.
   A free ballot and a fair count : the Department of Justice and the enforcement of voting rights in the South, 1877-1893 / Robert M. Goldman.
    p. cm. – (Reconstructing America ; no. 6)
   Originally published: New York : Garland, 1990, in series: Distinguished studies in American legal and constitutional history. With new front matter.
   Includes bibliographical references and index.
   ISBN 0-8232-2083-4 (hardcover) – ISBN 0-8232-2084-2 (pbk.)
   1. Afro-Americans—Southern States—Suffrage—History—19th century. 2. United States. Dept. of Justice—history—19th century. 3. United States—Politics and government—1865-1900. I. Title. II. Reconstructing America (Series) ; no. 6.

JK1929.A2 G65 2001
324.6′08996073075—dc21

00-059295

01 02 03 04 05   5 4 3 2 1

CONTENTS

Preface to the New Edition — vii

Preface — xv

Introduction — xxv

1. The Constitutional and Political Background of Fifteenth Amendment Rights Enforcement — 1

2. "A Meet Person Learned in the Law": The Attorney General and the Justice Department before 1877 — 25

3. The New Department and the New Departure: Voting Rights Enforcement under Hayes, 1877–1880 — 48

4. "A Free Ballot and a Fair Count": Voting Rights Enforcement and Independent Movements in the South, 1880–1884 — 83

5. Voting Rights and the Democratic Interregnum, 1884–1888 — 125

6. Revitalization Again: Harrison and Voting Rights Enforcement, 1888–1893 — 145

7. Bureaucracy, Sectionalism, and the Demise of the "Free Ballot and a Fair Count" — 180

Bibliographical Essay — 207

Index — 217

PREFACE TO THE NEW EDITION

While the reissue of one's book is an honor for any writer, it also presents something of a challenge, especially for an historian. On the one hand, a new edition suggests that one's work has withstood the historiographical test of time and can, therefore, stand on its own merits. At the same time, it obliges the author to provide readers of the new volume with a fair assessment of the relevant scholarship that has appeared in the intervening years, an endeavor that acknowledges the strengths but also the shortcomings of the original work. The study of our past is an ongoing process of discovery and interpretation, and nowhere is this better illustrated than with that period of American history in the years following the Civil War. It seems clear that over the nine years or so since it first appeared, *"A Free Ballot and a Fair Count"* demonstrates that the constitutional and legal struggles of African Americans during and after Reconstruction continues to be a vital and significant part of this process.

Although *"A Free Ballot and a Fair Count"* deals with the years after Reconstruction, it is inextricably connected to that earlier turbulent period. The enforcement of the political and civil rights of the newly emancipated African Americans in the South took place within the context of the many political, social, and constitutional changes that swept both that section and the rest of the nation in the years immediately following the Civil War. In his "coherent, comprehensive modern account"—*Reconstruction: An Unfinished Revolution, 1865–1877*—Eric Foner has laid to rest many if not most of the older views about Reconstruction. Most important, Foner restores the "centrality of the black experience" to the Reconstruction narrative. He demolishes the older view that saw the some four million freedpersons in the South as an ignorant and too easily manipulated group, put into positions of authority and political responsibility by "evil carpetbaggers" and white Southern sympathizers. Indeed, for Foner, African Americans' political participation, as a result of the Fifteenth Amendment and the Enforcement Acts, was "the most radical development of the Reconstruction years, a massive experiment in interracial democracy without precedent...."[1]

Both the federal government's commitment to protecting the civil and political rights of freedpersons and African Americans' own role in shaping their post–Civil War destiny has now become a standard theme in surveys and texts in constitutional and African American history. In Donald Nieman's *Promises to Keep: African-Americans and the Constitutional Order, 1776 to the Present*, the promise of social and political equality for southern blacks was among the most crucial changes envisioned by Republicans following Appomatox. While that promise may have been "deferred" after 1877, the struggle to achieve that envisioned equality did not cease. Similarly, Michael Les Benedict's *The Blessings of Liberty: A Concise History of the Constitution of the United States* affirms the Republican Party's commitment to racial equality. He also agrees that while the Supreme Court in the 1870s and 1880s did limit federal involvement in rights protections, it refused to accept the extreme states' rights constitutional arguments denying Congress "any power" to protect blacks' rights under the Reconstruction amendments.[2]

The basis of the federal government's attempt to protect voting rights in the South was the Fifteenth Amendment and the series of Enforcement Acts passed by Congress between 1870 and 1872. As when this book first appeared, the scope and meaning of both the amendment itself and the subsequent enforcement legislation continue to be matters of debate. The view that the Fifteenth Amendment itself was a flawed piece of work, intended by congressional Republicans to politically benefit their own selfish party interests, has most recently been challenged in Xi Wang, *The Trial of Democracy: Black Suffrage and*

Northern Republicans, 1860–1910. Meticulously examining the debates and votes on the amendment, Professor Wang has demonstrated that the final product did indeed reflect partisan concerns for "political advantages" on the part of its Republican drafters. But rather than a simple work of "political expediency," the Fifteenth Amendment reflected the very diversity of the Republican Party at the time, and the historical and constitutional constraints inherent in defining the nature of national citizenship. Wang has recognized that underlying the process was the fact that political and social equality was an important "ideological source" for Republicans' Reconstruction policies.[3]

The Trial of Democracy also confirmed Republicans' awareness that the mere passage and ratification of the Fifteenth Amendment would not by itself ensure freedpersons in the South full political participation. Thus Republicans passed the remarkable series of statutes known as the Enforcement Acts. These measures, as much as the Fifteenth Amendment itself, reflected Republicans' democratic values and their hopes for a true political revolution in the South. It also provided an entirely new kind of test for the federal government to actually implement and enforce the provisions of the measures. While *"A Free Ballot and a Fair Count"* did not completely reject earlier studies of federal voting-rights enforcement prior to 1877, its central argument was that enforcement efforts continued after that year. By implication, this challenged the earlier views of scholars like Everette Swinney, who saw the acts as essentially "dead letters" by 1874.[4] However, Professor Wang has concluded that the ending of Reconstruction "did not mean the ending of Republican commitment to black political rights, nor did it mean the ending of the vitality of the principles of federal protection of black rights as established by the Civil War amendments." Professor Wang has detailed the ongoing efforts of Republican leaders after 1877 to ensure equal access to the ballot box for African Americans. While those efforts ultimately proved futile in stemming the spread of state disfranchisement of African American voters, examining those efforts is crucial to understanding this revolutionary experiment.[5]

One concern expressed over *"A Free Ballot and a Fair Count"* was its lack of sufficient detail about the political, social, and economic context of voting-rights enforcement in each one of the southern states. Missing, as one reviewer put it, was any examination of the enforcement effort through the "lens of socioeconomic contextuality." Since the book's focus was the Justice Department's efforts across the entire South over an extended period, it was probably inevitable that some of the trees would be missed while describing the proverbial forest. Clearly, local conditions, developments, and personalities played important roles in the department's efforts to prosecute violations of the enforcement laws after 1877. As Professor Wang has noted, post-1877 enforcement remains a "neglected" topic that "still needs to be studied." Aside from Stephen Cresswell's work on northern Mississippi, such studies have yet to be done. Indeed, apart from Cresswell's work on southern and western federal law enforcement, the history of the Justice Department during the Gilded Age likewise continues to be a neglected topic. There has been, however, a renewed interest in violence in general in the late nineteenth century and anti-black violence in the South in particular.[6]

Although it involves enforcement efforts during Reconstruction, Lou Falkner Williams's monograph *The Great South Carolina Ku Klux Klan Trials, 1871–1872* provides the model for examining federal rights enforcement for specific states. In vivid and insightful detail Williams chronicles one of the federal government's most extensive and intensive prosecutions under the Enforcement Acts during Reconstruction. Williams describes all the factors that led white South Carolinians to resist racial equality with violence and the federal government's attempts to punish them, including the previously unexamined role of gender and violence against women. Despite the numerous indictments and convictions, however, the South Carolina Klan prosecutions proved a harbinger of things to come. They reflected the "determination" of white southerners to resist by any and all means what they saw as the federal government's attempt to impose on them a "standard of equality" they refused to accept. It also demonstrated the growing inclination on the part of that same federal government either to not use the power it did have or to interpret that power, derived from the three Reconstruction constitutional amendments, in such a narrow way as to undermine efforts to bring about a true revolution in race relations.[7]

Although the issues of black suffrage and civil rights in general continued to play an important role in American life, in recent times the struggle for racial political and social equality has acquired what might be called an historiographical dimension. The modern civil-rights movement is now often referred to as the "Second Reconstruction," and the use of this term inevitably invites comparisons with its historical predecessor. Beginning in the 1950s the federal government attempted to restore and protect suffrage rights for African Americans in the South, a campaign that ran parallel to the equally momentous struggle to end racial segregation and discrimination. As during the first Reconstruction, the basis of this campaign was the series of congressional civil- and voting-rights acts, most notably the Voting Rights Act of 1965. As in the earlier period, the Department of Justice was again assigned primary responsibility for implementing this legislation. This renewed effort, along with the many court cases generated by the legislation, has been fairly well documented by historians, political scientists, and legal scholars.[8]

What remains, however, is a debate over the actual effects and possible problems of the Second Reconstruction efforts by the federal government. One example of such a contentious issue is the phenomenon of "racial gerrymandering" and the drawing of legislative-district boundary lines. If states could not use race as a factor in legislative redistricting to dilute black voting strength, could the federal government now permit, if not encourage, predominantly black voting districts to increase African American voting power? Conservative critics of this and other similar policies argue that the federal government has gone way beyond its authority. These critics charge that the national government is now in the business of not merely ensuring fairness and nondiscrimination as far as "who votes," but is attempting to ensure that "whose votes count" is racially determined. It is argued that such policies are merely the political variation of "affirmative action" and are neither constitutionally justified nor truly helpful in furthering the integration of African Americans or other minorities into the American polity. Historian J. Morgan Kousser, who ironically chronicled the disfranchisement of black voters in the South at the end of the first Reconstruction, has provided one of the most effective responses to these complaints. In *Colorblind Justice: Minority Voting Rights and the Undoing of the Second Reconstruction*, Kousser uses the history of the "First Reconstruction" to defend the policies of the federal government today, while using the example of what happened at the end of the nineteenth century as a warning of the dangers of any diminution of efforts to enforce and protect the gains in minority voting rights resulting from the Second Reconstruction.[9] Moreover, at this time when the Department of Justice itself is under criticism for its actions and inactions, it seems especially important to understand the origins of that institution and its role in our constitutional system. At the beginning of a new century and millennium, the original idea and promise of a "free ballot and a fair count," along with the federal government's role in fulfilling that promise, remains as vital and relevant a topic as ever.

I would like to take the opportunity to express my gratitude to a number of individuals who have been instrumental in the publication of this new edition, especially Paul Cimbala and Don Nieman. Durrett Wagner clarified and fine-tuned both my writing and thinking, and I am only sorry we did not meet years ago. Dr. Mary Beatrice Schulte, Executive Editor of Fordham University Press, has been wonderfully supportive and has demonstrated patience above and beyond the call of duty. At long last, and in print, I would also like to thank my parents, Milton and Ruth; my stepmother, Bernice Zitter; and Jean and Paul Lewinson. And, of course, I have been most fortunate in having the help and support of Dr. Sandra Guerard, my wife, best friend, and ace reader.

Robert M. Goldman
Richmond, Virginia
September 2000

Notes

1. Eric Foner, *Reconstruction: America's Unfinished Revolution, 1863–1877* (New York, 1988) xxiv–xxvi. It should be noted that in my introduction to the first edition of this book I failed to credit Foner with recognizing the importance of black political participation and voting rights.

2. Donald G. Nieman, *Promises to Keep: African-Americans and the Constitutional Order, 1776 to the Present* (New York, 1991). Michael Les Benedict, *The Blessings of Liberty: A Concise History of the Constitution of the United States* (Lexington, Mass., 1996) 218. See also Melvin I. Urofsky, *A March of Liberty: A Constitutional History of the United States* (New York, 1988), 477–93.

3. Xi Wang, *The Trial of Democracy: Black Suffrage and Northern Republicans, 1860–1910* (Athens, Ga., 1997).

4. Everette Swinney, "Enforcing the Fifteenth Amendment, 1870–1877," *Journal of Southern History* 28 (May 1962) 293–96.

5. Wang, *Trial of Democracy*, 134–252.

6. Wythe Holt, "Review of 'A Free Ballot and a Fair Count' . . . ," *American Journal of Legal History* 36 (July 1992) 228. Wang, *Trial of Democracy*, xxii. Stephen Cresswell, *Mormons and Cowboys, Moonshiners and Klansmen: Federal Law Enforcement in the South and West, 1870–1893* (Tuscaloosa, Ala., 1991). An example of the studies in racial violence is George C. Rable, *But There Was No Peace: The Role of Violence in the Politics of Reconstruction* (Athens, Ga., 1988).

7. Lou Falkner Williams, *The Great South Carolina Ku Klux Klan Trials, 1871–1872* (Athens, Ga., 1996) 2–18, and generally.

8. The most recent example is Steven Lawson, *Black Ballots: Voting Rights in the South, 1944–1969* (Lanham, Md., 1999).

9. Abigail Thernstrom, *Whose Votes Count? Affirmative Action and Minority Voting Rights* (Cambridge, Mass., 1987). See also Stephen Thernstrom and Abigail Thernstrom, *America in Black and White: One Nation Indivisible* (New York, 1999) 462–92. J. Morgan Kousser, *Colorblind Injustice: Minority Voting Rights and the Undoing of the Second Reconstruction* (Chapel Hill, N.C., 1999).

PREFACE

In his 1951 *The Strange Career of Jim Crow*, C. Vann Woodward saw the years after 1877 as a period "still wrapped in a good deal of obscurity." The enforcement of voting rights in the South by the Justice Department took place within this dim context of the many political, constitutional, and social changes that swept both that section and the rest of the nation during the late nineteenth century. My *"A Free Ballot and a Fair Count"* attempted to make at least part of this era of history less obscure and to explore some of the "forgotten alternatives" Woodward believed existed with respect to the rise of racial segregation and disfranchisement in the South.[1]

Since its completion, a growing body of scholarly work has appeared, much of it confirming a number of themes presented. The traditional view of Reconstruction and its aftermath highlighted the extreme character of Republican constitutional policies and the equally harsh judicial repudiation of federal authority after 1877 in the name of states' rights and substantive due process. This view has largely been replaced by a more balanced approach to Republican achievements and principles, emphasizing the "conservative" nature of Reconstruction policy, and a Republican judiciary less intent on reviving antebellum states' rights dogma than a concern for, in the words of Michael Les Benedict, "preserving federalism." From this perspective "what is remarkable is the degree the Court sustained national authority to protect rights rather than the degree to which they restricted it."[2]

At the same time an increasing interest in the South's particular legal and constitutional tradition has manifested itself.

Several collections of essays, based on conferences devoted to these topics, have addressed the "ambivalent legacy" of southern legal development and the "uncertain tradition" of constitutionalism in Dixie. While these studies provide valuable insight into a variety of aspects and periods, the Redeemer years are virtually ignored.[3]

Edward L. Ayers's examination of crime and punishment in the South during the nineteenth century is an exception. Ayers sheds much-needed light on the development of southern state criminal justice systems, particularly the backgrounds of those convicted of crimes and the workings of the penal system under which they were punished. The culmination of this development by the end of the century was a "crisis of the New South." Racial fears and hostilities exposed the limitations and inadequacies of traditional rules and institutions. The result was a "lynching epidemic" which spread through the South in the 1890s, along with other forms of vigilante violence and blood feuds involving both races. Ayers paid little attention to federal law enforcement efforts in the late nineteenth century, however, except for conceding that violence in the upcountry mountain areas was often a response to federal efforts at eliminating moonshining activities. Other studies have likewise stressed the violent aspects of southern society and its role in Reconstruction and the years after. Southern resistance to federal law enforcement efforts was therefore perhaps not altogether different from similar responses to local efforts to control crime.[4]

While the starting point for Southern history and race relations after Reconstruction remains Woodward's work on Jim Crow and his *Origins of the New South, 1877–1913*, a number of his conclusions have been subjected to reexamination, qualification, and even challenge. James T. Moore's 1978 article, "Redeemers Reconsidered: Change and Continuity in the Democratic South, 1870–1900," critically appraised Woodward's characterizations of the Whig-Redeemers; while state studies of post-Reconstruction politics have likewise suggested more of the "old" in the New South, and recognized that Democrats were not always united in their opposition to black voting rights, or immediately successful everywhere in bringing about disfranchisement.⁵ Stephen Hahn's study of upcountry Georgia politics, for example, examined this diversity, particularly during the Independent revolt in the early 1880s. He concluded that for declining Republicanism after 1877, Independents' support for the "free ballot and a fair count" provided an "attractive alternative to Democratic attacks on black political rights." Thus, while the Independent-Republican alliance had little concern for the grievances of the black community, there remained an ongoing commitment to franchise protections.⁶

Increasing attention on race relations and the rise of Jim Crow in the Redeemer South is reflected in Joel Williamson's comprehensive history of southern race relations following emancipation. He acknowledges the continued political participation of blacks after Redemption. This participation took a variety of forms, from political activism in the black-belt regions where "Redemption had not thoroughly penetrated," to alliance with "white splinter movements" like the Independents, to what he calls the "echo Reconstruction" in parts of the upper South. As a result, southerners in the 1890s began the process of formal legal disfranchisement, using a variety of methods, and, according to Williamson, for a variety of reasons. The turning point was the failure of Henry Cabot Lodge's federal elections bill in the Republican-dominated Congress in 1891. The bill would have provided continued Justice Department protections in federal elections and would have meant "the beginning of another Reconstruction." Presumably, its failure provided states the motivation to act first through disfranchisement on the local and state level, since future Congresses might not still assert federal authority that the courts, in cases like *ex parte Yarbrough*, had affirmed.⁷

Charles F. Lofgren's *The Plessy Case: A Legal-Historical Interpretation* suggests a greater inevitability and acceptance of racial segregation in public facilities in the years after Reconstruction than Woodward had found. Moreover, the Supreme Court's decision in Plessy v. Ferguson was not crucial to acceptance of the "separate but equal" doctrine, since prior to 1896 lower federal courts had already "accepted the doctrine as part of the law of common carriers."⁸

Similarly, J. Morgan Kousser's 1985 Oxford University lecture on the development of racial discrimination in education describes a legal and intellectual environment by the late nineteenth century increasingly hostile to claims of black rights, but one not without victories for opponents of racism as well. Court decisions dealing with school segregation reveal a range of options and concern for local conditions, suggesting further that the last two decades of the nineteenth century provided the kind of alternatives and "choices" that Woodward had first claimed. Indeed, in a *festschrift* for Woodward, Kousser and co-editor James McPherson concluded that Woodward's "Jim Crow thesis" continued to "flourish."[9]

Both Lofgren and Kousser indicate a "promising" side to Gilded Age court rulings on racial segregation. These cases, they maintain, would provide a "useful tool" in what would become the twentieth century's attack on racial discrimination. So also, in the 1960s, Congress and the courts would return to the doctrines and language of the nineteenth century in crafting the voting rights legislation and decisions of the Second Reconstruction.

The success of the federal government's first attempt to protect voting rights in the South continues to generate debate. William Gillette's *Retreat From Reconstruction, 1869–1879* seriously questioned the effectiveness of federal enforcement efforts after the early years of Reconstruction. Where Everette Swinney had concluded that franchise protections were "virtually dead letters" by 1875, Gillette moves their demise back a year, arguing that the enforcement policy in the South "had collapsed by 1874." Indeed, for Gillette the entire enforcement policy was pretty much a failure, doomed from the start by congressional Republicans pinning their hopes on legislation—the Enforcement Acts of 1870–71—that promised more than it could ever deliver.[10]

Gillette did, however, focus on Justice Department activities and the various obstacles preventing department officials in the South from carrying out their duties. The incompetence and inertia, along with the effects of partisan political squabbles, would continue to hinder efforts after 1877. Gillette recognized the critical role played by the Justice Department in the "retreat" from Reconstruction, but like Swinney assumed that the struggle was over when the battle ended.[11]

If for Gillette the failure of Republican efforts to protect the civil and political rights of the freedman was a result of faulty legislation and overly sanguine politicians, for Robert Kaczorowski Reconstruction guarantees of equal rights were done in by the "politics of judicial interpretation." Federal judges, having first upheld national authority to protect Fourteenth and Fifteenth Amendment rights, reversed themselves by 1876. In doing so, the judiciary undercut Justice Department endeavors at the very moment that, for Kaczorowski, the department was achieving real success in the struggle against southern terrorism.[12]

Evidence of voting rights enforcement activities by the Justice Department are acknowledged in Stephen Cresswell's work on the Justice Department in the northern district of Mississippi between 1870 and 1890. While Cresswell concluded that voting rights enforcement overall in the district was a "notorious failure," he conceded that such factors as the presence of "energetic prosecutors" could and did result in successful prosecutions. At the same time, his intensive analysis of one particular district graphically illustrates the various institutional weaknesses within the department, as well as the external political pressures that ultimately brought failure to the government's policies.[13]

It may be that arguments about the success or failure of the Justice Department to ensure franchise protections is an exercise in futility, hinging as they do on one's definition of what success or failure represents when it comes to the protection of basic rights. Moreover, historians must work from the perspective of knowing that ultimately the vast majority of black voters in the South would be disfranchised. Nonetheless, it is also true that numbers of black citizens continued exercising their Fifteenth Amendment rights across the South. The fact makes worthwhile this attempt to explain and understand what did or did not happen.[14]

What these studies also confirm is acceptance of the important role played by the Justice Department in the events of the

Redeemer period in the South. Constitutional scholars have generally focused on the passage of legislation by Congress or the states and its interpretation by the courts, rather than executive branch implementation. And while much of the "new history" is concerned with economic and social factors and the lives of ordinary persons, there is also an increasing interest in reexamination of institutions and policies.

Morton Keller's *Affairs of State*, an examination of the effects of the Civil War on "public life" during the late nineteenth century, illustrates this trend. According to Keller, the Civil War resulted in a vast increase in the responsibilities and duties of national governance; yet, at least until 1900, government could not fulfill this expanded role. Echoing Walter Farnham's earlier notion of the "weakened spring of government," Keller describes how a combination of party politics, laissez faire attitudes, and what he calls "localism," worked against the development of a strong national state. The Justice Department was a prime example: it was created as an executive department in 1870 to handle the increased legal work brought on by the war, along with a variety of new responsibilities, but proved unprepared to do either well.[15]

Stephen Skowronek has demonstrated how attempts during the late nineteenth century to secure a more professional and efficient national administrative apparatus produced only "patchwork" results. Politicians, in part aided by judicial acceptance of laissez faire doctrines, managed to deflect any serious threat to continued control of the "party state." The Pendleton Act created a federal civil service system, but it in fact remained limited in the positions and agencies covered, while attempts to reform such government institutions as the army and the Interstate Commerce Commission likewise proved ineffectual.[16]

Skowronek ignores the Justice Department, but his model of national administrative capacities and reform reflects the department's experience during these years as well. Internal reforms often proved short-lived or unsuccessful, and the Pendleton Act covered only a few of the minor clerks in the Washington office. From the attorneys general to district attorneys and marshals, the Justice Department remained captive to the "party state" and, perhaps as much as any of the executive departments, continues to be so today.[17]

This body of valuable research in aspects of the Justice Department and voting rights in the South in the late nineteenth century leaves much to be done. As David Johnson has concluded, the history of federal law enforcement continues "virtually unexplored." John Conley's survey of the literature in criminal justice history noted that Cummings and McFarland's 1937 study, *Federal Justice*, constitutes the most recent and only comprehensive account of the department from its creation in 1870 up to the turn of the century.[18]

Little is known about the individuals who were part of or headed the Justice Department. Arthur Robb's 1946 brief sketches of the attorneys general remain a principal source of information for the 1877–1900 period; material on district attorneys and marshals is likewise meager. Lincoln Caplan's study of the solicitor general makes only passing reference to Samuel Field Phillips, who in fact held that position longer than anyone (1879–93), and who by statute and practice was acting attorney general for extended periods of time during these years.[19]

Finally, the attempt by the Justice Department to enforce franchise protections in the post-Reconstruction South reflected what Skowronek labeled the "unresolved tension" between expanding national authority on the one hand and the "localism" of partisan politics and economic and racial conflict on the other. Further studies are wanted of Justice Department involvement in specific states and districts, on the order of Cresswell's work on northern Mississippi, as well as research on the agency and law enforcement in other parts of the country. The Justice Department and law enforcement continue to provide a valuable window through which to shed more light on what Woodward found so obscure.

NOTES

1. C. Vann Woodward, *The Strange Career of Jim Crow*, 3d ed. (New York, 1975), xv.

2. Michael Les Benedict, "Preserving the Constitution: The Conservative Basis of Radical Reconstruction," *Journal of Southern History* 61 (June 1974): 65–90; Michael Les Benedict, "Preserving Federalism: Reconstruction and the Waite Court," *Supreme Court Review* (1978) 39–79. For the Reconstruction period generally, see Harold M. Hyman and William M. Wiecek, *Equal Justice Under Law: Constitutional Development, 1835–1875* (New York, 1982), 386–515; and Herman Belz, *Emancipation and Equal Rights* (New York, 1978). However, for a different approach to Reconstruction, see Eric Foner, *Reconstruction: America's Unfinished Revolution, 1863–1877* (New York, 1988). For understanding the "revolutionary" nature of Reconstruction, Foner emphasizes economic class issues, rather than race, as primary. In the process he downplays the significance of voting rights, and his treatment of this aspect reflects the older view that Supreme Court decisions like *Reese* and *Cruikshank* brought an end to black suffrage and federal protections immediately.

3. David J. Bodenhamer and James W. Ely Jr., eds., *Ambivalent Legacy: A Legal History of the South* (Jackson, Miss., 1984); Kermit Hall and James W. Ely Jr., eds., *An Uncertain Tradition: Constitutionalism and the History of the South* (Athens, Ga., 1989). While several of the essays in *Ambivalent Legacy* touch on the late nineteenth century, essays in *Uncertain Tradition* go from an essay on Reconstruction by Michael Les Benedict directly to the twentieth century. Perhaps the best indication of the growing interest in the South's legal and constitutional heritage is the inauguration of a journal, *The Georgia Journal of Southern Legal History*, dedicated to the topic.

4. Edward L. Ayers, *Vengeance and Justice: Crime and Punishment in the 19th-Century American South* (New York, 1984), 223–65. See, for example, George C. Rable, *But There Was No Peace: The Role of Violence in the Politics of Reconstruction* (Athens, Ga., 1984); and Joel Williamson, *The Crucible of Race: Black-White Relations in the American South Since Emancipation* (New York, 1984).

5. C. Vann Woodward, *Origins of the New South, 1877–1913* (Baton Rouge, La., 1951); James Tice Moore, "Redeemers Reconsidered: Change and Continuity in the Democratic South, 1870–1900," *Journal of Southern History* 44 (August 1978): 357–78. For recent state studies, see, for example, Jonathan M. Weiner, *Social Origins of The New South: Alabama, 1860–1885* (Baton Rouge, La., 1978); Dwight B. Billings Jr., *Planters and the Making of a "New South": Class, Politics and Development in North Carolina, 1865–1900* (Chapel Hill, N.C., 1979); and Steven Hahn, *The Roots of Southern Populism: Yeoman Farmers and the*

Transformation of the Georgia Upcountry: 1850–1890 (New York, 1983). For a defense of Woodward's work, see J. Morgan Kousser and James M. McPherson, "C. Vann Woodward: An Assessment of His Work and Influence," in Kousser and McPherson, eds., *Region, Race, and Reconstruction: Essays in Honor of C. Vann Woodward* (New York, 1982), xiii–xxxvii.

6. Hahn, *Roots of Southern Populism*, 204–38.

7. Williamson, *Crucible of Race*, 113, 224–58. Gerald Gaither, *Blacks and the Populist Revolt: Ballots and Bigotry in the New South* (Tuscaloosa, Ala., 1977) notes that southern blacks did not uniformly support the Lodge bill, and some leaders like Booker T. Washington even spoke out against it.

8. Charles A. Lofgren, *The Plessy Case: A Legal-Historical Interpretation* (New York, 1987), 199–200.

9. J. Morgan Kousser, *Dead End: The Development of Nineteenth-Century Litigation on Racial Discrimination in Schools* (Oxford, England, 1986); Kousser and McPherson, *Race, Religion, and Reconstruction*, xxvii.

10. William Gillette, *Retreat From Reconstruction, 1869–1879* (Baton Rouge, La., 1979), 45; Everette Swinney, "Enforcing the Fifteenth Amendment, 1870–1877," *Journal of Southern History* 28 (May 1962): 202–18.

11. Gillette, *Retreat From Reconstruction*, 45–54. Gillette marshals an array of charts and statistics to demonstrate the government's failure to "accomplish much that was substantial and enduring." (54) I am not a cliometrician, but it seems that what is to be proven is assumed, namely that protections ceased after 1877, so that statistics from after that date are simply ignored. Based on the 1894 *Annual Report* of the Attorney General, the following statistics have been calculated:

1870–1876	3,554 Election cases brought in the South
	1,180 Convictions (33% conviction rate)
1877–1893	3,387 Election cases brought in the South
	835 Convictions (24% conviction rate)

If one thus wants to play the "numbers game," then it could be argued that election law enforcement was at least as active after 1877 as before, and not that much less successful in terms of convictions.

12. Robert J. Kaczorowski, *The Politics of Judicial Interpretation: The Federal Courts, Department of Justice and Civil Rights, 1866–1876* (New York, 1985).

13. Stephen Cresswell, "Enforcing the Enforcement Acts: The Department of Justice in Northern Mississippi, 1870–1890," *Journal of*

Southern History 53 (August 1987) 421–40.

14. For the best account of continued black voting after 1877, see J. Morgan Kousser, *The Shaping of Southern Politics: Suffrage Restriction and the Establishment of the One-Party South, 1880–1910* (New Haven, Conn., 1974).

15. Morton Keller, *Affairs of State: Public Life in Late Nineteenth Century America* (Cambridge, Mass., 1977), 85–121; Wallace Farnham, "'The Weakened Spring of Government': A Study in Nineteenth Century American History," *American Historical Review*, 68 (April 1963): 662–80.

16. Stephen Skowronek, *Building A New American State: The Expansion of National Administrative Capacities, 1877–1920* (Cambridge, England, 1982), 39–84.

17. Robert M. Goldman, "The 'Weakened Spring of Government' and the Executive Branch: The Department of Justice in the Late 19th Century," *Congress & the Presidency* 11 (Autumn 1984): 166–77.

18. David R. Johnson, *American Law Enforcement: A History* (St. Louis, Mo., 1981), 87; John A. Conley, "Criminal Justice History as a Field of Research: A Review of Literature, 1960–1975," in *Law and Order in American History*, ed. J. M. Hawes (Port Washington, N.Y., 1979), 156. However, see Stephen Cresswell, "Resistance and Enforcement: The United States Department of Justice, 1870–1893" (Ph.D. diss., University of Virginia, 1986).

19. Arthur Robb, *Biographical Sketches of the Attorneys General* (Washington, D.C., 1946); Lincoln Caplan, *The Tenth Justice: The Solicitor General and the Rule of Law* (New York, 1987), 205.

INTRODUCTION

An important element in the traditional historical account of the end of the Reconstruction period in American history was its effect on the freedman in the South. The withdrawal of the remaining federal troops in the South signified the abandonment of the freedman to the control of his former masters. White southerners thereupon attempted to regain their absolute control through social segregation and political disfranchisement, this despite the guarantees of equality and political freedom promised in the three Reconstruction amendments to the Constitution. The implementation of separation of the races and political impotence was, by this account, immediate and complete. The period from 1877 to 1896 was characterized as the "nadir" in the history of the Negro in the United States.[1]

Yet, as C. Vann Woodward has shown with respect to segregation, the rise of Jim Crow in the South was not as simple or inevitable as historians, writing from the perspective of segregation and disfranchisement as an established fact, have generally assumed. The period from 1877 to 1896, Woodward concluded, was one of "forgotten alternatives" when "real choices had to be made" as to the future of the two races in the South. Indeed, "race relations after Redemption were an unstable interlude before the passing of . . . old . . . traditions and the arrival of the Jim Crow code and disfranchisement." To argue that the process was immediate and inevitable after 1877 was, in Woodward's view, to disregard a critical period in the history of race relations and the status of the Negro in the South.[2]

The present study is an attempt to examine the question of black voting rights in the South between the years 1877 and

1893. It will be argued that, like the "strange career" of Jim Crow segregation, the disfranchisement of the freedman in the South after 1877 was neither immediate nor inevitable. Between 1877 and 1893 the federal government, through the Department of Justice, attempted to enforce the rights granted the freedman by the Fifteenth Amendment and to implement congressional legislation designed to enforce the provisions of that amendment. That the attempt in the long run was indeed unsuccessful, and that by the beginning of the twentieth century southern blacks were to a great extent disfranchised, should not obscure the attempt that was made and the reasons why it was made and why it proved unsuccessful.

While the major focus of this work is the role of the Justice Department and the actual enforcement of franchise protections after 1877, consideration must be given to the constitutional and political framework for voting-rights protection for the freedman during this period. The constitutional basis of such voting rights was the Fifteenth Amendment, ratified in 1870, and the series of congressional measures passed in 1870 and 1871 known as the Enforcement Acts. The Fifteenth Amendment itself was a moderate measure since it did not provide for an outright grant of suffrage to Negroes, but prohibited discrimination at the ballot box on the basis of race, color, or previous condition of servitude. However, the Enforcement Acts spelled out in detail as crimes a wide variety of methods involving violence, intimidation, and fraud which might be employed to prevent blacks from voting. The Acts also provided for the actual enforcement of these sanctions by the federal government through the use of federal courts, Justice Department officials, and federally appointed election supervisors.[3]

A related element of the traditional historical account indicated above involves the decisions by the Supreme Court after 1870 as to the scope of protection afforded by the Fourteenth and Fifteenth Amendments and the supplemental civil rights legislation. Under this traditional interpretation the Supreme Court played a critical role in the abandonment of the freedman after Reconstruction by consistently striking down civil rights legislation and narrowing the scope and effectiveness of the

Fourteenth and Fifteenth Amendments. This was especially true, the interpretation maintains, with respect to the Fifteenth Amendment and voting rights. In 1876 the Supreme Court in *U.S. v. Reese* and *U.S. v. Cruikshank* declared sections of the Enforcement Acts unconstitutional and thereby left "Negro voters defenseless in the southern states."[4]

However, as is argued below, the *Reese* and *Cruikshank* decisions did not mark the demise of either the enforcement legislation or the attempts by the federal government to protect voting rights in the South. In those two decisions the Supreme Court struck down only several sections of the Enforcement Act of 1870, and a short time later Congress repassed the same sections using different wording. The legal and administrative basis for continued voting-rights enforcement by the federal government remained intact. Furthermore, between 1877 and 1898 virtually all federal court decisions in fact upheld the enforcement of voting rights through congressional legislation, the high point being the Supreme Court's decision in 1886 in *Ex Parte Yarbrough*.[5]

Along with the continued constitutional basis for the protection of black voting rights in the South was the political support for such protection. The enforcement of voting rights in the South after 1877 reflected the continued interest and concern by the Republican Party for the political rights of the freedman. Two important studies, by Hirshson and DeSantis, have clearly shown that Republican leaders continued to look to the South in the hopes of revitalizing the Republican Party in that section, which would in turn assure GOP national supremacy for years to come. One obvious aspect of this interest was the potential support and votes of the freedman. Thus, Republicans supported the enforcement of what they themselves came to call the "free ballot and a fair count." Republican Presidents Hayes, Garfield, Arthur, and Harrison attempted in different ways to build up southern Republicanism. They sought alliance with Conservatives, former Whigs and Unionists, Independent movements, and even the Populists. Yet, all these attempts began with the recognition of the critical importance of free and honest elections in the South. As a result, all of these presidents supported the active enforcement of the election statutes by the federal government.[6]

Given the continued constitutional and political support for the protection of franchise rights after 1877, how then was such policy actually translated into action? The primary focus of this study is an attempt to answer this question by dealing with the federal agency directly responsible for the enforcement of the election laws—the Department of Justice.

According to two historians of the Justice Department, Cummings and McFarland, "with district attorneys and marshals located throughout the country, the new Department of Justice had a potential network of agencies with which to enforce" the federal election statutes. However, as of 1877 the Justice Department's organization and administrative capacities were essentially decentralized and local in character. Although created a cabinet-level agency in 1870, the new department in this respect differed little from the Office of Attorney General in the beginning of the century. Between 1877 and 1893 a number of problems and factors, as much administrative as political or constitutional in nature, kept the department in much the some state. Thus, the enforcement of national policy and law was in the hands of a law enforcement agency still local in character with little effective centralized control.[7]

While these problems affected all aspects of the department's work during the last quarter of the nineteenth century, they were particularly apparent when it came to the protection of the "free ballot and a fair count." Among the most important factors that affected voting rights to be examined here were: corruption and inefficiency among local federal officials, the political nature of department appointments at the local level and the involvement of these officials in state and local politics, and the lack of sufficient financial and manpower resources on the part of the department and local officials to effectively enforce the federal election laws. When coupled with the active interference on the part of southern Democrats at every point of the enforcement process from the ballot box to the jury room, it may then be concluded that the disfranchisement of the freedman in the

South, when it came, was as much the result of administrative and bureaucratic failure as of political and constitutional abandonment.

The federal election statutes were not, as Professor Everrett Swinney concluded, "virtually dead letters" by 1874. Between 1877 and 1893 the Justice Department instituted over 1,200 election law prosecutions in the eleven states of the Confederacy. Only after Congress repealed the statutes in 1893 did prosecutions under these laws cease. At this same time southern states attempted to circumvent federal interference through revision of their state constitutions. These new constitutions contained provisions which in the long run were successful in disfranchising the vast majority of black voters in the South. Yet, in the last three decades of the nineteenth century such disfranchisement was not inevitable. Effective enforcement of constitutionally and politically supported voting rights might have precluded this process. In this sense, the "free ballot and a fair count" between 1877 and 1893 had its own strange career.

Notes

1. Rayford Logan, *The Betrayal of the Negro* (New York, 1954), chap. 5.

2. C. Vann Woodward, *The Strange Career of Jim Crow*, 3d ed. (New York, 1975), 32–33.

3. For discussion on the background and passage of the Fifteenth Amendment, see William Gillette, *The Right to Vote: Politics and the Passage of the Fifteenth Amendment* (Baltimore, 1969), and chap. 1 below.

4. *U.S. v. Reese*, 92 U.S. 214 (1876); *U.S. v. Cruikshank*, 92 U.S. 542 (1876). Loren Miller, *The Petitioners* (New York, 1966), 158.

5. For a complete discussion of these cases, see chap. 5 below.

6. Stanley Hirshson, *Farewell to the Bloody Shirt: Northern Republicans and the Negro, 1877–1893* (Chicago, 1968); and Vincent P. DeSantis, *Republicans Face the Southern Question: The New Departure Years, 1877–1897* (Baltimore, 1959).

7. Homer Cummings and Carl McFarland, *Federal Justice: Chapters in the History of Justice and the Federal Executive* (New York, 1937), 231.

"A Free Ballot and a Fair Count"

1

The Constitutional and Political Background of Fifteenth Amendment Rights Enforcement

THE ENFORCEMENT of voting rights in the South by the Department of Justice after 1877 took place within a constitutional, political, and administrative framework, the outlines of which had begun taking shape before the last federal troops were withdrawn from the South. The constitutional and political framework behind the protection of the "free ballot and a fair count" consisted of the politics and passage of the Fifteenth Amendment in 1870, congressional legislation over the following three years designed to enforce that amendment, the early Supreme Court rulings on the constitutionality of such legislation and the scope of the Fifteenth Amendment, and the attitudes and policies of the Republican party before and after the Reconstruction period. Finally, the actual enforcement of federal legislation dealing with voting rights by the Justice Department was affected by developments within the department itself before 1877. Thus, the first two chapters of this study elaborate on these pre-1877 factors influencing the subsequent history of the federal government, the Fifteenth Amendment, and the freedman in the South.

The importance of making some provision for black suffrage after the Civil War was clearly understood by northern Republican politicians even before the South had surrendered, although until 1865 the question of voting rights for the freedman had become crucial to northern Republicans both for humanitarian and practical reasons. It was agreed that emancipation for the black man in the South would become virtually meaningless unless he had the power of the ballot to protect himself. Yet, beyond this was also the simple calculation by northern Republicans that, with former slaves being counted for purposes of apportionment, a newly readmitted South would stand to gain fifteen additional seats in Congress. Republicans judged that if blacks were not enfranchised, these additional southern seats would endanger Republican control of Congress. As a result, "Republicans felt that security for both the Negro and the Republican party must be achieved at a time when they identified Republican victory with the national interest."[1]

The first effort on the part of Congress with respect to suffrage for the freedman involved the section of the Fourteenth Amendment dealing with congressional apportionment. The second section of the amendment provided for the reduction of representation in the House of Representatives for any state that "denied to any of the male inhabitants of such State, being twenty-one years of age, and citizens of the United States, or in any way abridged, except for participation in rebellion, or other crime" the right to vote at any national election.[2] No mention at all was made as to any positive right on the part of blacks to vote, nor was any provision or mention made of possible discrimination on account of race or color where such rights might be granted. As one writer has concluded, the second section was a "clumsy substitute for an outright grant of Negro suffrage." The section was clearly intended not so much to secure blacks in the South the franchise as to insure northern Republican hegemony in the House. It was, in addition, a holding action involving a reduction of southern representation until some point in the future when, so Republican politicians believed, the freedman "would be in a position to divide, if not dominate, the political power of the south."[3]

The election of 1868 helped convince even moderate Republicans in Congress that only further legislation, or perhaps a constitutional amendment, would suffice to settle the problem of black suffrage. Ulysses S. Grant, the Republican candidate for president, won by only a 300,000 vote plurality, and from the South came numerous reports of intimidation and violence against blacks attempting to vote. When the last session of the Fortieth Congress began in January 1869, proposals were immediately put forth for a voting rights amendment to the Constitution. Debate on these proposals continued until, on February 26, the Senate approved the final draft of the amendment hammered out by a conference committee of House and Senate members. The amendment as accepted by the Senate was then sent to the states for ratification. With the ratification by Georgia on February 2, 1870, the Fifteenth Amendment became part of the Republican party's answer to the "knot of reconstruction."[4]

The Fifteenth Amendment, as ratified, contained two sections. The first section declared, "The right of citizens of the United States to vote shall not be denied or abridged by the United States or by any State on account of race, color, or previous condition of servitude." The second section stated, "The Congress shall have power to enforce this article by appropriate legislation."[5]

As a result of the rather negative language of the first section of the amendment, there has developed a historical debate on the actual scope and intent of the Fifteenth Amendment. Did the amendment enfranchise blacks or did it merely prohibit discrimination in voting? Was the amendment, like the second section of the Fourteenth Amendment, designed to pressure southern states into granting blacks the franchise, while allowing northern states the choice of giving blacks the vote? Or conversely, was it intended primarily to secure the enfranchisement of northern black voters who would, hopefully, support the Republican party and its continued dominance of that section? To understand later enforcement of the provisions of the Fifteenth Amendment, a discussion of the historiographical debate on these questions would be relevant.

The first detailed study on the origins and background of the Fifteenth Amendment was a small monograph published in 1909 by John Mabry Mathews. According to Mathews, the amendment was the product of the interaction among four congressional factions that he designated as the humanitarians, the nationalists, the politicians, and the local autonomists. The humanitarian faction supported voting rights for blacks out of simple concern for the welfare and future of the newly freed slaves in the South. The nationalists were concerned with increasing the power of the federal government generally with respect to determining the qualifications of voters. Up to this time the Constitution had said almost nothing about the role of the federal government in this area, and the nationalists favored some change in this situation. On the other hand, the group that Mathews labeled the local autonomists represented the traditional values of states' rights and wanted to maintain state responsibility for elections and voting qualifications. The fourth faction, the politicians, was basically concerned with obtaining some sort of congressional control over southern elections.[6]

Though extremely vague as to which members of Congress belonged to which faction or factions, Mathews concluded that the deadlock in Congress that developed over the amendment among these four groups was ultimately broken by "an unpremeditated coalition between the humanitarians and the politicians." The amendment was thus regarded by Mathews as a moderate compromise measure reflecting a number of different viewpoints. The humanitarians could be satisfied because although the amendment did not directly confer on blacks the right to vote, it did prohibit "the three most obvious and easily administered tests by which the negro might be excluded from the suffrage." The local autonomists were not wholly ignored inasmuch as the amendment made no mention of limiting the constitutional prerogatives of the states in controlling local elections and determining qualifications for voters, especially property qualifications.[7]

The nationalists could also be content, to some degree, in the fact that the Fifteenth Amendment explicitly involved the federal government in the protection of voting rights. However, from the politicians' point of view, the amendment was a "very considerable gain," since the second section of the amendment gave Congress the authority to enforce its provisions through "appropriate legislation." Such authority could well be used to protect blacks from the rising level of violence and intimidation against them in the South. Thus, for Mathews the amendment was a moderate measure because it appeared to please just about everyone.[8]

Although Mathews ignored the question of possible selfish political reasons behind Republican concern for black voting rights, a 1918 study of suffrage in the United States by Kirk R. Porter suggested that northern Republicans "were not without ulterior motives in seeking to enfranchise the negro." According to Porter, "The principle of negro suffrage was popular, of course, but the Republican politicians were very likely to have something more in mind than justice to the black man when they fought to gain suffrage for him. They wanted to make sure of Republican majorities and permanently cripple the Democratic party."[9]

William Gillette's 1965 study of the politics and passage of the Fifteenth Amendment agreed with Mathews as to the moderate nature of the amendment. For Gillette, "The Fifteenth Amendment was . . . a moderate measure, supported by pragmatic moderates and practical radicals who understood the limits of their power and thus acted with limited purposes in mind, modest means in the articles, and practical results in securing ratification." Like Porter, Gillette discovered evidence of partisan political motivation behind the adoption of the amendment. However, after studying the congressional debates relating to the amendment as well as the legislative and newspaper accounts of the ratification process in the states, Gillette concluded that the Fifteenth Amendment was primarily designed to gain black voters in the North for the Republican party. Franchise rights for southern blacks was but an "important secondary objective," particularly since by 1859 Republicans generally believed that "Negro suffrage was accepted by many white southerners as a fixed fact that could not and, less frequently, should not be changed."[10]

The partisan political motivation of Republicans responsible for the Fifteenth Amendment was strongly challenged in a 1967 essay by John and LaWanda Cox. According to the Coxes, the radical and moderate Republicans in Congress secured the passage and ratification of the amendment at great political risk to themselves. This was especially true for those northern Republicans from states where both racial prejudice and Democratic opposition were strong. The Coxes also questioned Gillett's conclusions as to the importance of Republican concern for northern black voters. After examining post-1869 election returns in several northern states, the Coxes maintained that the enfranchisement of northern blacks had little effect on the fortune of the Republican party in the years following the ratification of the amendment. In their view the Fifteenth Amendment was primarily the victory of principle over considerations of party advantage.[11]

In the Epilogue to the 1969 edition of his work, Gillette responded to the Coxes' essay. For one thing, he pointed out that the Coxes' argument was mostly one of historical hindsight since they attempted to examine the motivation behind the amendment by looking at the "consequences" that followed its passage. Gillette felt this was invalid. "An argument that fails to come to grips with the evidence, an argument which obscures the real issue of intent in Congress and in the statehouses, an argument that avoids the only recent study, scarcely seems to be an argument at all."[12]

Gillette also defended both the moderate and partisan nature of the amendment, or what the Coxes termed the "expediency" argument about the origins of the Fifteenth Amendment. Gillette pointed out that the dichotomy the Coxes attempted to draw between "expediency" (Gillette's view) and "idealism" (the Coxes' view) was "misleading" because "there was no conflict at the outset between the interests of the black electorate and the interests of the Republican Party. Rather, the interests were mutual and not mutually exclusive. There was no necessary conflict between the immediate interest and the practical ideal, the achievable objective." Franchise rights for blacks, in other words, was not thought of as being incompatible with the future well-being of the Republican party.[13]

In attempting to reconcile the idealistic and partisan motives responsible for the Fifteenth Amendment, Gillette probably comes closest to getting at the "original understanding" behind the amendment. The Fifteenth Amendment was indeed a moderate measure: it was the outcome of compromises among various men and groups of men who had different ideas as to what a constitutional amendment involving voting rights should contain. As such, the amendment was the product of idealism and humanitarian concern, as well as partisan political planning.

That the amendment reflected concern for the future of the black man can be illustrated by the fact that the draft of the amendment as finally accepted by both houses was the work of Representative George S. Boutwell of Massachusetts. Boutwell firmly believed that voting rights were necessary for the freedman in order for him to protect his other rights. He wrote, "With the right of voting, everything that a man ought to have or enjoy of civil rights comes to him. Without the right to vote he is secure in nothing." On the other hand, to argue that the amendment reflected only the highest idealism of the Republicans, as the Coxes suggest, is to ignore the simple fact that perhaps the most idealistic Radical Republican of them all, Charles Sumner of Massachusetts, refused to support the amendment: rather than vote against it, he absented himself from every important vote on the measure in the Senate.[14]

What the Fifteenth Amendment did do was to commit the nation to the idea of "impartial" rather than "universal" male suffrage. This meant that instead of an outright grant of the elective franchise to blacks, as slavery had been abolished outright by the Thirteenth Amendment, the federal government would be concerned with preventing discrimination at the ballot box where such discrimination was racially motivated. A positive constitutional right was thus given through the negative prohibition of that right. The significance of this was that the future effectiveness of the amendment in securing black franchise rights would become dependent on the kinds of "appropriate legislation" Congress might pass to implement the first section of the amendment. And even more critical to the amendment's effectiveness would be the enforcement of such legislation. Hence, while the Fifteenth Amendment did represent an attempt at achieving the Radical goal of black suffrage, it also left open the possibility of the ultimate frustration of that goal if "appropriate" legislation was not provided or enforced.

The importance of additional legislation was understood by Republicans, and following the ratification of the Fifteenth Amendment in 1870, Congress passed a series of three acts commonly known as the Enforcement Acts. The general purpose of this legislation was to assure future compliance with the provisions of the Fourteenth and Fifteenth Amendments by providing the necessary administrative and legal machinery and procedures to accomplish that goal. The three measures covered a wide variety of political and civil rights problems confronting the freedman in the South as well as blacks and other minorities in the North. While all three acts involved voting rights, it was the first act that dealt especially with the Fifteenth Amendment and conditions in the South. Because of its importance this act will be discussed last and in greater detail.[15]

The second of the three acts—the Federal Elections Law of February 1871—was aimed primarily at election frauds in urban areas and as such was confined in the years 1877 to 1896 to northern cities. According to the most recent scholar of the February election law, the primary motivation behind its passage was the public reaction to the Tweed Ring vote fraud scandals of 1868 in New York City. Thus, rather than being generated by the problem of black voting rights, the Federal Elections Law was "in effect an urban reform measure instituted on a national level."[16] It was upheld by the courts as constitutional, but because of state and local reform measures, such as the Australian ballot, passed during the 1890s, the need for this particular federal law had for all practical purposes ceased by the end of the century.

The third law, passed in April of 1871, was known as the Ku Klux Act. According to the language of the act itself, the measure was aimed particularly at "conspiracies" against the execution of the laws of the United States and the hindrance or prevention "by force, intimidation or threats" of the lawful exercise of any citizen's civil rights on account of that citizen's race, color, or previous condition of servitude. In other words, the act was designed to outlaw the Ku Klux Klan. From the beginning of Radical Reconstruction in the South in 1867, instances of organized white terror against southern blacks had become more and more frequent. By 1868 "the Ku Klux conspiracy no longer lay within the power of most states to control. It was a sectional attempt to nullify the policy of Reconstruction which Congress had initiated in 1867, and Congress had to help put it down." The Ku Klux Act committed the national government to the arrest and punishment of southerners accused of organized harassment and intimidation of blacks. In 1871 federal marshals in the South began to enforce the act and to initiate prosecutions, particularly in South Carolina, Georgia, and Mississippi. These prosecutions continued through 1872, and by that year, as a most recent historian of the Ku Klux Klan has concluded, "the federal government had broken the back of the . . . Klans throughout most of the South."[17]

It was the first of the congressional Enforcement Acts, passed in May of 1870, that formed the basis of the federal government's enforcement policy of black voting rights in the South after 1877. The legislation was the result of the efforts of a joint House-Senate Conference Committee formed after various proposals for Fifteenth Amendment enforcement legislation by each house were rejected in the other chamber over a period of four months. The measure as finally approved by Congress was entitled "an act to enforce the rights of citizens of the United States to vote in the several states of this Union, and for other purposes."[18]

The act itself contained twenty-three sections. The first section stated that all citizens of the United States qualified to vote in any state or local election "shall be entitled to vote at all such elections, without distinction of race, color, or previous condition of servitude." This was the closest Congress got at the time to a direct and positive affirmation of the rights of blacks to vote. The next several sections provided penalties, including fines and prison sentences, for anyone convicted of preventing or attempting to prevent any citizen from exercising his voting privilege, or attempting to perform any of the prerequisites to the right to vote such as registering. Included in the categories of those subject to penalties were any election officers or officials who might "wrongfully refuse or omit to receive, count, certify, register, report or give effect to the vote" of any citizen lawfully entitled to the elective franchise.[19]

Sections 4 through 7 of the act defined in detail the various crimes against those attempting to exercise their franchise rights. Any person convicted of using force, bribery, threats, intimidation, or "other unlawful means" to prevent or hinder any of those rights guaranteed by the Fifteenth Amendment would be subject to a fine of not less than five hundred dollars, and/or imprisonment for not less than one month nor more than one year. In the case of two or more persons convicted of conspiring to prevent or hinder the voting rights of the freedman, the fine could be as high as five thousand dollars and the jail sentence up to ten years.[20]

The following sections set up the machinery and procedures whereby the act would be enforced. In terms of later enforcement of voting rights these were crucial sections, for responsibility for enforcement of the act was given directly to local Justice Department officials. District attorneys, their assistants, federal marshals and their deputies, and special commissioners of elections were all given authority to arrest, imprison, and set bail for those suspected of violating provisions of the act. These officials were subject to fines for failure to obey and execute any warrants issued under the act, and all were placed under the authority of federal district courts and district court judges. In addition, federal district and circuit courts were given exclusive jurisdiction over any and all crimes and offenses arising out of the enforcement legislation and any subsequent federal legislation in this area. Prosecutions in these courts would be brought either through indictment by a grand jury or by information filed by the federal district attorney in the court of appropriate jurisdiction.[21]

The final sections of the act dealt with a number of other possible methods of vote fraud and voter discrimination, such as impersonation of another person in voting or registering to vote, irregularities in the counting of ballots, and irregularities in the final certification of ballots by election officials. Except for candidates for presidential elector, Congress, or the state legislature, any person deprived of his office because of the denial to any citizen or citizens of the right to vote on account of race could bring suit to recover possession of that office in either the state or federal courts. In addition, section 18 of the Enforcement Act reenacted the entire Civil Rights Act of 1866, and the provisions of that measure were to be enforced along with those of the present act. Finally, the president was given the authority "to employ such part of the land or naval forces of the United States, or of the militia, as shall be necessary to aid in the execution of judicial process issued under this act." Federal district attorneys, marshals, and federal judges could also summon for aid and deputize any bystanders at any time to form a *posse comitatus*.[22]

In sum, this "conglomerate mass of incongruities and uncertainties," as one historian characterized the act, theoretically provided the basis for an impressive commitment on the part of the federal government to the protection of voting rights of blacks in the South. It covered virtually every practice and method then in use to prevent blacks in that section from voting or registering to vote, and provided the means and manpower to remedy the situation of increasing discrimination and harassment at the polls. The Enforcement Act of May 1870 gave the federal government, and in particular the Department of Justice, direct responsibility for making sure that the Fifteenth Amendment's goal of at least impartial suffrage in the South would be maintained. The next step would be how this legislation, along with subsequent enforcement acts, would be accepted by the courts.[23]

Though it was not until 1875 that judicial cases dealing with the constitutionality of the Enforcement Acts reached the United States Supreme Court, in 1871 Circuit Court Judge William B. Woods of Alabama upheld a series of indictments under the acts in *United States v. Hall*. However, in the *Hall* decision Woods used the "privileges and immunities" clause of the Fourteenth Amendment, and not the Fifteenth Amendment, in upholding the conviction of a group of white Alabamians accused of breaking up a political rally of blacks. According to Woods, the rights of free speech and assembly were federally enforceable rights protected under the first section of the Fourteenth Amendment.[24]

Between 1871 and 1875 numerous cases involving the Enforcement Acts were brought in the federal court in the South. In fact, "the very extent of the litigation under the enforcement acts soon overtaxed the capacity of the twenty-four district courts" in that section. As indicated above, the majority of these cases were part of the government's attempt to combat the Ku Klux Klan campaign of terror and intimidation against southern blacks. The success of this attempt was re-enforced by judicial acceptance of the enforcement measures on the circuit court level as in Judge Woods's decision in *United States v. Hall*.[25]

By 1875 several cases dealing with the constitutionality of the Enforcement Acts had reached the Supreme Court. The following year the Court in two separate decisions, *United States v. Reese* and *United States v. Cruikshank*, declared sections of the acts unconstitutional. Although these two decisions undeniably indicated judicial disapproval of congressional attempts at legislating complete civil and political protection for the freedman, they did not, as will be argued, mean the total rejection of the federal government's right to enforce "by appropriate legislation" the guarantees of the Fourteenth and particularly the Fifteenth Amendment.[26]

The *Reese* case involved indictments against several inspectors of a municipal election in Kentucky who had refused to accept and count the vote of one William Garner, "a citizen of the United States of African descent." The case was heard before the Supreme Court in January of 1875 and was considered of sufficient importance that both Attorney General George Williams and Solicitor General Samuel Phillips presented the oral arguments for the government's side. Counsel for the opposing side included former Attorney General Henry Stanbery. Although the Court heard the case in January, it did not announce a decision in the case until March of 1876, some fifteen months later.[27]

On March 27, 1876 the Supreme Court, in an opinion written by Chief Justice Morrison R. Waite, declared sections 3 and 4 of the May 1870 Enforcement Act unconstitutional. The basic issue confronted in the Court's decision was whether or not the two sections of the Enforcement Act went beyond the "appropriate legislation" necessary to enforce the provisions of the Fifteenth Amendment. Waite did not deny that Congress had the power to provide for such legislation. On the contrary, he stated, "Rights and immunities created by or dependent upon the Constitution of the United States can be protected by Congress. The form and the manner of the protection may be such as Congress, in the legitimate exercise of its legislative discretion shall provide."[28]

The problem, according to Waite, was that "the Fifteenth Amendment does not confer the right of suffrage upon anyone. It prevents the States, or the United States, however, from giving preference, in this particular, to one citizen of the United States over another on account of race, color, or previous condition of servitude." In other words, the only enforceable right set forth in the Fifteenth Amendment was the right of citizens to be free from discrimination in the exercise of their franchise rights because of their race or color. The issue then became whether or not the statutes being considered had in fact gone beyond the protection so afforded by the amendment.[29]

The Court ruled that they had, and that "the language of the third and fourth sections does not confine their operation to unlawful discriminations on account of race, &c." By "strictly" construing this "penal statute" to the specific crimes and punishments listed, the chief justice concluded that these sections were so "general" in their import that they went far beyond the intention and powers of Congress to punish those guilty of discrimination at the polls. The statutes, he concluded, encroached upon the traditional right of the state to determine the qualifications of its voters. Given the generality of the statute, it would be possible for the courts themselves to limit the meaning and scope of the statute's provisions, but this Waite humbly declined to do. For it would, he said, "substitute the judicial for the legislative department of government." Having decided, therefore, that Congress had not as yet provided for the crimes for which the defendants were charged in the indictments (discrimination based on race), the lower court was correct in finding the indictments faulty and giving judgment for the defendants.[30]

In light of the contemporary and historical view of the *Reese* decision as a landmark case in the repudiation of the promises of civil and political equality inherent in the three Reconstruction amendments, several aspects of the opinion should be noted. Given the various important issues with which the Court might have dealt, particularly the whole question of federal protection of black voting rights through the Justice Department and election supervisors, the *Reese* decision was both vague and narrow in its conclusions. The Supreme Court took fifteen months to strike down two sections of an act that contained twenty-three sections. And, in effect, the Court rejected these two sections because of a technicality in the wording of the sections, that is, that the crimes specified were not based on discrimination on account of race. The sections were not "explicit" enough in stating a punishable crime. "If . . . legislation undertakes to define by statute a new offence, and provides for its punishment, it should express its will in language that need not deceive the common mind." Thus, the rationale on which the two sections of the Enforcement Act were invalidated was based less on constitutional questions involving voting rights and the federal government than on the narrow issue of statutory construction.[31]

This aspect of the Court's decision was directly challenged in a dissenting opinion by Justice Ward Hunt. Hunt accurately pointed out that the purpose of the entire Enforcement Act being considered was to protect blacks against violations of their right to vote, and that this purpose was clearly set forth in the first two sections of the act, sections the Court chose to ignore. Hunt further noted that while sections 3 and 4 did not mention race, the crimes listed referred directly back to similar crimes listed in the first two sections, which were in fact based on discrimination on account of race. Yet, as one historian has stated, "Despite the force of . . . [Hunt's] contention, the majority decided instead to notify Congress that unless it crossed every 't' and dotted every 'i' the Court would not sustain its civil rights legislation."[32]

The question of the constitutionality of the Enforcement Acts was also confronted by the Supreme Court the same term in *United States v. Cruikshank.* The case had arisen from what became known as the Colfax Massacre or the Grant Parish Riots in Louisiana in April 1873. A number of blacks had been besieged and then burned out of the Colfax courthouse and then "callously shot down." On the basis of Justice Department investigations ninety-six men, including W. J. Cruikshank, were indicted for conspiracy and murder under the provisions of the May 1870 Enforcement Act. Of those indicated only nine were brought to trial, and they were found guilty only of conspiracy. The convictions were appealed finally to the Supreme Court, where counsel for the defendants included former attorney general and United States Senator Reverdy Johnson, and David Dudley Field, the brother of Supreme Court Justice Stephen J. Field.[33]

Attorney Field, who presented the defendants' oral arguments before the Court, maintained that the war amendments did not give Congress the power to pass positive legislation "in areas where possible state discrimination might occur." The amendments, he argued, merely set limits on possible state discriminatory legislation that could only be enforced through congressional provision of judicial remedies. Field, as had the attorneys for the defendants in *Reese*, thus argued against the acts on the broadest possible constitutional grounds.[34]

Yet, despite the persuasiveness of Field and a government brief that was "uninspired," the Supreme Court refused in *Cruikshank* to declare the Enforcement Acts unconstitutional. Indeed, the final result of the majority opinion, again written by Chief Justice Waite, was even narrower than the *Reese* decision. The final outcome in *Cruikshank* was simply a reversal of the convictions of the defendants, and not even the relevant sections of the Enforcement Act were declared void, as had been the case in *Reese*.[35]

Waite began his opinion in *Cruikshank*, as he had done in *Reese*, with a general discussion of the nature of the federal system and the meaning of national citizenship. In *Reese* Waite admitted that one attribute of national citizenship, because of the Fifteenth Amendment, was the right to vote free from discrimination on account of race. He now stated that "the right of the people peaceably to assemble . . . is an attribute of national citizenship, and, as such, under the protection of and guaranteed by the United States." While it is the right of the state to protect persons in the enjoyment of their right of life and liberty, Congress has the power to enforce this guaranty if it is abridged by the state on the basis of racial discrimination. At this point Waite brought up his earlier decision in *Reese* to illustrate his point. "The right to vote in the States comes from the States; but the right of exemption from the prohibited discrimination comes from the United States. The first has not been granted or secured by the Constitution of the United States, but the last has been."[36]

According to Waite, the right of persons peacefully to assemble was the same as the right to vote, and Congress had the power to protect citizens from injury or intimidation in the exercise of that right if it was done because of race. Congress had in fact done this in section 6 of the May 1870 Enforcement Act. The issue then became, as in *Reese*, whether or not the indictments under which the defendants were prosecuted were sufficient in law to sustain this accusation. The Court held that they were not, since the indictments did not allege that the murder of blacks in Grant Parish by Cruikshank and others was committed because of the victims' race. "We may suspect that race was the cause of the hostility; but it is not so averred." For the Court this was a mortal flaw in the indictments, because "[e]verything essential must be charged positively, and not inferentially. The defect here is not in form, but in substance." Hence, "the conclusion is irresistible, that these counts [of the indictment] are too vague and general. . . . It follows that they are not good and sufficient in law. They are so defective that no judgment of conviction should be pronounced upon them."[37]

Given the limited result of the *Reese* and *Cruikshank* decisions it is hard to accept the conclusion of Charles Warren, as well as many other historians and scholars, that "the practical effect of these decisions was to leave the Federal statutes almost wholly ineffective to protect the Negro." In the first instance only two sections out of a comprehensive body of prohibitory legislation were voided, and in the second case only the indictments based on other sections of the same legislation were dismissed by the Court. As one commentator accurately stated, "While the *Cruikshank* case drastically narrowed the scope of permissible civil rights legislation, the decisions (in *Reese* and *Cruikshank*) seemingly left intact congressional power to prevent voting discrimination."[38]

That the *Reese* and *Cruikshank* decisions did leave intact congressional power to protect black voting rights in the South is evidenced by the fact that two months after the two decisions were handed down Congress repassed the two sections voided in *Reese* along with all of the other sections of the May 1870 Enforcement Act. The two new sections, 5506 and 5507, of the Revised Statutes, were more specific in their wording than the original sections of the first Enforcement Act, but were still based on "the right of suffrage, to whom that right is guaranteed by the Fifteenth Amendment to the Constitution of the United States." Thus, in effect, Congress ignored the Court's decisions and passed a virtual fourth enforcement act.[39]

Even more important, however, than the two revised sections was the reenactment of the other sections of the 1870 Enforcement Act, which set up the machinery and procedures for federal protection of the political rights of the freedman in the South. Though parts of the Revised Statutes relating to crimes against the "elective franchise" were repealed by Congress in 1893, sections 5506 through 5532 provided the legislative basis for the enforcement of voting rights of blacks to the end of the century. Included were those sections that gave federal courts jurisdiction over voting rights cases, which gave the President authority to use troops or state militia to help enforce federal guarantees, and most important, which gave the Department of Justice the power and responsibility to enforce all of the provisions relating to the "elective franchise." To portray accurately the course of black voting rights in the South after 1877 it is thus necessary to go beyond the pronouncements of the Supreme Court and examine how those laws that did exist to secure franchise rights for blacks were actually enforced in the South and within the governmental agency most responsible for that enforcement—the Justice Department.[40]

With the approach of the presidential election of 1876, the disfranchisement of southern blacks was neither so inevitable nor immediately at hand as later historians, working from a twentieth-century perspective of black disfranchisement as an accepted given, almost unanimously believed. Although the "seeds of failure" in the Radical Republican hopes for black civil and political equality in the South may have indeed been planted, in 1876 it was clear that their growth might yet at least be delayed. The critical factors in this process were the politics and policies of northern Republicans and the expression of these policies in the enforcement of the federal election laws through the recently created Department of Justice.[41]

Notes

1. Herman Belz, *Reconstructing the Union: Theory and Policy During the Civil War* (Ithaca, N.Y., 1969), 136–37; William Gillette, *The Right to Vote: Politics and the Passage of the Fifteenth Amendment* (Baltimore, 1969), 21–22.

2. U.S. Constitution, Amendment 14, sec. 2.

3. Richard Claude, *The Supreme Court and the Electoral Process* (Baltimore, 1969), 50. See also Joseph B. James, *The Framing of the Fourteenth Amendment* (Urbana, Ill., 1956). The most extensive analysis of the politics behind the passage of the second section can be found in W. W. Van Alstyne, "The Fourteenth Amendment, the 'Right' to Vote, and the Understanding of the Thirty-Ninth Congress," *Supreme Court Review* (1965): 33–86. According to Van Alstyne, the section was passed due to the efforts of Charles Sumner even before the important "due process" section was proposed by Senator John A. Bingham. Van Alstyne agreed that the second section was meant to insure continued Republican dominance in Congress, and that Republicans had "considerable reason to suppose that it would succeed" in accomplishing this. (44)

4. Gillette, *Right to Vote*, chaps. 1 and 2.

5. U.S. Constitution, Amendment 15.

6. John Mabry Mathews, *Legislative and Judicial History of the Fifteenth Amendment* (New York, 1971), 20–36 and passim.

7. Ibid., 33.

8. Ibid., 36.

9. Kirk R. Porter, *A History of Suffrage in the United States* (reprint, New York, 1971), 179.

10. Gillette, *Right to Vote*, 170, 172, 93, and passim.

11. John and LaWanda Cox, "Negro Suffrage and Republican Politics: The Problem of Motivation in Reconstruction Historiography," *Journal of Southern History*, 33 (August 1967): 303–30. The Coxes' work must be read in light of recent "revisionist" writings on the Reconstruction period. An important element in this revisionist writing has been the favorable reevaluation of the Radical Republicans. Once thought to be narrowly partisan and vindictive in their attitudes and actions toward the South and the post-War problems of the freedman, the Radicals are now viewed as rather idealistic and honestly committed to ensuring the civil and political equality of the freedman. See Bernard Weisberger, "The Dark and Bloody Ground of Reconstruction Historiography," *Journal of Southern History*, 25 (1959): 427–47. For examples of revisionist studies, see Kenneth M. Stampp, *The Era of Reconstruction, 1865–1877* (New York, 1967); William R. Brock, *An American Crisis: Congress and Reconstruction, 1865–1867* (New York, 1963); and LaWanda and John Cox, *Politics, Principle, and Prejudice, 1865–1866* (New York, 1969). For recent support of the Coxes' view of the Radical Republicans' idealism and constitutional conservatism, see Michael Les Benedict, "Preserving the Constitution: The Conservative Basis of Radical Reconstruction," *Journal of American History*, 62 (June 1974): 65–90; and Glenn M. Linden, "A Note on Negro Suffrage and Republican Politics," *Journal of Southern History*, 36 (August 1970): 411–20. Although Linden's study provides statistical evidence of "a marked consistency among Republican senators and representatives" in supporting measures designed to protect the civil and political rights of blacks during and after the Civil War, it does not explain the reasons behind the form these measures took, for example, the Fifteenth Amendment. Nor does either essay appear to preclude possible selfish motives that might have been present in the minds of those Republicans who were responsible for the Fifteenth Amendment.

12. Gillette, *Right to Vote*, 166 n. 1.

13. Ibid., 175.

14. George S. Boutwell, *Reminiscences of Sixty Years in Public Affairs* (New York, 1902), 2:40. David Donald, *Charles Sumner and the Rights of Man* (New York, 1970), 352–54. One aspect of the debate on the origins of the amendment remains unresolved, at least for the purposes of this

study: whether the amendment was to aid northern or southern blacks. In this, both the Coxes and Gillette appear to agree: the Fifteenth Amendment's primary concern was northern blacks. According to Gillette, there was little conflict over the ratification of the amendment in the southern states. In fact, "The very moderation of the Fifteenth Amendment appealed to some Democrats and annoyed some Republicans." (104) While it is hard to fault the evidence Gillette uses to support his contentions, several things might be pointed out with respect to this argument and later enforcement of voting rights in the South. For one thing, Gillette virtually disregards the fact that the southern states were still under the control of the Radical regimes at the time, and that this as much as anything else explains why the amendment was so easily ratified in the South. A few years later and there would have been at least as much opposition to the amendment in the South as Gillette claims there had been in the North. For both humanitarian and practical reasons it is also hard to accept southern blacks as being a "secondary," if "important," concern of the Fifteenth Amendment. It was in the South where intimidation and violence against the freedman was becoming widespread, and where the future success of Reconstruction lay. From a practical standpoint, it was also in the South where the greater number by far of potential black Republican voters lived. Finally, and perhaps most important, even given the correctness of Gillette's view, it is also the case that after 1877 the focus of concern by the federal government and the Republican Party as to the Fifteenth Amendment was directed toward the freedman in the South. Hence, history itself makes Gillette's conclusions in this specific area almost irrelevant.

15. W. W. Davis, "The Federal Enforcement Acts," in *Studies in Southern History and Politics*, ed. William A. Dunning, (New York, 1914), no. 9; Mathews, *Legislative History*, chap. 5; Everette Swinney, "Enforcing the Fifteenth Amendment, 1870–1877," *Journal of Southern History*, 28 (May 1962): 202–4.

16. Albie Burke, "Federal Regulation of Congressional Elections in Northern Cities, 1871–1894," *American Journal of Legal History*, 14 (January 1970): 17–34.

17. Allen Trelease, *White Terror: The Ku Klux Klan Conspiracy and Southern Reconstruction* (New York, 1971), 383. Section 6 of the May 1870 Enforcement Act had contained provision for making it a felony for two or more persons to conspire to commit acts of intimidation or violence against black voters. And, as Trelease indicates, this section provided the basis for most federal prosecutions of Klan members.

However, lack of such efforts by federal officials before 1871 prompted Congress to pass specific legislation dealing with the Klan conspiracy in the South. (See Trelease, 385–87, and chaps. 24 and 25, generally.)

18. *U.S. Statutes at Large*, 16, 140–46 (17 vols., Washington, D.C., 1850–73). For discussion of the details of the passage of the act, see Mathews, *Legislative History*, chap. 5; Davis, "Enforcement Acts," 205. For the debate on the act, see Alfred Avings, ed., *The Reconstruction-Amendments Debates* (Richmond, Va., 1967), 437–63.

19. 16 *Statutes at Large*, 140.

20. 16 *Statutes at Large*, 140–41.

21. 16 *Statutes at Large*, 142–43.

22. 16 *Statutes at Large*, 143–46.

23. Homer Cummings and Carl McFarland, *Federal Justice: Chapters in the History of Justice and the Federal Executive* (New York, 1937), chap.12; Swinney, "Enforcing the Fifteenth Amendment," 202–4. Even William Davis, who was strongly critical of the Enforcement Acts, conceded that they were "remarkable" statutes. According to Davis, the May 1870 law provided "both minutely and broadly for the protection by the Federal government of all citizens in the enjoyment of both civil and political rights so far as they are guaranteed directly or indirectly by the Constitution of the United States. . . . It defines as misdemeanors some 26 offenses; as felonies some 5 offenses; and as crimes merely, some 87 offenses." (Davis, "Enforcement Acts," 209.)

24. Fed. Cas. 79 (1871). Woods was an Ohio Republican who had settled in Alabama after the war, and was appointed in 1869 by President Grant to the Circuit Court for the Southern District of Alabama. Before being appointed to the Supreme Court by President Hayes in 1880, Woods did uphold the power of the federal government to punish anyone intimidating a voter in a federal election, in *U.S. v Goldman*, 25 Fed. Cas. 1350. According to Louis Filler, Wood's "liberalism" with respect to the protection of blacks by the federal government "was virtually spent in these two decisions." Wood's interpretation of the "privileges and immunities" clause was rejected by the Supreme Court in the *Slaughterhouse* cases, 16 Wall. 36 (1873), and in 1883 Woods authored the Supreme Court's decision in *U.S. v. Harris*, 106 U.S. 629 (1883), declaring the Ku Klux Act unconstitutional. Louis Filler, "William B. Woods," in *The Justices of the United States Supreme Court, 1789–1966*, ed. Fred Israwl and Leon Friedman (New York, 1969), 2:1329–47.

25. Davis, "Enforcement Acts," 209–15; Felix Frankfurter and James

M. Landis, *The Business of the Supreme Court* (New York, 1927), 65. See also Trelease, *White Terror*, chap. 25; and Cummings and McFarland, *Federal Justice*, chap. 12.

26. *U.S. v. Reese*, 92 U.S. 214 (1876); *U.S. v. Cruikshank*, 92 U.S. 542 (1876).

27. Charles Warren, *The Supreme Court in United States History* (New York, 1922), 2:601–4; Cummings and McFarland, *Federal Justice*, 245–46. According to Cummings, Attorney General Williams suspended prosecutions in the South under the Enforcement Acts in October 1874, expecting a decision by the Court that term on the constitutionality of the acts. That decision was never given, and during the same term Williams and Solicitor General Phillips argued the *Reese* case. No reason can be discovered as to why the Supreme Court took fifteen months to render its decision in the case. Warren suggests that it reflected "the care with which the Court considered the case." This explanation is not especially persuasive. However, see note 31 below.

28. *U.S. v. Reese*, 217.

29. Ibid., 217–19.

30. Ibid., 220–23.

31. Ibid., 220. According to Waite's biographer, C. Peter Magrath, the chief justice had originally intended to write the decisions in the *Reese* and *Cruikshank* cases when he thought they would be decided on constitutional grounds. "But since the judges 'decided not to have any intimation in the opinion upon constitutional questions,' he preferred not to take the cases." He then assigned them to Justice Nathan Clifford, who Waite felt had more knowledge of "criminal law." Clifford's draft opinions were rejected by the Court. "Thereupon Waite took back the cases and began preparing opinions deciding *Reese* and *Cruikshank* essentially on *constitutional grounds*" (emphasis mine). What is interesting, in light of the analysis presented above and of Hunt's dissent, is that the *Reese* decision was not based on broad constitutional grounds, but on criminal statutory construction, and a strained one at that. The same is true for the *Cruikshank* decision, discussed below. Further evidence of the inconsistencies in Magrath's analysis of the *Reese* decision appear in his discussion of the "three-pronged assault" on the act launched by the defendants' attorneys in their briefs to the Court. The first and third "prongs" took issue with the constitutionality of the entire Enforcement Act and with the right of Congress, through the Fifteenth Amendment, to regulate state elections. Both of these broad constitutional arguments were not used at all by Waite. The "prong" that *was* incorporated into Waite's opinion

was the second, which contended that the two sections were too general and were not limited to actions based on racial discrimination. This was the narrowest argument presented, and further shows the limited character of the *Reese* decision. C. Peter Magrath, *Morrison R. Waite* (New York, 1963), 119–29.

32. *U.S. v. Reese*, 239–56. Magrath, *Waite*, 129. Justice Clifford wrote a separate concurring opinion, agreeing that the indictments were bad, "but for reasons widely different from those assigned by the Court." (*U.S. v. Reese*, 223)

33. *U.S. v. Cruikshank*, 542. Cummings and McFarland, *Federal Justice*, 244–46; Warren, *Supreme Court*, 603–4; Magrath, *Waite*, pp. 119–29. See also Charles Fairman, *Reconstruction and Reunion, 1864–1880*, Part 1 (New York, 1971), 1377–80. The case reached the Supreme Court, Justice Joseph P. Bradley wanting to void the indictments, and Judge Woods, based on his previous decision in *U.S. v. Hall*, voting to sustain them. (Fairman, 1378–79)

34. Magrath, *Waite*, 124. Field's arguments on the role of the courts and the war amendments would become more frequent as the years progressed. For by "suggesting that courts, not legislatures were to enforce the amendments, Field—a noted corporation lawyer—allowed the judiciary ample scope to protect property interests even as he denied that the amendments could do much for the Negro." (Magrath, 124)

35. Ibid., 124–25; 92 U.S. 559.

36. 92 U.S. 554–55.

37. 92 U.S. 556–59.

38. Warren, *Supreme Court*, 604; Magrath, *Waite*, 130–31. Both Warren and Magrath discuss the public reaction to the two decisions, reaction that was generally favorable, even among northern Republicans. For example, according to Magrath, "The Republican New York *Times*, which three years earlier had blasted the Grant Parish Riot as a 'fiendish deed,' endorsed the decisions and spoke of 'the admirable clearness and emphasis of the opinions.'" (130) Both authors attribute the favorable response to the decisions to a growing weariness with the southern race question and with the increasing desire on the part of northerners, especially Republicans, to facilitate reconciliation between the sections following the horrors of the Civil War and Reconstruction. Neither author acknowledges the possibility that the mild response might also have been due to the realization that the decisions in and of themselves did not mean the total repudiation of the federal government's commitment to the protection of black vot-

ing rights in the South. As will be seen, Republican concern for the freedman voter did not cease by any means in 1876. For other historians and writers who share Warren's view of the decisions, see especially Loren Miller, *The Petitioners* (New York, 1966), chaps. 7 and 10; also Rayford Logan, *The Betrayal of Legislative History*, 107–8.

39. *U.S. Revised Statutes*, 5506–32. As will be discussed later, when the constitutionality of the revised sections came before the Supreme Court again, the Court reversed itself by holding that the Fifteenth Amendment did confer a positive right of suffrage. *Ex parte Yarbrough*, 110 U.S. 651 (1884).

40. *U.S. Revised Statutes*, 5506–32.

41. C. Vann Woodward, "Seeds of Failure in Radical Race Policy," in *American Counterpoint: Slavery and Racism in the North-South Dialogue* (Boston, 1971), 163–83.

2
"A Meet Person Learned in the Law": The Attorney General and the Justice Department before 1877

THE RESPONSIBILITY for enforcing the Fifteenth Amendment and the congressional legislation supplementing that amendment lay with the federal Department of Justice, officially organized as an executive department in 1870. In the years following Reconstruction, implementation of national policy with respect to the protection of black political rights in the South was thus in the hands of an administrative agency that was not only relatively new but for the most part decentralized in its organizational structure and bureaucratically unprepared to handle efficiently such an important and complex task. Thus, along with Supreme Court pronouncements, congressional legislation, and the policies of the Republican party, a significant factor in the enforcement of franchise rights for the freedman after 1877 were developments involving the centralization and bureaucratization of the Justice Department during these years.

The term "bureaucratization" as used in this study refers to the increased systematization and rationalization of procedures and policies of that branch of the federal government involved in the administration and enforcement of governmental policy and laws.[1] In this instance, the specific segment of the federal government being considered is the Department of Justice and the administration of federal policy and laws with regard to voting rights in the South.

With few exceptions, administrative history of the nineteenth century in the United States has generally been a neglected area of critical study. This neglect is especially evident in considering the role of the administration of justice in American constitutional history in the last quarter of the nineteenth century. In his work, usually considered definitive, on administrative history in the years between 1876 and 1900, Leonard White does not even mention the Justice Department and makes only one minor reference to the office of the attorney general. Although political scientists and lawyers have begun to deal with such relevant questions as how laws are enforced, and the actual impact of judicial decisions, historians have for the most part ignored dealing with law enforcement in its constitutional setting, and with the development agencies and organizations, such as the Justice Department, involved in the law-enforcement process.[2]

The present study also maintains that the administration of justice is an important indicator of the degree of complexity of the governmental bureaucracy. Despite increasing nationalization of economic, social, and political variables in late nineteenth-century America, the administration and enforcement of federal law and federal justice, particularly in matters of a political nature such a voting rights, remained to a great extent in a state of decentralization. Or, in other words, the activities of the Justice Department and local department officials after 1877 continued to be guided and influenced as much by local conditions and pressures in the South as by factors of national politics and federal constitutional law. The eventual disfranchisement of black voters in the South by the twentieth century is not only of political and constitutional significance then, but of administrative significance as well. And the burden of administering the laws guaranteeing the political rights of the freedman after the end of Reconstruction rested directly with the Justice Department. Therefore, in attempting to understand how the department carried out its responsibilities in this area, it is necessary to examine the development of the office of attorney general up to 1870, and the creation that same year of the Department of Justice as an organized federal executive agency.

The Constitution of 1787 made no explicit provision for either a presidential cabinet or a federal administrative bureaucracy. The Constitution did, however, provide Congress with the obligation of creating an entire judicial system for the new nation. This mandate was fulfilled with the passage of the Judiciary Act of 1789. This act created the Supreme Court, consisting of a chief justice and five associate justices, an entire system of lower federal circuit and district courts, and the jurisdictional boundaries of these various courts. In addition, the Judiciary Act called for the appointment by the president of

> a meet person learned in the law to act as attorney-general for the United States, who shall be sworn or affirmed to a faithful execution of his office; whose duty it shall be to prosecute and conduct all suits in the Supreme Court in which the United States shall be concerned, and to give his advice and opinion upon questions of law when required by the President of the United States, or when requested by the heads of any of the departments, touching any matters that may concern their departments, and shall receive such compensation for his services as shall by law be provided.[3]

The same section of the act creating the office of the attorney general also provided for the appointment of a government attorney for each of the federal court districts. To be selected would be "a meet person learned in the law to act as attorney for the United States . . . to prosecute . . . all delinquents for crimes and offenses, cognizable under the authority of the United States, and all civil actions in which the United States shall be concerned." To assist these district United States attorneys in enforcing the legal processes of the federal government, a marshal was also to be appointed for each district. It is important to note, however, that in this legislation the attorney general was not given any sort of control over the district attorneys and marshals. Finally, the appointment of all these officials, as was true for federal judges, was in the hands of the president, with the advice and consent of the Senate.[4]

President George Washington appointed Edmund Randolph

of Virginia as the first attorney general. As attorney general, Randolph had absolutely no staff to assist him and received a salary of only fifteen hundred dollars, which he had to supplement with continued private legal practice in order to earn a living. The Judiciary Act did not give the attorney general cabinet-level status. Indeed, the presidential cabinet was itself an extraconstitutional development, begun under Washington's first administration, and not recognized as a body until 1793. At first, the attorney general was responsible for assisting cabinet members as well as the president. However, upon Washington's invitation Randolph began attending cabinet meetings, and from then on attorneys general were considered part of the president's cabinet. Despite cabinet status, Randolph had no illusions about the importance of his office. In 1790 he described the attorney general as "a sort of mongrel between the State and the U.S.; called an officer of some rank under the latter, and yet thrust out to get a livelihood in the former."[5]

During the next sixty years following Randolph's appointment as the first attorney general, changes in the operation and organization of that office were the result of the initiative and efforts of several individual attorneys general. Although at various times during these years Congress considered legislation aimed at creating a centralized legal department for the federal government, such measures more often than not simply became piecemeal additions to the duties and responsibilities of the attorney general himself. In 1800, for example, the fifteen hundred dollar salary enjoyed by Randolph and his successors was increased to three thousand dollars. Yet, it was not until the 1850s that the salary of the attorney general was put on a par with that of the other cabinet officers.

The first incumbent to make a significant contribution to the development of the attorney general's office was William Wirt, who, like Randolph, was from Virginia. Wirt was appointed attorney general in October of 1817 by President James Monroe. Upon assuming office, Wirt discovered that in the twenty-seven years that had passed since Randolph had been attorney general, the office had continued to remain a "one-man operation." There was no office staff to assist the attorney general, no system of record keeping, and no provision for the preservation of letters and documents. There was nothing, in fact, to tell Wirt how past attorneys general had performed their duties, or to aid him in guiding future office holders in their activities. Wirt wistfully concluded that "the gentlemen who have held this office in succession, have been in constant danger of being involved themselves, and involving the departments which depended on their counsel, in perpetual collisions and inconsistencies; exposing the government to that kind of degradation which never fails to attend an unsteady and contradictory course."[6]

Attempting to bring some order to his office, Wirt secured from Congress authorization to hire a clerk to assist him in his duties, as well as a sum of money to be used for stationery and office expenses. He also instituted a system of letter-books, in which correspondence to and from the attorney general would be recorded. Wirt was particularly concerned with the fact that the various opinions given by past attorneys general to the president and department heads had never been preserved in any orderly fashion. To remedy this situation he sketched out a plan whereby the official opinions of the attorney general would be recorded, along with the requests and documents for such opinions by the president and the other department heads. Wirt's system became the basis for the official publication of the attorney general's opinions, although the first published volume of such opinions was not until 1841, seven years after Wirt had died.[7]

Wirt also recognized that the actual functions of the attorney general had expanded far beyond the original duties for that office set out by law in the Judiciary Act of 1789. According to that act the attorney general was limited in his right to give official opinions to cases where he was requested to do so by the president and the heads of the various other cabinet departments. However, in the years since the act was passed, requests for legal advice and direction had been received from a variety of other sources, including the district attorneys and marshals, collectors of customs, collectors of public taxes, and even by military courts martial. Wirt felt that opinions should be given in these instances as a matter of right on the part of the attorney general, and that to make it a matter of right it would be "expedient to have it provided for by law."8

Although Wirt favored the expansion of the attorney general's responsibilities in some circumstances, he was unwilling to see such extensions in certain other cases. In 1820 Wirt refused a request for a legal opinion by the House of Representatives, basing his refusal on the duties of his office as set forth in the 1789 act. By the terms of that act, Wirt now argued, the duties of his office were quite specific and definite. To be

> instrumental in enlarging the sphere of . . . official duties beyond that which is prescribed by law, would, in my opinion, be a violation of this oath [of office]. Under this impression I have, with great care, perused all the documents which have been handed to me in this case, for the purpose of ascertaining whether this order with which I have been honored from the House of Representatives falls under either head of my official duties; and it appears to me that it does not. A reference to the law will show, I think, that this is indisputably clear.9

Congress had provided legislation in the 1820s requiring the attorney general to reside in Washington, although Congress did not prevent the attorney general from engaging in private legal practice to supplement his income. Wirt was explicit in his criticism of this situation. He complained that "even under the duties, as they now exist, very *little time* is left to the Attorney General to aid the salary of his office by individual engagements," and believed that this explained why a good number of his predecessors had resigned. Wirt himself maintained as much of his own private practice as possible, though as the duties of the office increased he was less and less able to do so. In some instances he was able to supplement his income by representing the federal government in lower courts outside of Washington.10

Another area where Wirt was not willing to see an expansion of the duties of the attorney general was in regard to the direction and control of the district attorneys. Once again going back to the 1789 Judiciary Act, Wirt contended that his duties did not include giving advice and opinions to the district attorneys "touching any matters that may concern their departments."

Wirt also based his refusal to control the district attorneys on another piece of legislation passed by Congress in May of 1915. This legislation created the office of "agent," to serve in the Treasury Department. This agent was responsible for overseeing the activities of the district attorneys, particularly in matters involving the collection of money or property in the name of the United States.[11]

Wirt thus refused to direct suits conducted by the district attorneys, as he was "very unwilling to create a precedent which shall incumber this burdensome office with duties foreign to it, and which seem to me to surpass the power of any human being to perform." Wirt felt that the responsibility for directing the district attorneys as to which suits should be brought on behalf of the government lay with the Treasury Department. He wrote:

> The Treasury Department sends to the district attorneys all orders for suits, and puts them in possession of all the facts and evidence necessary for the prosecution of these suits. But here, I apprehend, the duties of the Department stop; and it is no part of these duties to prescribe to the district attorney *the form of the action*, or the *form of the pleadings*: these are referred exclusively to his own learning; and it is for this reason that he is required to be a person *learned in the law*.[12]

Wirt served as attorney general for seventeen years, and when he resigned he left a substantial body of precedents upon which future attorneys general would build. Although it might be an exaggeration to say that Wirt "had chopped his way through a wilderness," it is nonetheless true that he was the first attorney general to recognize and appreciate the importance of that office, though he kept its bureaucratic organization to a minimum. Although he was hesitant about enlarging the powers of the attorney general, he was successful in defining and systematizing the developments in the office up to that time.

While Congress during these years did not give the attorney general statutory power to render opinions to all those officials and agencies that had requested them, it did, through a number of legislative acts, increase the various legal and administrative responsibilities of the attorney general. These new duties included such activities as advising treaty commissioners, validating titles to land purchased by the federal government, approving pension and land claims against the United States, and representing the government in the court of claims.[13]

However, other congressional legislation during this same period limited the authority and responsibilities of the attorney general. The most important example of this was the creation in 1830 of the office of the Solicitor of the Treasury. As discussed above, Congress had, in 1815, established the post of agent of the Treasury Department. The responsibility of that office was to direct the district attorneys in cases involving monetary claims for and against the federal government. The 1830 act transformed the position of agent into that of solicitor, and made the solicitor responsible for instructing the district attorneys, marshals, and other judicial officers in all matters in which the United States had an interest, pecuniary and otherwise. The solicitor of the Treasury was also given charge of all the financial accounts of these local officials, as well as those of all lower federal courts.[14]

Although "the Attorney General and the Solicitor of the Treasury conducted their business most amicably," the fact remained that the legal business of the federal government on the local level was being directed by an official other than the chief legal officer of the nation. This resulted in a tradition of independence on the part of district attorneys and marshals from any sort of centralized control by the attorney general's office in Washington. Even after the creation of the Justice Department and the reversion of most of the functions of the solicitor to the attorney general, the problem of central control by the attorney general over local federal officials would become an important one, particularly with respect to such questions as the enforcement of voting rights in the South. The tradition of local independence died slowly, and, as is argued below, this helped neutralize effective enforcement of black franchise rights after 1877.[15]

The other attorney general to make important contributions to the development of that office in the years before 1870 was Caleb Cushing. Appointed to the office in 1853 by President

Franklin Pierce, Cushing firmly believed that the position of attorney general of the United States was a fulltime job. In addition to taking up permanent residence in Washington and remaining there during the entire time he served, Cushing was the first attorney general to hold himself entirely to the duties of his office and not engage in private legal work. Part of the reason for this may have been that by 1853 the salary of the attorney general had been increased to four thousand dollars, a level equal to that of the other cabinet members.[16]

A year after his appointment, Cushing submitted to the president a full historical discussion of his office and the developments that had taken place with respect to that office to date. He began with an analysis of the Judiciary Act of 1789, and the duties of his office as prescribed by that legislation. There were only two. The first was to represent the United States in the Supreme Court, and the second was to give advice on questions of law. However, Cushing explained, since that time the office of the attorney general had expanded a great deal in terms of activities for which he was responsible. Though this expansion had been the result of rather piecemeal legislation by Congress, Cushing nevertheless concluded that the attorney general was "either directly, and by statute, either express or implied, the administrative head, under the President, of the legal business of the government."[17]

With such responsibility, Cushing felt that more comprehensive legislation was necessary to put the office of the attorney general on at least an organizational par with the other executive and cabinet departments. To this end Cushing made a number of suggestions for possible congressional action. He recommended that the attorney general be required to make "a periodic report" to the president and Congress on the activities and needs of the office. He also proposed that the attorney general be given the responsibility for granting pardons, and be in charge of the commissions of all public officers of the federal government whose office was of "a judicial character or relation." Finally, Cushing called for the attorney general to be given the responsibility of prosecuting all suits where the United States was involved, even if it was not a party of record in such a suit. The aim of all these proposals, Cushing explained, was "such modifications in the office as may render it really and effectively, as well as in theory, responsible for the law business of the Government."[18]

Cushing, like Wirt, was not always in favor of expanding the responsibilities of his office. While Cushing considered himself the "administrative head" of the government's legal business, he was unwilling to involve the office in matters affecting what he considered to be questions of "public policy and executive determination." In reply to a request by Secretary of War Jefferson Davis for an opinion as to whether some federal property seized by the city of Kenosha, Wisconsin, might be recovered by the government, Cushing explained that the attorney general had no power to decide whether or not the government should act. "The relation of the Attorney General to any one of the Executive Departments, in such questions, is that of counsel to client, to give advice as to the legal right, and instruct procedure, if desired, leaving all considerations of administrative exigency or expediency to the decision of the proper Department." In other words, the attorney general could determine if the government had the right to recover the land and how to go about doing so, but he could not decide on whether or not an attempt at recovery should be made.[19]

Cushing's most important contribution as attorney general was his body of official opinions. These opinions were both more numerous and more comprehensive than those of any attorney general who either preceded or followed him. In these opinions Cushing did not simply give a brief statement in reply to the questions presented to him, as had been the practice. Instead, he "usually presented a careful examination of the subject from every point of view." The result was that Cushing's opinions fill three entire volumes of over seven hundred pages each of the published *Official Opinions*. But perhaps more important, the scope of these opinions would provide future attorneys general with useful and complete precedents upon which to guide their own decisions. This too was a further step in the bureaucratization of the attorney general's office.[20]

Despite the efforts of individuals like Wirt and Cushing, the role of the attorney general and the organization of his office had not undergone much fundamental and comprehensive change during the first half of the nineteenth century. As of 1860 the attorney general "still maintained a very modest office on a slender budget." Other executive departments continued to seek advice and counsel from their own legal staffs in many instances, and whenever possible handled their own court proceedings. Since the district attorneys and marshals were by statute subject to the direction of the solicitor of the Treasury, these officials could expect little assistance from the attorney general's office, and often in seeking such help or information they were referred to other departments for instructions. This kind of thing worked both ways, as letters to local representatives of the federal government from the attorney general were often returned to Washington unanswered. In addition, the attorney general and his staff had no permanent offices of their own and were "housed first in one department then in another."[21]

The need for some basic and comprehensive change in the office and functions of the attorney general was made particularly apparent with the completion of the Civil War and the reconstruction of the nation which followed. During this period, the legal business of the national government increased markedly, due in part to the large number of pension, confiscation, and revenue cases brought about as a result of the war. Beginning in 1867, proposals for reform of the attorney general's office were introduced in Congress, and discussion, along with a congressional investigation, continued for three more years. Finally, on June 22, 1870, Congress approved an "Act to Establish A Department of Justice."[22]

The act creating the Justice Department reaffirmed the traditional functions of the attorney general, while giving him some "sweeping" new powers. The former duties for which the attorney general would maintain responsibility included such activities as approving public building plans; restoring destroyed federal court records; maintaining federal courthouses; promoting public health; codifying federal statutes; and naming, with congressional approval, the membership of federal boards and commissions. The department was also responsible for settling claims by or against the United States; supervising the use and sale of federal lands; handling internal revenue and customs matters; enforcing federal criminal and civil regulations; supervising all legal matters involving Indian affairs, the mail, immigration, and naturalization; and, generally, the "enforcement and protection of the rights and property of the United States."[23]

Along with a broader and more specific definition of the functions and areas of jurisdiction of the new department, the act provided for a substantial increase in the size of the attorney general's office. In addition to two new assistant attorneys general, provision was made for the appointment of "an officer learned in the law, to assist the Attorney General in the performance of his duties, to be called the solicitor-general, and who, in case of a vacancy in the office of Attorney General, or in his absence or disability, shall have power to exercise all the duties of that office." The solicitor-general was also given the responsibility of presenting oral arguments in the government's cases before the Supreme Court, a function formerly limited to the attorney general. In cases of particular interest or importance, the attorney general could still choose to appear before the Court himself to argue the case.[24]

The act also set out, and in some instances increased, the salaries for the various department officials, and directed that rooms in the Treasury building be made available to "accommodate the officers and clerks of the . . . Department." As proposed by Cushing earlier, the attorney general was now required to submit an annual report to Congress each January "of the business of the said Department Of Justice, and any other matters appertaining thereto that he may deem proper, including the statistics of crime under the laws of the United States, and, as far as practicable, under the laws of the several states."[25]

However, the most important change in the organization of the Justice Department was the supervisory powers given to the attorney general over the "conduct and proceedings" of the various district attorneys and their offices throughout the country, powers previously held by the solicitor of the Treasury. Not only did this supervisory power extend to legal matters, but the attorney general was also given control over the financial accounts of the district attorneys, marshals, their assistants, and the clerks and other officers of the courts of the United States.[26]

In sum, the 1870 act constituted a comprehensive and definite attempt at the increased centralization and organization of the attorney general's office. A "legal department" had been created and expanded, and the powers and duties held by a number of different executive departments had been placed under the authority of one central office. Yet, as Cummings and McFarland conclude, "the readjustments contemplated by the Department of Justice Act were disregarded. . . . [A] mere statute could not create a Department of Justice." According to these historians of the department, there were three problem areas which continued to plague the Justice Department in the ensuing years: interdepartmental relations; the supervising of the field forces; and the development of an efficient central organization.[27]

The problems of interdepartmental relations and the development of a central organization were mainly due to the fact that the various other executive departments, such as Interior and Treasury, refused completely to accept the idea of using the Justice Department for all legal matters. In many instances these departments continued to rely on their own legal staffs for advice. And despite statutory provisions to the contrary, district attorneys and their assistants would continue in many cases to seek advice and instructions from the various other departments, and the "departments were also disposed to retain their former practice of supervision over district attorneys."[28]

The lack of supervision by the attorney general over the activities of the local federal officials was the most crucial problem facing the department as it attempted to enforce voting rights in the South. Seventy years of independence had created an organizational resistance on the part of local authorities to any effective outside, centralized control. A good portion of the energies of the various attorneys general after 1870 would be directed at combating inefficiency, corruption, and simple inertia among district attorneys, marshals, and their staffs. These conditions, as will be seen, were widespread in the South. As a result, the

Justice Department was never entirely able to apply its full resources and powers to such important problems as voting rights enforcement.

In theory, the organizational structure of the Justice Department as of 1876 provided a clear framework within which the department could carry out federal policy and law enforcement at the local level. The jurisdictional boundaries of department officials in the states were based on federal circuit and district court lines. This was not a new arrangement, as the appointment of one federal attorney for each judicial district had originally been determined by the Judiciary Act of 1789, and Congress in 1870 had seen fit to continue that system. Each district had one district attorney and one federal marshal. Depending on the size and importance of the district, most districts also had one assistant district attorney and at least one deputy marshal. All southern states except Tennessee and Alabama had two federal districts; those two states had an additional middle district. The Fifth Judicial Circuit Court comprised the states of Texas, Louisiana, Mississippi, Alabama, Georgia, and Florida. Tennessee was part of the Sixth Circuit, along with Kentucky, Ohio, and Michigan. Virginia, North Carolina, and South Carolina were part of the Fourth Circuit, along with West Virginia and Maryland.

When it came to the enforcement of political rights by the federal government, local Justice Department officials could be supplemented with additional personnel. The Enforcement Act of May 1870 provided for the appointment of special election "commissioners" who would have the same powers of arrest, imprisonment, and bail as the district attorneys and marshals. No specific number of commissioners was set for any one district, but the circuit courts were authorized "from time to time, to increase the number of commissioners, so as to afford a speedy and convenient means for the arrest and examination of persons charged with violation of this [Enforcement] act." These commissioners were also empowered to appoint one or more persons to assist them in the execution of any warrants or other process. The commissioners and their deputies could also, to aid in the performance of any of their duties, call together a *posse comitatus* or summon such military or naval aid "as may be necessary to the performance of the duty with which they are charged."[29]

The establishment of the new department in 1870 and the enactment of the various enforcement laws within a short period of time created general optimism about the future success of government policies aimed at protection of black civil and political rights in the South. Under Attorney General Amos Akerman and "with district attorneys and marshals located throughout the country, the new Department of Justice had a potential network of agencies with which to enforce the provisions of the new law[s]."[30]

After the passage of the first Enforcement Act in May of 1870, prosecutions in the South by the department began almost immediately. According to Everette Swinney, the Justice Department made a "determined effort" between the years 1870 and 1877 at enforcing the voting rights granted the freedman by the Fifteenth Amendment. During these seven years approximately 3,600 cases were instituted by the department in the eleven states of the Old Confederacy. At least up until 1874 the department was fairly successful in securing convictions in these cases. In 1870 the government won seventy-four percent of its enforcement cases, and over the next three years was able to secure convictions in forty-one, forty-nine, and thirty-six percent respectively, of its cases involving the Fifteenth Amendment and the Enforcement Acts.[31]

In his study of the Justice Department and the enforcement of voting rights of blacks in the South between 1870 and 1877, Swinney concluded, "By 1877 the Negro vote had been largely neutralized and a solid Democratic South assured." Like many of the historians who preceded him, he used the presidential election of 1876 and the famous "Compromise of 1877" as a somewhat arbitrary cutoff date to end a particular period of historical development. The implicit conclusions of Swinney's arguments were that after 1877 the Justice Department no longer attempted to enforce voting rights in the South, and that after that date Republicans in the North and South were convinced of the inevitability of a South completely controlled by an all-white

Democratic party. However, as is argued in the succeeding chapters, the Justice Department continued to make an active attempt at the protection of black voting rights in the South after 1877, and this attempt was a reflection of the fact that at least up until the 1890s, Republican politicians continued to believe in the possibility and importance of a viable biracial Republican party in the South.

While the final outcome of the presidential election of 1876 would be determined ultimately by Congress and Republican and Democratic politicians, the Department of Justice was continually involved in the protection of voting rights in the South both during and after the campaign. As had been the case in the previous national elections of 1872 and 1874 since the passage of the Enforcement Acts, the approach of the 1876 presidential contest was marked by letters and reports to the attorney general from district attorneys and marshals in the South on the volatile conditions there. In general, these letters expressed concern for the safety of Republicans—black and white—at the upcoming elections, and usually included requests for additional marshals and even troops.[32] Intimidation and force against Republicans in the South began long before election day. In May 1876, U.S. Commissioner J. S. Waterman reported that a group of Democratic "roughs" had entered the offices of a Republican candidate in Petersburg, Virginia. Seeking a Republican politician by the name of "Books," the mob mistook one Daniel Butts, a black man and tenant of the building, for him and proceeded to "Beat and stamp[ed] him in an unmerciful manner; crying, 'Kill the d—d negro,' while they were beating him!" According to Waterman such incidents had made the negroes in that district "despondent"; further daily threats led them to believe "that the Democrats intend to override by force all civil authority and that no force of U.S. Marshals or Deputy Marshals will suffice to preserve order and protect the lives of the voters."[33]

As November approached, such violence continued. U.S. Marshal Charles P. Ramsdell reported that an October meeting of Virginia Republicans had been broken up by a gang of "Democratic toughs." Both the Republican congressional candidate Joseph Segar and a fellow speaker were beaten, and the latter was "burned by a pistol discharged at his head." Ramsdell noted that previous elections in Virginia "have been anything but orderly," and suggested that "troops can do no harm to well-disposed citizens, and in light of experience I am of the opinion that they will be needed. Their presence will be, I think, promotive of good order."[34]

Responding to such reports and requests for information and directions from federal officials in the South, Attorney General Alphonso Taft issued a Circular Letter to all United States marshals as to their responsibilities in the forthcoming elections. Taft, an Ohio attorney and father of William Howard Taft, had been appointed attorney general by President Ulysses S. Grant on May 22, 1876, after serving two months as Grant's secretary of war. Taft began his letter by explaining the jurisdiction of federal officers at elections generally. He noted that there was a difference between elections for state and local officials and those for members of Congress and presidential electors. Only in the latter kinds of elections did the United States government "secure voters against whatever in general hinders or prevents them from a free exercise of the act of voting."[35]

The Circular Letter also reminded the marshals and deputies of their responsibility of being present at places of registration and voting, and their right to call a *posse comitatus* should they have reason to believe that the peace was about to be, or had in fact been, threatened. One problem for which the attorney general provided a solution in his letter was the question of additional deputy marshals. The revised federal statutes passed after the *Reese* decision in 1873 allowed the appointment of special deputy marshals for election purposes in cities of over twenty thousand inhabitants. However, there were few such places in the South that could qualify for such extra deputies, despite the fact that it was in the South where such men might be needed the most.[36]

Taft's solution was based on an ingenious interpretation of the election statutes. He indicated that special deputies could be appointed to handle duties set out in other sections of the revised statutes, which did not include cities of twenty thousand or more inhabitants "in all states in which Sheriffs have a similar power." In other words, marshals in southern districts that did not include such urban areas could appoint deputies in those states where no state law limited the number of deputy sheriffs that could be appointed. Since the kinds of duties required of deputies in the sections of the revised election statutes concerned generally with federal elections were almost the same as those presented in the particular sections of those statutes dealing with elections in areas of twenty thousand or more inhabitants, these extra deputies would have almost the same responsibilities and powers as their counterparts in urban areas.[37]

The attorney general ended his letter of instructions to U.S. marshals with a strong affirmation of the supremacy of federal laws and federal officials over state law and state officials. He also expressed optimism about the ability of federal officials to secure peaceful and honest elections, and that in discharging the duties of their office these officials would "doubtless receive the . . . support of all good citizens of the United States in your respective districts."[38]

Despite the attorney general's optimism, and the presence of federal troops and extra deputy marshals, instances of intimidation, fraud, and violence against Republican voters in the South during the 1876 canvass were common. This was true for those southern states where final election returns were in doubt, particularly South Carolina and Louisiana.[39] According to U.S. Marshal Pitkin of New Orleans, only large numbers of troops in that city prevented massive violence during the election. Pitkin reported that due to the number of extra deputies appointed in the state at large, "the election proceeded quietly save in 5 parishes where intimidation had been an organized institution for months."[40]

Irregularities in these five Louisiana parishes shed doubt on the slim majority received by Democratic presidential candidate Samuel J. Tilden and Democratic gubernatorial candidate Francis T. Nicholls. This situation became critical when it was made evident that the results of the presidential contest hinged on Louisiana's electoral votes. As a recanvassing of the votes began, both Republicans and Democrats set up their own state governments almost side by side in New Orleans, with each claiming to be the rightfully elected government of Louisiana.[41] This condition continued throughout December and January, while Justice Department officials in Louisiana called for federal troops to protect the Republican "government" under Stephen Packard, which was in a "state of siege" in the State House. The troops were never sent, and, with the report of the special Electoral Commission, the government of the state was peacefully relinquished to Nicholls and the Democrats, and all federal troops left New Orleans.[42]

Despite the intimidation, violence, and obvious violations of federal laws in not only Louisiana but most of the other southern states as well, the Justice Department was hesitant in the pursuance of prosecutions arising out of the November election. There are perhaps two reasons that explain this inaction on the part of the department. For one thing, between November and the inauguration of the new president in March, it was still uncertain as to whether a Democratic or Republican administration would be taking office. Amid this uncertainty, there was sufficient motivation for not taking such politically charged actions by a department connected with the Republican party. Furthermore, if the Democrats should win, then such prosecutions might well be discontinued anyway.

A second reason for the department's inaction can be found in the attitudes of Attorney General Taft. In early January 1877, Taft submitted his annual report to Congress. In his report he described "the spirit of insurrection in South Carolina, and in some other states in which colored voters are numerous." Taft blamed this spirit on the notion of the people in those states that the Fifteenth Amendment was a "blunder" and that southerners were "not bound to recognize or submit to it."[43]

While Taft did not believe that the amendment was a blunder or that southerners were not bound to obey its provisions, he was not convinced that what had taken place in the South was entirely the fault of those who did believe this. The vote of the freedman was being perverted, he maintained, because the freedman himself was insufficiently educated to exercise his rights intelligently. He explained:

> Without denying the inconvenience of having a large population of unintelligent voters, it is enough to say that the colored citizens have, under the Constitution, a clear title to the ballot, of which I know no fair or practicable way to deprive them. It is the duty of those who are more intelligent to aid in putting into operation a system of popular education which shall reach every class in every state. Universal education of the voting people, both white and colored, is essential to the safety of our republican government. No time should be lost in furnishing ample opportunities to every American citizen, of whatever complexion, race, or condition, to acquire sufficient mental and physical training to vote and to fight with intelligence.[44]

The abandonment of concern for black political rights implicit in Taft's report was not yet to be. Events in the winter of 1876–77 culminated in the election of a Republican, Rutherford B. Hayes, and an administration committed to the continued protection of the franchise rights of the freedman. In addition, the specific responsibility for this protection through the enforcement of the federal election laws rested still with the Department of Justice and the federal executive department official whose office Edmund Randolph had once characterized as a "sort of mongrel between the State and the U.S."

Notes

1. Peter Woll, *American Bureaucracy* (New York, 1963), chaps. 1 and 2; Max Rheinstein, ed., *Max Weber on Law and Economy and Society* (Cambridge, Mass., 1954), chaps. 5, 11, and passim.

2. Leonard White, *The Republican Era* (New York, 1964). White also ignores the office of attorney general in all his earlier studies of nineteenth-century administrative history. Aside from the general survey provided by Homer Cummings and Carl McFarland's *Federal Justice: Chapters in the History of Justice and the Federal Excutive* (New York, 1937), the only major recent work dealing with the question of law enforcement before the Civil War is Stanley W. Campbell, *The Slave Catchers: Enforcement of the Fugitive Slave Law, 1850–1860* (New York, 1970). For studies dealing with post-Civil War law enforcement and

the federal government, see, as well as Cummings and McFarland's *Federal Justice*, Everette Swinney, "Enforcing the Fifteenth Amendment, 1870–1877," *Journal of Southern History*, 27 (May 1962); Albie Burke, "Federal Regulation of Congressional Elections in Northern Cities, 1871–1894," *American Journal of Legal History*, 14 (January 1970); and Allen Trelease, *White Terror: The Ku Klux Klan Conspiracy and Southern Reconstruction* (New York, 1972). This neglect of nineteenth-century administrative and constitutional history has not been the case in English history. For a comprehensive review of the literature in this area, see Roy McLeod, "Statesmen Undisguised," *American Historical Review*, 78 (December 1973), 1386–1405.

3. *U.S. Statutes at Large* 1 (1789): 75.

4. Ibid., 75–76.

5. Quoted in Henry B. Learned, *The President's Cabinet* (New Haven, Conn., 1912), 109. For discussion of the development of the presidential cabinet, see C. C. Thach, *The Creation of the Presidency, 1775–1789* (Baltimore, 1969); and Carl B. Swisher, *American Constitutional Development*, 2d ed. (New York, 1954), 61–63.

6. William Wirt to Hugh Nelson (chairman of the House Judiciary Committee), in John P. Kennedy, *Memoirs of the Life of William Wirt* (Philadelphia, 1850), 2:59.

7. Learned, *The President's Cabinet*, 171–72. The first volume of published opinions began with those given out by Wirt during his tenure in office.

8. Kennedy, *Memoirs*, 69.

9. 1 *Official Opinions of the Attorneys General of the United States* (Washington, D.C., 1852), 335. (Hereafter cited as *Opinions*.)

10. Kennedy, *Memoir*, 61.

11. 1 *Opinions*, 611.

12. 1 *Opinions*, 611–13.

13. Cummings and McFarland, *Federal Justice*, 153–54.

14. 4 *Statutes at Large*, 414–16.

15. Cummings and McFarland, *Federal Justice*, 147.

16. Clause M. Fuess, *The Life of Caleb Cushing* (New York, 1923), 2:137; Learned, *The President's Cabinet*, 177–78.

17. 6 *Opinions*, 349.

18. 6 *Opinions*, 326–55.

19. 7 *Opinions*, 576–78. According to Cushing's biographer, however, Cushing had a rather "lofty" conception of the office of attorney general, and as the "mouthpiece" of Pierce's administration made the attorney general the "great, controlling, supervising office" of that

administration. (Fuess, *Life of Cushing*, 137.)

20. Ibid., 137 and 178.

21. Cummings and McFarland, *Federal Justice*, 219–22. See also Lloyd M. Short, *The Development of National Administrative Organization in the United States* (Baltimore, 1923), 184–95; and Luther Huston, "History of the Office of Attorney General," in *Roles of the Attorney General of the U.S.*, ed. Luther Huston, et al. (Washington, D.C., 1968), 5–6.

22. 16 *Statutes at Large*, 162; Cummings and McFarland, *Federal Justice*, 222–29.

23. Ibid., 225.

24. 16 *Statutes at Large*, 162.

25. Ibid.

26. Ibid. In 1851 the management of the accounts of local federal officials was taken from the solicitor of the Treasury and given to the newly created Department of Interior. Cummings and McFarland, *Federal Justice*, 148–49, and 225.

27. Ibid., 487.

28. Ibid., 260–61. During the 1870s and 1880s, the problem of interdepartmental relations was especially the case with respect to the Justice Department's handling of unauthorized removal of timber from federal lands and the prosecution of illicit distillers. In these cases the interests and activities of the department often collided with those of the Interior and Treasury departments, which also claimed some authority in these matters.

29. 16 *Statutes at Large*, 142–43.

30. Cummings and McFarland, *Federal Justice*, 231.

31. Swinney, "Enforcing the Fifteenth Amendment," 204. It should be noted that Swinney's percentages included convictions in Kentucky, Maryland, West Virginia, and Missouri as well. According to Swinney, and based on the annual reports of the attorneys general for the years 1870 to 1877, the breakdown of prosecutions instituted by state are:

South Carolina	1,387	Florida	41
Mississippi	1,175	Texas	29
North Carolina	559	Virginia	16
Tennessee	214	Louisiana	4
Alabama	134	Arkansas	3
Georgia	73		

32. U.S. Attorney Lewis to Attorney General Taft, Sept. 16, 1876,

Source-Chronological Files, R G 60, National Archives. (Hereafter cited as *Source Files*.)

33. Waterman to Taft, May 24, 1876, *Source Files*; U.S. Marshal J. H. Pierce to Taft, Sept. 13, 1876, *Source Files*; Samuel Phillips to W. H. Smith, Oct. 9, 1876, *Source Files*.

34. Ramsdell to Taft, Oct. 23, 1876, *Source Files*.

35. Robert Sobel, ed., *Biographical Directory of the United States Executive Branch, 1774–1971* (Westport, Conn., 1971), 313. Attorney General Taft to U.S. Marshals, Sept. 4, 1876, *Letters Sent by the Department of Justice: Instructions to U.S. Attorneys and Marshals*, RG 60, National Archives. (Hereafter cited as *Instructions*.)

36. *U.S. Revised Statutes*, 5506–32.

37. Taft to U.S. Marshals, Sept. 4, 1876, *Instructions*.

38. Ibid.

39. George B. Tindall, *South Carolina Negroes, 1877–1900* (Baton Rouge, La., 1966), 11–14; William I. Hair, *Bourbonism and Agrarian Protest: Louisiana Politics, 1877–1900* (Baton Rouge, 1969), 3–13. See also Albert D. Kirwan, *Revolt of the Rednecks: Mississippi Politics, 1876–1925* (New York, 1961), 5–8; and Frenise Logan, *The Negro in North Carolina, 1876–1894* (Chapel Hill, N.C., 1964), 10.

40. Pitkin to Taft, November 1876, *Source Files*.

41. Pitkin to Taft, Dec. 14, 1876, *Source Files*; H. Dibble to Attorney General Devens, March 7, 1877, *Source Files*; Hair, *Bourbonism*, 5–8.

42. Pitkin to Taft, Dec. 14, 1876, Jan. 9, 1877, *Source Files*; Packard to Pitkin, Jan. 29, 1877, *Source Files*; Hair, *Bourbonism*, 8–13.

43. U.S. Congress, House Executive Documents, *Report of the Attorney General*, 44th Cong., 2d sess., 1877, pt. 20:13.

44. Ibid. For Taft's activities during the disputed election crisis, see C. Vann Woodward, *Reunion and Reaction: The Compromise of 1877 and the End of Reconstruction* (New York, 1951), 115–16.

3

The New Department and the New Departure: Voting Rights Enforcement under Hayes, 1877–1880

THE POLITICAL BACKGROUND and events of the presidential election of 1876 and the resulting Compromise have been extensively examined by historians. Democrats, along with dissident Republicans, accepted Rutherford B. Hayes's election as president in return for the removal of the remaining federal troops in the South, the appointment of a southerner or of southerners to Hayes's cabinet, and the promise of federal money for a program of internal improvements in the South, particularly money for Mississippi River levees and subsidies for the construction of the Texas & Pacific Railroad.[1] The principal participants in this "bargain" were northern Republican politicians and southern conservative Democrats, or Bourbon Democrats as they were more often called. These Bourbon Democrats, for the most part the lineal descendants of Henry Clay and the southern Whigs, comprised the leadership of the Redeemer movement, which by 1876 had recaptured political control from the Reconstruction carpetbagger governments in every southern state except Florida, Louisiana, and South Carolina.[2]

What these Redeemers in the South shared with their Republican counterparts in the North was a "middle-class, industrial, capitalistic outlook." This outlook aimed at the economic, as well as political, normalization of the South now that the war and Reconstruction were over. For Republicans this did not mean that the freedman in the South was to be abandoned. On the contrary, many believed along with then Congressman James A. Garfield that "the constitutional rights of the negro shall be as safe in the hands of one party as it is in the other; and that thus in the south as in the north men may seek their party associates on the great commercial and industrial questions rather than on questions of race and color."³ Thus, as C. Vann Woodward has suggested, the Compromise of 1877 "did not mean that the Republicans had given up the hope of controlling the voting strength of the freedman for party advantage. It only meant that the Carpetbaggers had proven an ineffective means of controlling those votes and that it was hoped that the old masters might be more resourceful in accomplishing the same end."⁴

The combination of sectional conciliation and concern for the rights of the freedman on the part of Republicans was known as the "New Departure." The major architect of the New Departure policies was Hayes. Both as candidate and president, Hayes supported the enforcement of the three Civil War amendments and believed that no enduring peace between the sections was possible unless the rights of the freedman were safeguarded. As a young attorney in Cincinnati, Hayes had defended fugitive slaves seeking their freedom. By 1866 Hayes supported the franchise for blacks in the South. He stated that "universal suffrage is sound in principle, the radical element is right." And while he had had reservations about the "ultra measures" of the Radicals of his party during Reconstruction, he was sympathetic to their goals of political and civil equality for blacks.⁵

After his election as president, Hayes continued to stress the themes of sectional conciliation and protection of black rights. In his inaugural address he declared: "[T]he permanent pacification of the country upon such principles and by such measures as will secure the complete protection of all its citizens in the free enjoyment of all their constitutional rights is now the one subject in our public affairs which all thoughtful and patriotic citizens regard as of supreme importance." And in his diary he wrote that the American people "want peace—they long for repose. What is required is First that for the protection and welfare of the colored people the 13th, 14th and 15th amendments shall be sacredly observed and faithfully enforced according to their true interest and meaning."[6]

However, during the early part of his administration Hayes was apparently more concerned with conciliation between the sections and fulfilling his part of the Compromise. He withdrew the remaining federal troops from Louisiana and South Carolina, and appointed David Key, a Democrat from Tennessee, as his postmaster general. In addition, Hayes was also aware of the need to consolidate his support from within his own party. In this regard he was "determined" to include in his cabinet a Massachusetts man as well as a southerner. Therefore, the president was sympathetic to the recommendations of Massachusetts Republican and former attorney general, Ebenezer R. Hoar, that Charles Devens of that state be given a place in the cabinet. Though Devens rejected Hayes's initial offer of the position of secretary of war, he did accept the post of attorney general and took office on March 12, 1878.[7]

As attorney general, Devens supported the New Departure policies which called for the protection of the freedman in the south.[8] With his very first instructions to local federal officers in the South, Devens called for a vigorous enforcement of franchise rights and directed that "violators of the election laws where they have made themselves amenable to punishment under the Statutes of the United States should be brought to trial." He also indicated that it would be the duty of all district attorneys "to prosecute all persons charged according with the forms of law with criminal violations . . . and that in these prosecutions he is to know no sect or party and have nothing to do with any political considerations in the trial of such offenses. He must look to the law and by that he must be guided."[9]

The attorney general was well aware of the fact that the election laws were considered by many to be highly political and "that no case under them can be tried without inciting more or less political feeling." He continually reminded local officials that their actions and prosecutions should appear to be as nonpartisan as possible, and that there should be "no grounds to reproach the Government with acting in a severe or vindictive spirit towards any citizen or party." However, he also made it equally clear that "the law must not be disregarded and made of no effect."[10]

Although willing to provide assistance in the prosecution of franchise violations, Devens also put district attorneys in the South on notice that the major responsibility for the prosecution of such cases rested with them. "I have always thought," Devens wrote, "instructions to officers of the Government unnecessary in cases of plain and palpable violations of the law." District attorneys were advised to carry through on those prosecutions they felt had the best chance of success, and in those cases where the evidence was strongest. The decision as to which cases might succeed and which had the strongest evidence to support the government's case was left to the district attorneys. "They cannot be tried in the office of the Attorney General. In these cases and generally the United States Attorney must take the responsibility of their management and disposition."[11]

Between the time that Devens took office in March of 1877 and the congressional elections of 1878, the Justice Department was involved in one major series of prosecutions in the South which did arise out of the 1876 election. These prosecutions originated in Mississippi from a number of incidents collectively known as the "Kemper County outrages." The fact that in the 1875 state elections the Democrats virtually captured the state government did not preclude the massive use of fraud and intimidation against blacks and white Republicans in the November 1876 presidential contest. Largely as a result of such fraud and intimidation, Tilden carried the state by over 50,000 votes, and all six Democratic candidates for Congress were victorious. Under Luke Lea, United States district attorney for the Southern District of Mississippi, indictments were brought against approximately fifty persons from Kemper County for violation of the federal election laws. Between November, when the indictments were handed down by the circuit court in Jackson, and the beginning of March, almost nothing more was done by Lea with respect to the cases.[12]

Shortly after taking office as attorney general, Devens informed Lea that the latter's diligence and competence in protecting federal rights had come under serious question, and that Lea's continuance in office would "depend in a great measure upon the energy with which the interests of the United States are hereafter protected by you." Devens ordered Lea to stop bombarding Washington with appeals for directions and advise and to get on with those duties and responsibilities "which properly belong to your office," particularly the prosecution of the pending election cases.[13]

Having upbraided the district attorney for not taking more vigorous action, Devens issued a Circular Letter in early April to all district attorneys informing them of the failure of Congress to make sufficient appropriations to defray the department's expenses for the remainder of the fiscal year. Devens directed that "the expenses for the United States Courts for the remainder of the year . . . be reduced to the lowest practicable limit." Complying somewhat eagerly with this letter, Lea had all pending cases under his direction, including the election cases, continued until the November term of the circuit court.[14]

In late April the Justice Department again became actively involved in Kemper County, this time as the result of the "barbarous" murders of Judge W. W. Chisolm and a man named Gilmer. At the time of their murders both men had been under arrest and were being held by the county sheriff because of their supposed involvement in the November election cases. The evidence indicated that they were murdered in order to prevent them from testifying on behalf of the government when the cases came up for trial. Devens hoped that state authorities would take action in finding and prosecuting the murderers since the two men were not under federal control at the time of their slayings. When no such action appeared forthcoming, Devens concluded that it had become necessary "for the United States to do that which is proper for the protection of parties who were witnesses in its own courts."[15]

Anxious to secure convictions in at least these cases, Devens authorized the appointment of a special assistant attorney, R. A. Hill, to aid Lea in the prosecution of the murder cases.

Meantime, Lea maintained that further effort on the election cases was worthless, and "that a trial of them would generally be regarded as in mischievous conflict with the pacificatory policy of the Administration" and "would produce more evil than good." Thus, Lea had the November election cases continued until the following January. At that time the cases were finally brought to trial, and after a month-long trial they terminated in a verdict of not guilty for all defendants. Despite the verdict, Lea seemed to think that the result was a victory for the administration because the trial "was so conducted that the defendants gained no popular sympathy and it is hoped that more good than evil will result from it."[16]

If Devens thought that appointment of a special prosecutor to assist the district attorney would facilitate the prosecution of the Kemper County murder cases, he was mistaken. It was not until almost two years after the crime, on February 12, 1879, that indictments were finally issued against fourteen "of the more prominent actors" thought to be involved in the murders of Chisolm and Gilmer. Even then, Devens constantly had to prod Lea to arrest those indicated and bring them to trial. The cases were ultimately tried in 1881, unsuccessfully, after Devens had left office and by the time prosecutions arising out of the elections of 1878 and 1880 had become more important.[17]

Although the 1877 Mississippi cases were the only major involvement of the Justice Department during the first year of Devens's tenure as attorney general, they are a good illustration of some of the factors and problems relating to the enforcement of voting rights in the South after 1876. The attorney general was committed to a policy of enforcement of the election laws, and was even willing to provide extra assistance to local officials to effect such a policy. That he was reluctant to provide detailed direction in the handling of cases involving the violation of election laws was due less to his lack of commitment than to his probably logical assumption that local attorneys and marshals, almost all of whom were southerners, were closer to the situation and better aware of circumstances and how to handle them than the attorney general in Washington. Thus, with respect to voting rights enforcement, the problem of supervision of the field forces by the attorney general, discussed above, was a very real one. When confronted with a district attorney like Luke Lea, who was not only "totally inefficient . . . and unfit for his place" but openly dubious of the validity and usefulness of the election law prosecutions, the result was most often delay, inaction, and few convictions. However, as will be seen, both the commitment and attempts to enforce such protections continued.[18]

What one historian has termed the "acid test" for the New Departure policies of Hayes and many of his fellow northern Republicans came in the congressional elections of 1878. By this time, not only were all southern states in the hands of Democratic-Redeemer regimes, but Hayes and his policies toward the South were under attack from members of his own party. Much of this criticism came from former carpetbaggers and Republican stalwarts like Roscoe Conkling, James G. Blaine, and James A. Garfield, who accused the president of abandoning Republicans in the South with his policies of conciliation and noninterference, and of likewise abandoning the freedmen to their masters.[19]

Hayes was "most sensitive" to charges that his policies meant the end of federal protection of black civil and political rights in the South. His trip through the South in late 1877, as well as supportive communications from prominent blacks in the South, served only to further reinforce his views in these matters. However, events before and during the 1878 canvass helped convince even Hayes that southerners were responding to his attempts at sectional conciliation with simply more intimidation and violence against black and white Republicans, and that only more active federal protection would put an end to this situation. Indeed, "By the end of 1878 practically all major Republican leaders realized that the President's Southern policy had collapsed and that only a Solid North could prevent the Democrats from controlling the Nation."[20]

Prior to the November 1878 elections, the attorney general issued what by now had become a regular Circular Letter of instructions to local district attorneys and marshals as to their duties in the upcoming contest. Devens again called for the energetic enforcement of the federal election laws and suggested that all warrants issued for violations of the franchise laws be made returnable where the district attorney or his assistant could be present at the hearing to make sure that such warrants were indeed carried out.[21]

The 1878 elections also marked the first appearance of standardized instructions issued by a district attorney to local commissioners, election supervisors, and deputy marshals. A week after Devens issued his Circular Letter of election instructions, Charles E. Mayer, district attorney for the Northern and Middle Districts of Alabama, issued a general letter of instructions to all local federal officials in the state and a special letter directed to the United States deputy marshals. Election commissioners were ordered to give "prompt notice" to the district attorney of any offence committed "without regard to the supposed interest of any political party or candidate." Deputy marshals were also warned of the "delicate nature" of their duties and the fact that though they were to enforce the election laws vigorously, they must appear as nonpartisan as possible. According to Mayer, the purpose of the federal election laws was to enable every qualified voter the opportunity to cast his vote and to insure that that vote be counted honestly and fairly. "If this purpose be substantially obtained, slight and trivial violations of the law may be overlooked."[22]

Mayer was not specific as to what slight violations might be overlooked. He was, however, determined that the elections in November be honest and fair. Like a number of other southern district attorneys, Mayer felt that overt violence and intimidation would be less important than fraud as a means of controlling the freedman's vote. He believed that violation of the laws "will be confined to refusals to receive lawful voters; challenging voters with *intent* to delay *and* prevent voting; obstructing registration with like intent; placing false ballots in the boxes; falsely counting the ballots for false election returns and the willful and fraudulent throwing out by the County Supervisors, upon frivolous pretexts, of returns from the several precincts."[23]

Although Mayer was correct in thinking that fraud would become more common as a means of controlling the Negro ballot, physical intimidation of blacks and Republicans continued to occur. In late October district attorneys from Texas and South Carolina reported on instances of violence in their respective states, and prosecutions were begun before the first ballots were even cast.[24]

In Texas, seventeen citizens of Montgomery County were arrested for intimidation or what was called "bulldozing." The term bulldozing covered just about any crime from murder to simple verbal insult and intimidation. The only requirement was that it be directed at those men who refused to support the Democratic party and its candidates. As such, bulldozing was not confined to blacks or Republicans. Indeed, the Montgomery County outrages were directed against the Texas Greenback Party, which was organized for the most part by dissident white Democrats.[25]

On November 5, 1878, elections for members of Congress were held throughout the nation. The election results in the South were a bitter disappointment to northern Republicans. All Republican candidates for governor were defeated, and Republican representation in Congress from the South decreased from ten to three members. Despite hopes to the contrary, the Democratic party continued to be the party of the white man, and few of these were persuaded to switch their allegiance to the Republican banner. Compared to the 1876 results, Republicans showed a decrease in electoral strength in all parts of the South. This included the so-called Black Belt counties of the South where blacks comprised a solid majority of the population. In a newspaper interview shortly after the election, Hayes was forced to admit that his New Departure "experiment" had failed. "The first election of importance held since it was attempted has proved that fair elections with free suffrage for every voter in the South are an impossibility under the existing condition of things."[26]

The Democratic victories and the decline of Republican electoral strength in the South could be explained in large part by the numerous instances of intimidation, fraud, and violence against Republicans during the 1878 canvass. Reports on election law violations and various outrages were sent in to the attorney general from almost every southern state. Devens advised all district attorneys to proceed at once with all prosecutions in such cases. Although he cautioned district attorneys to select for special attention those cases where evidence was most clear, Devens intimated that the department would provide local officials with as much financial support as necessary to ensure the effective enforcement of the election statutes. To District Attorney Mayer of Alabama he indicated, "I have no doubt I can furnish ample means to try all the cases."[27]

While prosecution of election cases took place in every southern state after the 1878 elections, those in North Carolina, Texas, Georgia, Florida, Tennessee, Mississippi, Arkansas, and Virginia were on a smaller scale than prosecutions in Alabama, Louisiana, and South Carolina. In Madison County, North Carolina, use of fraud was reported to prevent blacks from voting. Old men were refused a ballot because they could not recall their exact age. Others were refused because they could not name *all* the candidates for office, or because they were paupers or inmates of the local poor house. And one man was not allowed to vote because his wife was out of town at the time. District Attorney J. M. Albertson promised prosecution of those election officials who engaged in such practices, as well as those officials responsible for secretly changing the boundaries of the polling stations and further preventing a number of registered voters from casting their ballots. However, by April of 1879 he had yet to find "sufficient evidence" even to begin prosecutions, and was certain that further effort was probably not warranted.[28]

Although the attorney general refused to instruct Albertson to press on with what the latter felt to be unnecessary investigations, he did make known his disapproval of the district attorney's views. Devens told Albertson not to "believe that such cases cannot be brought to a practical result, for I fear if you entertain this opinion, they will not reach one. You may rely upon it that the time has come in such States as North Carolina where there are many good men of both parties who see the danger to which they are drifting if they turn over their ballot boxes to ruffians who intimidate and to swindlers who cheat the people out of their votes." Despite the attorney general's warning, prosecution of election law violators in North Carolina did not come for some time.[29]

In Texas, prosecutions that arose out of the Montgomery County riots before the elections continued, along with additional ones based on election day incidents. District Attorney Baldwin was passionate in his desire to enforce the law and pledged that he would prosecute "those Montgomery County Bulldozers, until the highest law of the land says they are not amenable to U.S. law." A short time after making this promise, Baldwin died and his assistant, Colonel J. R. Burns, assumed control of the election cases. For his part, Burns promised a "prompt trial" of the cases he could easily handle "*alone.*"[30]

During the trials of those arrested for rioting, or bulldozing, Burns used arguments based not on the Fifteenth Amendment or the federal election laws, but on the right to free speech and its application to individual violations of that right through the Fourteenth Amendment. On this premise the sections of the Revised Statutes dealing with conspiracy to prevent the exercise of franchise rights were constitutional. If Congress could make no law abridging the freedom of speech and assembly, they could certainly make it a crime for individuals who might attempt to abridge those rights on their own. The Fourteenth Amendment provided that no state might abridge the "privileges and immunities" of its own citizens. According to Burns, the protections of free speech and assembly were among those privileges and immunities that the state could not abridge and that Congress could legislate to protect. This Congress had done—in those sections of the election laws that make it illegal for one or more persons to conspire to prevent or hinder "the free exercise or enjoyment of any right or privilege" secured by the Constitution. Burns argued that in addition to the specific right upon which the statute was based, the right to vote, free speech, and freedom of assembly were also covered. However, Burns's unusual constitutional arguments evidently made little impact on the judges and juries in East Texas in 1879. All thirty-six of the Montgomery County bulldozers were acquitted.[31]

In Arkansas, the practice of bulldozing seems to have crossed over state lines from East Texas. The 1878 elections in Arkansas were described by the U.S. marshal as a "farce" in which the only counties and districts where fraud was not practiced were those in which "Democratic majorities are so large as to render fraud unnecessary." Unfortunately, no prosecutions were ever brought by either of the two district attorneys in the state. Likewise, in Mississippi and Tennessee few warrants were ever issued against election law violators and even fewer cases were brought to trial.[32]

Prosecutions were carried through in Virginia and Florida, and in the latter state a number of convictions were obtained. The most important of the Virginia cases involved the removal of a special deputy marshal from a polling place by a policeman acting under the orders of state election officials. Since no fraud or any wrong doing was alleged to have been committed as a result of the deputy marshal's removal, the circuit court decided that the presence of such a deputy was not required by law except when called in for aid and protection by an election supervisor.[33]

In Jacksonville, Florida, the three members of the Brevard County returning board were convicted of certifying false returns in favor of the Democratic candidates. Both the district attorney and the attorney general were pleased that convictions in election cases had been obtained. Alva Knight, a Republican attorney from Jacksonville, predicted that the results of the Brevard County cases will have a "good effect" in that it might make "our friends in the North . . . arrive to the fact that there is no hope of a fair election in Florida only as the U.S. Courts are vigorous in punishing violations of the laws relating to the elections." The attorney general praised the efforts of District Attorney Stickney and directed him to urge the court to impose a prison sentence upon the defendants. "These offenses," Devens wrote, "were of unusual gravity and were evidently deliberately committed and if these persons escape with the lighter penalty which the fine inflicts, they would not seem to have received the punishment adequate to their desserts or sufficient to prevent a repetition of the crime should the occasion arise."[34]

In Alabama, prosecutions growing out of the 1878 elections

were somewhat more extensive than in the states discussed above. In that state fifty indictments covering about a hundred persons were handed down for violation of the federal election statutes. The major portion of the Alabama indictments were against Democratic election officials for secreting ballot boxes when the polls closed, and making the final count in locked quarters, where invariably a Democratic winner was announced. Because of the flagrant nature of the violations, District Attorney Mayer was optimistic about securing convictions in these cases. However, defendants' attorneys were able to hold up the trial of those indicted through the use of various dilatory pleas and motions.[35]

Although Mayer was able to have the trials begun, and to prevent the defendants' counsel from learning the names of the government's witnesses, he was not able to prevent the arrest of both himself and U.S. Marshal Turner by state authorities. Mayer was immediately released, but a writ of habeas corpus had to be obtained from the federal circuit court to secure the release of the marshal. The ostensible reason for their arrest was a number of minor debts owed by both men to local merchants. However, it was clear that the arrests were really only further attempts by local Democrats to obstruct the trial of the election cases.[36]

The first series of trials of these Alabama cases finally ended in May of 1879. They were a "great disappointment" to the district attorney. The jury had been unable to reach a verdict, and all of the defendants were discharged. In attempting to explain the result, Mayer blamed the outcome on "race prejudice." The defendants were all white men and the government's witnesses were all black men. The jury was composed of ten white men and two Negroes. Because the white men on the jury belonged to both political parties, according to Mayer, "I therefore thought that I had reason to expect a verdict in accordance with the evidence. The arguments for the defence showed that race prejudice was their main reliance and the result proved that their judgement was better than mine."[37]

Trials involving the Alabama election cases continued for the rest of the year under Mayer's direction and the attorney general's support. Convictions in these cases were unfortunately rare, despite the obvious efforts of the district attorney. The major reason for the lack of convictions was the impossibility of getting the entire jury to agree on a guilty verdict. While Mayer admitted that the juries were generally impartial, he also agreed with defendants' supporters claims that the juries were "fucked," although for opposite reasons. For the defendants, Republicans on the juries made the panels suspect. For Mayer, the presence of Democrats prevented the unanimity needed for convictions. By the end of 1879 the once optimistic district attorney was convinced that the obstacles to successful prosecution of violators of the election laws were "insufferable." Although he pledged continued efforts in obtaining convictions, he did so in the knowledge that a guilty verdict in such cases in his district was a near hopeless thing.[38]

Yet, the most important prosecutions arising from the congressional elections of 1878 were those in Louisiana and South Carolina. The outrages against blacks and Republican voters in these two states were of such proportions as to call for a congressional investigation, and in his annual message on December 2, 1878, President Hayes made specific mention of events in South Carolina and Louisiana as supporting the conclusion that "the rights of the colored voters have been overridden and their participation in the elections not permitted to be either general or free."[39]

In Louisiana, the 1876 elections had not meant total victory for the state's Democrats. Republicans still held a number of state offices, as well as local parish positions, and they made up a "sizeable minority" in the state legislature. As a result, the ensuing eighteen months after the 1876 elections were marked "by frenzied activity as the Democrats organized their forces for the election of 1878, by means of which they planned to regain control of other branches of the State government." Given these conditions, it was only natural that voter manipulation, peaceful or otherwise, might be expected.[40]

Incidents of violence and intimidation against Republicans began long before election day. Three months before the election the attorney general was made aware of what was happening and directed the district attorney in New Orleans, A. H. Leonard, to investigate possible crimes already committed and prepare for future violations of the election laws. Reminding Leonard of the Supreme Court's decision in *U.S. v. Reese*, Devens noted that "the great difficulty since the recent decision of the . . . Court is [establishing] the proof that the outrage was committed on account of race, color, or previous condition of the person injured, but it would seem that when so many occurrences of this nature takes [sic] place where the parties outraged are always black, in some cases evidence might be found to bring the cases under the United States laws."[41]

The results of the November 5th canvass was a Democratic landslide. All six Democratic candidates for Congress were victorious, and Democrats regained control of almost all local and parish governments, and further increased their majority in the state legislature. The largest Democratic victories were in parishes where black voters outnumbered whites, and it was argued by some that blacks in these parishes had simply supported the Democratic ticket. Any evidence of this is nonexistent. What really took place in these areas was "a carefully planned and relentlessly executed political 'reign of terror.'"[42]

Letters to the attorney general's office in Washington indicated the degree of fraud and violence practiced against Republicans. Henry Adams, a black Republican leader from Shreveport, reported that "they are killing our race by the hundreds every day and night and the white Southern Republicans are not allowed any more showing about political matters than the poor colored peoples." And a petition from the Citizens Conservation Association detailed instances of violation of the election laws and claimed there was enough evidence for between two and three thousand instances of fraud. The association blamed not only the Democrats for the fraud committed, but also criticized the U.S. marshals and their deputies for disregarding "plain violations" of the laws and refusing to make arrests of those even suspected of engaging in fraud or intimidation.[43]

Devens responded by directing District Attorney Leonard and U.S. Marshal Wharton to begin immediate and extensive investigations of the reported outrages, which Devens believed to be "of the most open and infamous character." He felt that there should be no problem in securing evidence, and suggested that the district attorney and the marshal concentrate their efforts on those "who have been leaders rather than those who have been followers." Finally, Devens reminded them that "large sums of money have been furnished you to obtain a fair election in Louisiana. If it has not been obtained there should be at least sufficient evidence in your possession to bring to justice those who have violated the elective franchise. . . . I expect of you resolution in vindication of the laws of the United States."[44]

Marshal Wharton immediately began his investigations into the alleged outrages. To assist in these investigations, the attorney general authorized the hiring of several private detectives and special deputies. In some of the parishes, the investigations by the marshal and his assistants were hampered by local quarantines "established for various purposes." However, by December 1st, the marshal was able to complete his report detailing the evidence found of the various violations of the election laws, and the district attorney forwarded a copy to Washington.[45]

Although fraud was practiced throughout the state, much of it centered in six parishes and the city of New Orleans. In Caddo Parish, fifty to seventy-five blacks were reported killed, many others and their families were driven from their homes, and widespread fraud and intimidation was used to keep them away from the polls. "The parish should have gone Republican by over 2000 majority but the Democrats openly took the election by force and fraud." In Natchitoches and Ouchita parishes, similar instances occurred and similar methods were used to overcome Republican majorities. In Morehouse Parish, intimidation was so intense that Republicans there were forced to abandon the canvass. In one instance a Republican candidate from Jackson Parish was simply driven out of the parish; Tansas Parish was "invaded by armed forces from Mississippi," resulting in the murder of several blacks and dispossession of many Republicans. Finally, in New Orleans it appeared that "fraud was substituted for violence and very little pains taken to conceal the fact."[46]

Shortly after the marshal's investigations were completed, a grand jury was convened in New Orleans to consider issuing indictments for violations of the federal election laws. But even while the grand jury met, efforts were made to hinder the proceedings. Two important government witnesses on their way to give testimony in New Orleans were taken off a steamboat near Caledonia, Louisiana, by a mob and then murdered.[47]

Acting on evidence "of a nature such as could not be disregarded," the grand jury issued indictments against 120 residents of New Orleans and the parishes noted above. The charges included preventing the special deputy marshals from discharging their duties, resisting registration of persons entitled to register, securing illegal votes and refusing legal votes, bribery, refusing to permit the attendance of U.S. supervisors at the polls, intimidation of voters, and conspiracies to drive Republican leaders from the parishes and keep Republican voters from the polls.[48]

Although District Attorney Leonard was confident that the cases could be brought to a successful conclusion and the guilty parties brought to justice under the election laws, he realized that the government's attempts would be "resisted" and that it was probable some of the witnesses summoned would be killed, as had happened near Caledonia. He asked for, and received, the assistance of a special prosecutor to aid him in the preparation and handling of the election cases.[49]

However, Leonard was wrong about the use of violence. The defendants were able to hire the "ablest" attorneys to represent them and these attorneys proceeded to pack the juries with Democrats and delay the trials with all manner of pleas, motions, and other dilatory tactics. Killing witnesses was no longer necessary. Despite a forceful and able prosecution by the district attorney, the first election case trials in March of 1879 ended in a "not guilty" verdict for all defendants. Devens was disappointed with the results of the trial but praised the district attorney for his honest efforts. In fact, none of the persons originally indicted by the grand jury was ever convicted. By 1880 the cases arising out of the 1878 congressional election were quietly allowed to be dropped, while new prosecutions were begun based on violations occurring during the 1880 presidential contest.[50]

In South Carolina, as in Louisiana, the 1876 elections had ended in the victory of a Democratic regime, but had not meant the end of the Republican party in the state. As governor, Democrat Wade Hampton pursued a policy of moderation with respect to Republicans and blacks, and appointed a number of Negroes to various state and local offices. Although Hampton's conciliatory policies converted some blacks to the Democratic party, the South Carolina freedmen for the most part remained loyal to the party of Lincoln. After 1876, however, the state Republican party began to be riddled with internal problems, and in 1878 did not even put forth a slate for state officers. Yet, national offices would be contested. In any case, the critical factor in the survival of the Republican party in South Carolina was the continued protection of black voting power and franchise rights.[51]

One of the major hindrances to effective enforcement of the federal election statutes in South Carolina, and thereby a factor in the further decline of the Republican party there, was the district attorney for the state, former Circuit Court Judge Lucius Northrup. Northrup was appointed to the post in August of 1877 by President Hayes, over the objections of many state and national Republican leaders. One of the most outspoken of Northrup's detractors was Assistant District Attorney William E. Earle. Claiming that he would be unable to serve under a man he described as "incompetent," Earle resigned two days after Northrup took office. Indeed, throughout his tenure in office Northrup would be subject to constant criticism, and much of it by members of his own Republican party.[52]

Troubles began in South Carolina before the 1878 election day. U.S. Marshal Wallace reported the arrest of several men involved in riots in Charleston at the beginning of October, and later that month a meeting of Sumter County Republicans was broken up by a band of Democratic "Red Shirts." According to Wallace, the situation in South Carolina was uncertain; although the Democrats had become "more circumspect" in their campaign activities, they were also becoming "more defiant in expressing their determination to crush the Republican party out of existence by force if necessary." The marshal expressed his determination to protect Republicans against outrages "whenever we can." The district attorney also promised faithfully to enforce the federal laws, though Attorney General Devens cautioned him to go carefully and not contribute to whatever political tensions might already exist. Northrup replied by telegram that he knew "the people with whom I deal and will be firm and prudent. Medicine strong but patient needs it. I will be very careful but not let anybody here know it."[53]

The prosecution of the early election law violations was badly handled; the marshal characterized the process as a "blunder from beginning to end." At the hearing for the defendants before the federal commissioner, the warrants were found to be too "indefinite" and the defendants were released. In addition, the deputy marshal had trouble locating and bringing in the government's witnesses, and in one instance brought in the wrong man who happened to have had the same last name as the witness sought.[54]

However, the elections of 1878 in South Carolina were held with little of the fatal violence that marked the elections in Louisiana. According to Northrup, the election was "not such an election as you would call peaceful; but peaceable for this climate, at this season." Instead of violence, massive fraud was used to secure Democratic victories. At one place in Charleston, where Northrup himself had voted, the polls were open from six in the morning until six in the evening, and the final count showed more than 3,500 votes for the Democratic ticket. Northrup figured that this meant someone had voted every thirteen seconds continuously throughout the day. However, the district attorney was not particularly enthusiastic about responding to this situation. "A great many complaints reached me," he reported to Washington, "and I suppose we shall do something in the way of arrest. . . . I shall try and put the government to no further expense than possible."[55]

Based on reports and information received by Northrup, warrants were issued and arrests made in Charleston, Sumter, Barnwell, Orangeburg, and Hampton counties. In the midst of these arrests, Northrup complained that the Republican press in the North was abusing him for not making enough arrests, and the local Democratic papers were castigating him "for making them by the wholesale." He thereupon asked the attorney general for permission to turn over the handling of all election cases to his assistant, E. W. MacKey, on the grounds that the district attorney had other important government cases to complete. Devens promptly refused this request and ordered Northrup to keep the election cases under his personal supervision. The attorney general also sent Northrup a special assistant prosecutor from Washington to assist in the election cases, and gave Northrup permission to hire a stenographer to take care of all the clerical work involved in the cases.[56]

Along with the hesitancy of the district attorney to deal with the election cases, active interference on the part of local Democrats also hindered enforcement of the election statutes. Witnesses and federal officers were subjected to harassment and worse. U.S. Commissioner Samuel Lee was arrested in Sumter on the charge that he had not kept his office as probate judge open every day as required by law. Having anticipated such a move against Lee, U.S. Marshal Wallace had an earlier warrant made out against Lee as a witness in the federal court. Lee was then removed from the jail in Sumter and taken to the jail in Columbia where he could be protected by federal deputies. In Kingstree, Camden, Columbia, Orangeville, and Blackwell counties, witnesses in the election cases were also placed under arrest by state authorities, most often on a charge of perjury. Wallace described the situation as one of "open rebellion" on the part of South Carolina Democrats, and vowed for his part to "keep up the fight" by securing writs of habeas corpus to have the jailed witnesses released.[57]

Throughout November, Northrup, MacKey, and Wallace spent almost as much time attempting to free witnesses and combat local opposition to their activities as they did in the actual prosecution of election crimes. As a result, few further warrants were finally issued compared to the number of crimes supposedly committed. The whole trouble, according to MacKey, was that "almost every democrat in the State approves and sanctions the frauds committed, believing that the end justifies the means, and violations of the election laws are not regarded as very serious offenses in this State—at any rate not sufficiently serious to warrant the arrest of any one." MacKey himself was arrested by state authorities on a charge of libel, and the district attorney had to go to the state court to plead his defense and obtain his release.[58]

In early December, 1878, the federal grand jury was convened in Charleston to consider whether or not to issue indictments against those charged with violations of the election laws at the November canvass. After meeting for almost two weeks, the grand jury handed down one series of indictments out of two "major" cases presented by the district attorney, and most of the minor cases presented were either continued until the following April term of the circuit court or dismissed. Northrup saw nothing particularly discouraging about these results, and contended that it was really too soon after the elections for these kinds of cases to be brought. Since new frauds were coming to light all the time, the district attorney felt confident that many more indictments would be issued at future terms of the court.[59]

The trial of those who were indicted began the following month, lasted two days, and ended in a mistrial. The defendants were Democratic election managers accused of permitting the use of "tissue-paper" ballots to secure an unusually large Democratic vote, larger in fact than the number of registered Democratic voters in the district. The "tissue ballot," or "kiss ballot" as it was more commonly known, was perhaps one of the most widespread and ingenious methods of fraud used by the Democrats in South Carolina and the South generally to secure a large Democratic vote. Essentially, a tissue ballot looked like a single normal Democratic ballot, but in reality was a number of thin identical ballots made of tissue and stuck loosely together. After the polls had been closed, it was contrived at some point to make sure that the ballot box was vigorously shaken or handled, causing the tissue ballots to separate. One hundred Democratic ballots, for example, suddenly became five hundred Democratic votes. To combat this type of fraud, federal election supervisors were required to make sure that the number of votes in the ballot box did not exceed the number of registered voters on the poll lists. When it did, they were blindfolded and drew out of the box only that number of ballots for which there were registered voters. However, this procedure was ineffective generally because the large number of tissue ballots cast guaranteed a substantial Democratic majority in any case.[60]

Because of the transparent nature of this fraud, Northrup was certain that convictions in such cases could easily be obtained. "The law," he declared, "seemed to be made for the tissue ballots and the tissue ballots for the law." In reality, the opposite was true. Convictions after the fact involving such methods were almost impossible to achieve. To rephrase the district attorney's own words, it seems that fraud was made for the tissue ballots and the tissue ballots for fraud.[61]

Having had little initial success in fulfilling his promise to enforce the election laws, the district attorney was pleased with the arrival in South Carolina of the special Senate committee investigating fraud and violence in the 1878 elections in the South. As indicated above, in his annual message to Congress on December 2, 1878, President Hayes had discussed the recent outrages against the election laws in the South, and had made specific reference to events in Louisiana and South Carolina. Hayes called for Congress to examine the conduct of the elections in these two states "as may be appropriate to determine the validity of the claims of members from these states to their seats." The same day as Hayes's speech, the attorney general issued his annual report, in which he discussed the various outrages that had taken place in the South against Republicans and blacks, particularly ballot-box stuffing, and asked Congress for increased appropriations with which to prosecute offenses committed against the federal election laws.[62]

On the same day as well, Senator James G. Blaine introduced a resolution in the Senate calling for an investigation of the alleged frauds in Louisiana and South Carolina. After some debate, the resolution passed on a straight party vote, and a committee was formed under the chairmanship of Republican Senator Henry M. Teller of Colorado. The committee left immediately for Louisiana, where it spent the next month taking exhaustive testimony and gathering data on the violence and fraud that had occurred in that state. The committee's findings of fact closely paralleled those made by Justice Department officials in that state.[63]

On January 20, 1879, the Teller Committee began its investigations in South Carolina. A week prior to this time, District Attorney Northrup sent out a printed statement to all United States election supervisors ordering them to forward to Northrup "the names and post office address of such persons, as you may know, who can give *material testimony, such as can be used in court,* concerning the conduct of the recent Congressional election in your district." The supervisors were also asked for their personal knowledge of facts concerning fraud, violence, intimidation, or any other unlawful means that may have been used to affect the outcome of the election. The district attorney intended to share this information with the committee, as well as use it for his own prosecutions.[64]

In addition to supplying the committee with information and witnesses, Northrup attended many of the sessions of the committee's hearings. Each day he would also send to the attorney general clippings from the local newspapers summarizing the day's proceedings and testimony. The committee finished its investigations at the end of January and, as was true in Louisiana, found widespread use of fraud by Democrats in order to achieve their electoral victories. Indeed, the committee determined that ballot-box stuffing had occurred in practically every county in South Carolina, and that this was probably the single most important factor in explaining the Democratic victories. They concluded: "There is great unanimity among the Republicans, both white and black, as to the fidelity of the colored people to the Republican party; and there is no testimony before the committee that will justify the conclusion that the Democrats, or that the Democratic vote can have been increased to the proportions claimed for it, and that must exist if the returns made of the late election are honest."[65]

Armed with the committee's findings and those of his own investigations, the district attorney prepared for the April trials of the election cases. Though Northrup was more confident of obtaining convictions in these cases, he admitted his frustrations in dealing with the whole question of the enforcement of the election statutes. He would have liked to have kept as "aloof" from politics as possible in these matters, and yet he stated that "I am not one of those who believe the Republican party is dead here. . . . Every vote is there yet. The thing necessary is to count it." Nor could he keep politics out of the courtroom, "The law is plain—the facts are plainer, but I can't make a white democratic juror believe colored witnesses nor force him to vote. I can't keep politics out of the human mind and I can't make the jury commissioners select more impartial men."[66]

In addition to the political problem, Northrup continued to be faced with intimidation and arrest of witnesses and Republicans by Democratic state officials in an effort to block the prosecution of the election cases. Of particular concern was the arrest and conviction of a black Republican by the name of Pendergrass. Pendergrass was convicted in the state courts of perjury growing out of testimony he had given before the grand jury in the election cases. Pendergrass was given a large fine, and in the event he could not pay the fine would have to spend two years in the state prison. In order to pay the fine and have him released, Northrup obtained a mortgage on the home of another local Republican leader. Similar instances of harassment occurred for as long as the prosecution of the election cases continued.[67]

The trials conducted during the April term of 1879 were not very successful. Of three election cases tried, convictions were obtained in only one. In one case, District Court Judge Hugh Bond had directed the jury to return a verdict of not guilty, but Northrup made a motion, which was accepted, to have the case continued until the following November. The district attorney again blamed the Democratic juries for the lack of convictions. The November 1879 trials of the election cases were even less successful; no convictions were obtained. The trials left Northrup with "little hope" that the election laws of the federal government could ever be enforced and "little probability of our ever securing a jury for the next four years, in which the defendants' right of challenge would not leave an entire Democratic panel." So convinced, Northrup finally resigned as district attorney in March 1881.[68]

Northrup's pessimism reflected the sentiments of many federal officials in the South, especially after the 1878 elections. While a good amount of time and energy had been expended in the enforcement of the federal election laws, the actual results in terms of convictions were not encouraging. Evidence was hard to secure. Witnesses, and officials as well, were persecuted and sometimes prosecuted by state and local authorities and private citizens. Juries refused to convict violators of the election statutes, and when they did, the maximum penalties allowed by the law were never inflicted.

Yet, the attorney general was insistent on the responsibility of the federal officials in the South to enforce the election laws vigorously and fairly. In cases where convictions were secured, Devens directed district attorneys to refrain from making any sort of bargain with defendants or their lawyers and to urge upon the judge "the propriety of giving imprisonment as the punishment." The constitutionality of the laws he was to enforce was not for him to decide. "No one but the Supreme Court has authority to pronounce a statute unconstitutional. Until it has distinctly decided the question it is in my opinion the duty of all inferior courts to hold the statute constitutional." Likewise it was the duty of all "prosecuting officers" of the United States to "proceed upon the theory that the statutes are constitutional."[69]

Devens was sensitive to the problems of enforcing the politically charged election laws in the South. Although willing to supply southern district attorneys with special assistant prosecuting attorneys to aid in the election cases, the attorney general was reluctant to send in such help from outside the South. Responding to a request from District Attorney Northrup of South Carolina for a "Northern lawyer" to assist in arguing the election cases before the court, Devens replied that sending a lawyer from the North "would tend to increase rather than allay any excitement against the prosecutions. We are not attempting with the ordinary forces of the United States in South Carolina, all of whom are natives of the State, to enforce on the soil of

South Carolina, the laws of the United States."[70]

The lack of sufficient funds also hampered Devens's attempts at enforcing franchise rights. The attorney general had promised several district attorneys that there would be ample funds to proceed with whatever prosecutions they thought necessary, while in fact the department had no such funds. Although the department in several instances did authorize money for the hiring of extra personnel and the like, the attorney general could just as often be found refusing such requests, and even calling for local department officials to reduce or be more careful in their expenditures because of the department's lack of sufficient appropriations from Congress.[71]

However, the problems of enforcement and the lack of convictions in election cases also reflected the failure of Hayes's New Departure policies. Events and developments in the South in late 1879 and the first months of 1880 were evidence of the fact that neither conciliation nor franchise rights protection had proven effective in rejuvenating southern Republicanism. And the final report of the special Senate committee investigating election frauds in Louisiana and South Carolina gave further convincing proof that the New Departure had not been working as it was supposed to.

The report concluded that elections in the two states were "neither fair nor free" and "that by violence and fraud the honest expression of the will of those entitled to vote was prevented, and thousands of citizens of those states deprived of the elective franchise." The committee believed that the critical issue was not one of home rule or reaction against carpetbag rule, but simply the refusal of the Democratic party "to tolerate opposition in any form." To achieve their ends, "by whatever means, and at whatever cost," they resorted to widespread violence, intimidation, and fraud. The committee also castigated the state governments of the two states for their total failure to punish those "who have thus wantonly murdered or outraged their citizens," and for their efforts at hindering federal officials and witnesses in federal election cases by arrest and the threat of arrest.[72]

The report called for the strengthening of the election laws by virtue of Congress's power under the Constitution to regulate elections for members of Congress. Such a power, the committee contended, "implies" the power to punish violations of such laws as Congress might pass to regulate these elections. "It will scarcely be contended—certainly it cannot be fairly claimed—that the national government is compelled to rely for the punishment of offenses against its own laws upon the laws of the several States. The statement of such claim is sufficient to show its absurdity."[73]

Both the committee's report and the results of the 1878 election had an effect on Congress, the president, and the Republican party. In Congress, during the months of January and February in 1879, a number of proposals were discussed with respect to the strengthening of the election laws and the reaffirmation of the three Civil War amendments. The only result of these debates was the passage of two resolutions, proposed by Senator George Edmunds of Vermont, which dealt with these two issues and which pledged Congress to some sort of future action.[74]

Congress did take action, but not in the way anticipated in Edmunds's resolutions. Thanks to the victories in the 1878 elections, the new 48th Congress that convened in March of 1879 had a Democratic majority. Using this majority, the House attached riders to the Army appropriations bill repealing those sections of the federal statutes that dealt with federal supervision over the elections. The president responded vigorously by vetoing the measures each time they were passed by the House. Although part of the reason for Hayes's vetoes involved the question of presidential prerogative, the major factor was his determination that the national government was responsible for the honesty of federal elections and for the safety of voters at these elections. The Constitution, he argued, grants Congress "ample powers" to provide laws with which to secure free and fair elections in every state, and in fact Congress has done so. "But to repeal these laws without substituting better—especially if it be done on the principle that the National authority is to be subordinate to the State—is in my judgement wholly inadmissible." While Hayes was not totally satisfied with the present laws, he was certainly not willing to see them repealed.[75]

In his third annual message to Congress, Hayes repeated many of the arguments he had previously stated in regard to the protection of voting rights and elections in the South. He could find "no reason to qualify the opinion I expressed in my last message, that no temporary or administrative interests of the government, however urgent or weighty, will ever displace the zeal of our people in defence of the principal rights of citizenship." He called on the American people to respect and obey the election laws and urged Congress "to supply any defects in these laws which experience has shown and which it is within its power to remedy."[76]

However, Hayes spent the largest portion of his message discussing civil service reform. As his administration drew to a close, he concerned himself less with southern matters and more with governmental reform. His policies had not prevented the use of violence or fraud by Democrats in the South to gain and retain political control and reduce or eliminate Republican votes and voters in that section. In July 1880, Hayes wrote: "It could clearly be proved that by a practical nullification of the 15th Amendment the Republicans have for several years been deprived of a majority in both the House and the Senate. The failure of the South to faithfully observe the 15th Amendment is the cause of the failure of all efforts towards pacification. It is on this hook that the bloody shirt now hangs." Perhaps a new president and a new attorney general might have better success at protecting voters and keeping southern Republicanism alive.[77]

Notes

1. C. Vann Woodward, *Reunion and Reaction: The Compromise of 1877 and the End of Reconstruction* (New York, 1951), especially chaps. 3, 9, and 10; Paul Buck, *The Road to Reunion* (Boston, 1937). See also Woodward's *Origins of the New South, 1877–1913* (Baton Rouge, La., 1951), chap. 2. For a critique of Woodward, see Allan Peskin, "Was There a Compromise of 1877?" *Journal of American History*, 60 (June 1973): 63–75; however, see Woodward's reply in the same issue, 215–23.

2. Woodward, *Origins*, chap. 1.

3. Garfield to Hayes, Washington, Dec. 12, 1876: quoted in Stanley Hirshson, *Farewell to the Bloody Shirt: Northern Republicans and the Negro, 1877–1893* (Chicago, 1968), 25.

4. Woodward, *Reunion and Reaction*, 229.

5. Hirshson, *Bloody Shirt*, 24-26; Vincent P. DeSantis, *Republicans Face the Southern Question: The New Departure Years, 1877–1897* (Baltimore, 1959), 32–33; T. Harry Williams, ed., *Hayes: The Diary of a President, 1875–1881* (New York, 1961), 77–85; Kenneth E. Davidson, *The Presidency of Rutherford B. Hayes* (Westport, Conn., 1972), 207–14. During his successful gubernatorial campaign in Ohio, Hayes had endorsed a suffrage amendment for blacks in the state constitution, although the amendment was ultimately voted down. George Sinkler, *Racial Attitudes of American Presidents from Lincoln to Roosevelt* (New York, 1971), 109 and 201–7; and Davidson, *Hayes*, 11–12.

6. U.S. Congress, *Inaugural Addresses of the Presidents of the United States from Washington to Kennedy* (Washington, D.C., 1961), 136; Williams, *Hayes*, 77.

7. For details on the policies of the early part of the Hayes administration, see Hirshson, *Bloody Shirt*, 21–44. According to Hirshson, it was only after the outrages committed during the 1878 congressional elections revealed the South as unwilling to go along with their part of the Compromise, that Hayes began emphasizing protection over conciliation. It appears that Devens inclusion in the cabinet had more to do with his geographical and political suitability than his views on law enforcement and the southern question. Richard E. Welch Jr., *George Frisbie Hoar and the Half-Breed Republicans* (Cambridge, Mass., 1971), 74.

8. Biographical material on Devens, as well as the other attorneys general discussed in this study, is slim. See Arthur Robb, *Biographical Sketches of the Attorneys General* (Washington, D.C., 1946), 46, private copy in Department of Justice Library; Robert Sobel, ed., *Biographical Directory of the United States Executive Branch, 1774–1971* (Westport, Conn., 1971), 86; Davidson, *Hayes*, 97–99. Devens was born in Charleston, Massachusetts, April 4, 1820. He was serving on the Supreme Judicial Court of Massachusetts when nominated for attorney general. After graduating from Harvard Law School in 1838, he practiced law until 1840, when he was elected to the state senate. After serving in the senate for two years, he became U.S. marshal for the district of Massachusetts. While marshal in Boston, Devens obtained some minor notoriety in 1850 when he participated in escorting to the ship wharfs a black fugitive slave by the name of Sims. Sims had been

tried under the recently passed fugitive slave law, and despite protests by the citizens of the city, was the first fugitive slave sent back to the South from Boston since the Revolution. Ironically, after the Civil War, Sims made his way to Washington, and in 1877 was given a job as a messenger in the Justice Department by newly appointed Attorney General Devens. During the war, Devens served in the state militia along with other Harvard graduates like Oliver Wendell Holmes Jr. Afterward, he was appointed to the state superior court, and in 1873, to the supreme judicial court. Homer Cummings and Carl McFarland, *Federal Justice: Chapters in the History of Justice and the Federal Executive* (New York, 1937), 177–78. See also, Stanley W. Campbell, *The Slave Catchers: Enforcement of the Fugitive Slave Law, 1850–1860* (Chapel Hill, N.C., 1968), 117–20. Besides being a very handsome man, Devens was known as a first-rate orator. Hoar, at one time Devens's law partner, always urged Devens to enter politics. Evidently, Devens had no such desire. After his service as attorney general, he went back to Massachusetts and the supreme judicial court, on which he served until his death in 1891. Robb, *Biographical Sketches*, 46.

9. Devens to L. L. Lewis, March 23, 1877, *Letters Sent by the Department of Justice: Instructions to U.S. Attorneys and Marshals*, RG 60, National Archives (hereafter cited as *Instructions*); Devens to Luke Lea, April 2, 1877, *Instructions*; Devens to Charles Mayer, May 12, 1877, *Instructions*; Devens to George M. Duskin, May 18, 1877, *Instructions*. See also Charles Boothby to Devens, March 17, 1877, *Source-Chronological Files*, RG 60, National Archives (hereafter cited as *Source Files*).

10. Devens to Mayer, May 12, 1877, *Instructions*; Devens to Duskin, May 18, 1877, *Instructions*.

11. A. R. Sutton (chief clerk of attorney general) to William Stone, March 28, 1877, *Instructions*; Devens to Lea, April 11, 1877, *Instructions*; Devens to Mayer, May 12, 1877, *Instructions*.

12. Albert D. Kirwan, *Revolt of the Rednecks: Mississippi Politics, 1876–1925* (New York, 1961), 5–6; Vernon L. Wharton, *The Negro in Mississippi, 1865–1890* (Chapel Hill, N.C., 1947), 200; George T. Swann (chief superintendent of elections) to Taft, Jan. 11, 1877, *Source Files*; J. L. Lake to Devens, Jan. 4, 1877, *Source Files*; Lea to Devens, March 27, 1877, *Source Files*; J. A. Orr to Devens, April 5, 1877, Oct. 24, 1877, *Source Files*.

13. Devens to Lea, March 6, 1877, April 11, 1877, *Instructions*.

14. Lea to Devens, April 18, 1877, *Source Files*; Devens to District Attorneys, April 5, 1877, *Instructions*.

15. Devens to Lea, August 8, 1877, Confidential Letter, *Source Files*; Brannigan to Devens, May 26, 1877, *Source Files*.

16. R. A. Hill to Devens, Oct. 27, 1877, *Source Files*; Lea to Devens, Oct. 9, 1877, Feb. 9, 1878, *Source Files*.

17. Lea to Devens, Feb. 12, 1879, Jan. 10, 1879, May 13, 1879, *Source Files*; Devens to Lea, Nov. 28, 1877, Jan. 26, 1878, *Instructions*.

18. Attorney General A. Garland to President Cleveland, Nov. 7, 1885, *Appointment Files*, Box 383, RG 60, National Archives (Washington, D.C.).

19. DeSantis, *Republicans Face the Southern Question*, 104–32; Hirshson, *Bloody Shirt*, 33–44.

20. Williams, *Diary*, October 26, 1878; DeSantis, *Republicans Face the Southern Question*, 130–32; Hirshson, *Bloody Shirt*, 45.

21. Devens to District Attorneys, Oct. 4, 1878, *Instructions*. According to Assistant U.S. Attorney J. W. Gurley of Louisiana, this would not be a practical policy in his state as it would mean that all such warrants would be returnable in New Orleans, which at that time was in the midst of a malarial epidemic and under quarantine restrictions. Gurley to Devens, Oct. 10, 1878, *Source Files*.

22. Mayer to Supervisors and Marshals (copy to Devens), Oct. 12, 1878, *Source Files*.

23. Mayer to Devens, Sept. 12, 1878, *Source Files*. See also Devens to Mayer, Oct. 3, 1878, *Instructions*.

24. Edward Callaway to Devens, Oct. 27, 1878, *Source Files*; Phillips to Devens, Oct. 23, 1878, *Source Files*; Wallace to Devens, Oct. 17, 1878, Oct. 21, 1878, *Source Files*.

25. Burns to Devens, Oct. 24, 1878, *Source Files*; Phillips to Devens (enclosed newspaper clipping), Oct. 23, 1878, *Source Files*; Edward Callaway to Devens, Oct. 27, 1878, *Source Files*; Wallace to Devens, Oct. 17, 1878, Oct. 21, 1878, *Source Files*. See also Lawrence D. Rice, *The Negro in Texas, 1874–1900* (Baton Rouge, La., 1971), 106. For a discussion of the origins of the term "bulldozing," see William I. Hair, *Bourbonism and Agrarian Protest: Louisiana Politics, 1877–1900* (Baton Rouge, La., 1969), 5.

26. For a complete discussion of the 1878 election results, see DeSantis, *Republicans Face the Southern Question*, 99-101; Hirshson, *Bloody Shirt*, 49.

27. Devens to Jack Wharton, Nov. 12, 1878, *Instructions*; Devens to Mayer, Dec. 9, 1878, *Instructions*.

28. U.S. Commissioner McGiness to Albertson, Aug. 15, 1878, *Source Files*; Albertson to Devens, Aug. 21, 1878, Jan. 2, 1879, Jan. 10, 1879,

March 6, 1879, and April 3, 1879, *Source Files*.

29. Devens to Albertson, Jan. 7, 1879, *Instructions*.

30. Baldwin to Devens, Nov. 21, 1878, *Source Files*; Burns to Devens, Dec. 4, 1878, *Source Files*.

31. Burns to Devens, Feb. 3, 1879, *Source Files*.

32. U.S. Marshal Torrans to Devens, Dec. 5, 1878, *Source Files*; District Attorney Chandler to Devens, Dec. 15, 1878, June 30, 1879, *Source Files*.

33. Special U.S. Attorney Lyons to Devens, Feb. 17, 1879, *Source Files*. Although there were reports of Ku Klux Klan activity, it appears that no prosecutions were ever undertaken with respect to such activity. See U.S. Marshal James Ballam to Devens, Feb. 24, 1890, *Source Files*.

34. For details on the trial, see clipping from *Jacksonville Daily Sun and Press*, sent to Devens from Stickney, Jan. 3, 1879, *Source Files*; Knight to Devens, Jan. 3, 1879, *Source Files*; Devens to Stickney, Jan. 3, 1879, *Instructions*.

35. Mayer to Devens, Dec. 13, 1878, *Source Files*.

36. Mayer to Devens, Dec. 13, 1878, Dec. 30, 1878, Jan. 2, 1879, Jan. 4, 1879, *Source Files*. For details on the arrest of Mayer and Turner, see series of telegrams between Mayer and Devens, Jan. 1879, *Source Files*.

37. Mayer to Devens, May 5, 1879, *Source Files*.

38. Mayer to Devens, Jan. 2, 1879, Oct. 6, 1879, *Source Files*. According to Mayer, the situation with respect to juries would be made worse in the future by the expected passage of a new state jury law, which would require the jury commissioner to be of the other principal political party to which the district clerk belonged. In northern Alabama this would mean a Democratic commissioner, and "people will be on the jury who cannot be convinced by the evidence of the guilt of the accused and especially not by 'negro evidence'." If even a supposedly impartial jury would not return satisfactory verdicts, Mayer felt, it was clear that a jury chosen by a Democratic jury commissioner would be even less inclined to do so.

39. Fred Israel, ed., *The State of the Union Messages of the Presidents* (New York, 1966), 2:1350–51.

40. Hair, *Bourbonism*, 76; Otis Singletary, "The Election of 1878 in Louisiana," *Louisiana Historical Quarterly*, 40 (April 1957): 47.

41. Devens to Leonard, Aug. 7, 1878, *Instructions*.

42. Singletary, "Election of 1878," 49–50.

43. Adams to Devens, Nov. 11, 1878, *Source Files*; George D. Hite and others to Devens, Nov. 12, 1878, *Source Files*.

44. Devens to Wharton, Nov. 12, 1878, *Instructions*.

45. Wharton to Devens, Nov. 20, 1878, *Source Files*.

46. Leonard to Devens, Dec. 1, 1878, Source Files. See also Hair, *Bourbonism*, 78–82; and Singletary, "Election of 1878," 51–53.

47. Leonard to Devens, Dec. 14, 1878, Dec. 21, 1878 (telegram), *Source Files*.

48. Leonard to Devens, Source Files Dec. 25, 1878.

49. Leonard to Devens, Dec. 25, 1878, Jan. 31, 1879, *Source Files*. Devens to Leonard, Feb. 2, 1879, *Instructions*.

50. Leonard to Devens, Feb. 8, 1879, *Source Files*; E. D. Webster to Devens, March 6, 1879, *Source Files*; "G. H. V." to Devens, May 21, 1880, *Source Files*. Devens to Leonard, March 7, 1879, *Instructions*.

51. George B. Tindall, *South Carolina Negroes, 1877–1900* (Baton Rouge, La., 1966), 24–40.

52. Earle to Devens, Oct. 3, 1877, *Source Files*. Earle also indicated that another reason for his resignation was the fact that he had been passed over for the appointment, though he considered himself better qualified than Northrup. Earle's candidacy was supported by Chief Justice Waite and Circuit Court Judge Hugh Bond. Indicative of the bad feelings between the two men was the fact that in November of 1878, Earle served as counsel for several defendants charged in the murder of a federal revenue agent. Earle did this solely to oppose Northrup, who was the prosecuting attorney in the case. Even more unusual was the fact that as assistant attorney, Earle had participated in the arrest of the defendants. Wallace to Devens, Nov. 11, 1878, *Source Files*. After the 1876 election, the department in South Carolina began prosecutions in what were known as the "Ellerton County outrages." Both white and colored citizens were indicted for participation in riots. Given the attempts by Hampton at racial conciliation in the state, the prosecutions were generally unpopular, and were eventually dropped by Northrup. This further alienated the district attorney from state Republicans who wanted a more vigorous enforcement of the election laws. William Stone to Devens, April 23, 1877, *Source Files*; Robert Aldrich (chairman of the State House Judiciary Committee) to Devens, April 24, 1878, *Source Files*.

53. Wallace to Devens, Oct. 17, 1878, Oct. 21, 1878, *Source Files*; Northrup to Devens, Oct. 15, 1878, Oct. 17, 1878, Nov. 2, 1878, *Source Files*.

54. Wallace to Devens, Oct. 21, 1878, *Source Files*.

55. Northrup to Devens, Nov. 5, 1878, *Source Files*; MacKey to Devens, Nov. 5, 1878, Nov. 1, 1878 (telegram), *Source Files*.

56. Northrup to Devens, Nov. 11, 1878, *Source Files*; Devens to

Northrup, Nov. 16, 1878, *Instructions*.

57. Wallace to Devens, Nov. 20, 1878, Nov. 9, 1878, *Source Files*.

58. MacKey to Devens, Nov. 20, 1878, *Source Files*; Northrup to Devens, Nov, 16, 1878, *Source Files*; editorial in the *Charleston News and Courier*, Nov. 20, 1878.

59. Northrup to Devens, Dec. 3, 4, 10, and 14, 1878, *Source Files*.

60. Northrup to Devens, Jan. 4, 1879, Jan. 8, 1879, *Source Files*.

61. Northrup to Devens, Jan. 4, 1879, *Source Files*.

62. Israel, *State of the Union Messages*, 2:1357; "Annual Report of the Attorney General for 1878," U.S. House *Executive Documents*, 46th Cong., lst sess., vol. 1852 (1878).

63. *Congressional Record*, 45th Cong., 3d sess. 1878, p. 2; Hirshson, *Bloody Shirt*, 51; Singletary, "Election of 1878," 44–62.

64. Northrup to Supervisors and Commissioners of Election (copy to Devens), Jan. 13, 1879, *Source Files*.

65. Northrup to Devens, Jan 20, 1879, *Source Files*; U.S. Senate, *Report of the U.S. Senate Committee to Inquire into the Alleged Frauds and Violence in the Elections of 1878*, 45th Cong., 3d sess., 1879, S. Rept. 855, xxiv–xxviii.

66. Northrup to Devens, Feb. 24, 1879, *Source Files*.

67. Northrup to Devens, March 6, 1879, March 20, 1879, Nov. 13, 1879, *Source Files*.

68. Northrup to Devens, "Report on April Term Cases," April 23, 1879, Nov. 11, 1879, Nov. 17, 1879, Dec. 3, 1879, *Source Files*. In addition to Democratic juries as a reason for the lack of convictions in election cases, Northrup also blamed the Supreme Court's recent decisions on the Fourteenth and Fifteenth Amendments. "I believe it is my duty to say that Reese et al. and Cruikshank et al. leaves the citizen of the United States nothing to stand on but his race, color, or previous condition and that it is absolutely impossible to prove that element of the case. Indeed, there are colored democrats and white republicans." Interestingly, Northrup proposed an alternative rationale for the election laws and their enforcement based on Article 1, sec. 4 of the Constitution. Three years later, as discussed below, the Supreme Court upheld the revised election statutes on this basis in its decision in *ex parte Yarbrough*.

69. Devens to Chandler, Jan. 28, 1979, *Instructions*; Devens to H. R. Ware, March 26, 1879, *Instructions*.

70. Devens to Northrup, April 7, 1879, *Instructions*.

71. See, for example, Devens to Farrow, March 25, 1879, *Instructions*; Devens to Wharton, April 12, 1879, April 26, 1879, May 5, 1879,

Instructions; Devens to Mayer, May 10, 1879, *Instructions*; Devens to Duskin, May 20, 1879, *Instructions*; Devens to Turner, May 22 and 23, 1879, *Instructions*; and Devens to Hill, May 26, 1879, *Instruction*.

72. Senate Committee, *Report on Elections of 1878*, xlii–xliv.
73. Ibid., xlv–xlvi.
74. For details on the debate, see Hirshson, *Bloody Shirt*, 53–54.
75. James Richardson, ed., *A Compilation of the Messages and Papers of the Presidents* (New York, 1897), 7:523–47; Hirshson, *Bloody Shirt*, 55; DeSantis, *Republicans Face the Southern Question*, 85–86; Williams, *Hayes*, March 22, 23, 25, 26, 27, 28, 29, 30, 1879, and April 7, 1879.
76. Richardson, *Messages and Papers*, 7:560–61.
77. Williams, *Hayes*, July 21, 1880.

4

"A Free Ballot and a Fair Count": Voting Rights Enforcement and Independent Movements in the South, 1880–1884

BETWEEN 1880 and 1884, Republicans shifted the focus of their attentions in their efforts to build up a viable southern wing of the Republican party. Whereas President Hayes had attempted to do this by appealing to the more conservative elements of southern society, President Garfield and President Arthur sought to disrupt the solid South through support of economic radicals in that section. However, the common element running through the programs of all three of these presidents was their support of voting rights for blacks in the South and the enforcement of the federal election laws to protect those rights.

After thirty-six ballots, the 1880 Republican nominating convention choose James A. Garfield of Ohio as its compromise candidate. The platform of the Republican party indicated that during the 1880 campaign the party would resort once again to "waving the bloody shirt." The platform charged the Democrats with the "habitual sacrifice of patriotism and justice to a supreme and insatiable lust for office." To this end the Democratic party had "obstructed all efforts to promote the purity and to conserve the freedom of the suffrage." The Republicans called for the division of the "Solid South . . . by the peaceful agencies of the ballot" and for the protection of honest voters against "terrorism, violence, or fraud." The use of the sectional issue and the "bloody shirt" was successful. Garfield was elected president, but his margin of victory was only 9,464 votes out of some 9 million votes cast.[1]

In the days prior to the 1880 election, Attorney General Charles Devens responded continually to requests for directions and special instructions from southern district attorneys regarding their duties and responsibilities at the upcoming elections. Just before election day, Devens sent a Circular Telegram to all federal district attorneys telling them to "see that all alleged election frauds in your District are vigorously prosecuted. Send report promptly, even if only preliminary." He also assured them that they might "use all necessary force to execute the law and arrest offenders promptly," and that "all reasonable expenses for assistance can be paid."[2]

Devens received a number of requests from southern district attorneys for instructions as to the duties and powers of the special deputies, particularly in areas of fewer than twenty thousand inhabitants. The most frequent question raised was whether or not such deputies could make arrests of election officials without first securing a proper warrant or other legal process. Although Devens admitted that this question "presents some difficulties," he maintained that arrests without warrants should be made against such individuals as party election managers "when they do distinct acts, clearly subversive of the right to register to vote (such as stuffing the ballot box in the presence of the marshal) and acts of a character in which they could not of necessity have any right to discretion or judgement." The attorney general suggested that warrants should be obtained whenever possible, but that "it would still be your duty to take those steps for the enforcement of the laws by proper preparation, speedily to execute process, which the information gives you should show to be sufficient or necessary."[3]

Another problem anticipated by southern district attorneys was the refusal of lower federal court judges to issue or uphold warrants. In the past such southern judges, almost always Republican appointees, were sometimes reluctant to uphold attempts by district attorneys to obtain what the judges thought were wholesale indictments in election cases. The attorney general had definite views on such judges, as well as on federal judges who also doubted the constitutionality of the election laws. Devens ordered that "if any judge of the United States courts plants himself upon the ground [refusing numerous indictments or doubting the constitutionality of the election laws] take care that the evidence is preserved for he will clearly subject himself to impeachment on account of the decision of the Supreme Court of the United States which it is his bounded duty to obey."[4]

Although reports of election law violations were received by the attorney general from almost every southern state during and after the 1880 elections, the most numerous were reported in South Carolina, Alabama, Louisiana, Mississippi, and Florida. In a letter to District Attorney Stickney of Jacksonville, Florida, Devens elaborated on how the district attorneys in the South should respond to election law violations. Two considerations were of primary concern:

> I desire in every case an arrest and vigorous prosecution with the purpose of obtaining the punishment of the offenders. It seems to me that a moderate number of cases properly prepared with the evidence made close and definite, rather than a multiplication of cases, which tends not only to be expensive (which is only a secondary matter), but to confusion and weakness which is unwanted, may prove the most effective means of enforcing the laws.
>
> Do not let cases be instituted unless you yourself or some person in whom you have confidence examines into the facts which can be proved. . . . A few cases that will really result in punishment will mean more to the proper execution of the law than a vast number of cases where no conviction can be had, especially if in such cases, proper proof shall be wanting.
>
> Of course details must be left to yourself.[5]

Devens was also willing to supply district attorneys with special assistant attorneys to prosecute election cases. However, he rejected the suggestion of one marshal that a corps of detectives be organized under the attorney general's direction to "work up [election] cases." Devens dismissed such a proposal as being "simply impracticable." Prosecution of election cases in the South went on through December and January 1881, and convictions were obtained in Mississippi, Florida, and South Carolina. Aside from expressing his appreciation for these convictions, Devens spent his remaining months as attorney general with internal department administrative matters. He attempted to arrange and bring up to date the financial accounts of the Justice Department and local offices around the country, and in general to smooth the transition of his office into the hands of the new attorney general and a new president.[6]

The views of President Garfield on the race question and the enforcement of the federal election laws had undergone a series of changes during the late 1860s and the 1870s. Following the ratification of the Fourteenth and Fifteenth Amendments, Garfield, then a Congressman, had expressed doubts about the efficacy of both these additions to the Constitution. Basically, he felt that both of these amendments gave Congress too much power over the states. By the late 1870s Garfield had become one of the strongest supporters of the Fifteenth Amendment and the Enforcement Acts. In 1879 he participated in a forum in the *North American Review* along with other prominent American politicians: James G. Blaine, L. Q. C. Lamar, Wade Hampton, Alexander H. Stephens, Wendell Phillips, Montgomery Blair, and Thomas A. Hendricks. The forum was directed to the question: "Ought the Negro to be Disfranchised? Ought He to Have Been Enfranchised?" Garfield's comments expressed complete support for the continued enforcement of the political rights of the freedman under the provisions of the Fifteenth Amendment. In his opinion there was no compromise position between slavery and full citizenship. Once slavery had been abolished and citizenship given to the black man, then all those rights attendant on such freedom and citizenship had to be granted as well.[7]

Garfield believed that the Fifteenth Amendment would not only aid the social and economic progress of the freedman, but it was the best means the freedman had at his disposal to protect himself. "Suffrage," he wrote, "is the sword and shield of our law, the best armament the liberty offers to the citizen." Without the protection of the ballot, the re-enslavement of the Negro was a very real possibility. Garfield added that despite the importance of the ballot to the freedman's future, it should not be assumed that the black man would always exercise that franchise honestly and intelligently. The influence of corrupt leaders at times was to be expected. What was more important in the long run was that greater educational opportunities and the accumulation of property by blacks in the South would eliminate the influence of such leaders, and both races would be free to choose their political parties on the basis of real issues. Real issues in Garfield's mind meant economic issues.[8]

Although Garfield emphasized racial harmony, he was not above "waving the bloody shirt" as well. He laid the blame for the outrages against black voters in the South directly in the lap of the Democratic party, and warned that if such invasions of constitutional rights were to continue, the nation might once again witness a bitter sectional struggle. Such a result, he felt, could only inflict serious injury to the social and economic prosperity of the South, and have harmful effects on all races in that section of the country.[9]

Garfield devoted a good portion of his inaugural address to the race issue in general and the question of Negro voting rights in particular. "The free enjoyment of equal suffrage is still in question, and a frank statement of the issue may aid its solution." Garfield noted the numerous instances in the South in which blacks were denied the freedom of the ballot. However, the president was not less willing to lay the blame for this problem directly on the Democrats and the white citizens of the South. He maintained "that in many places honest local government is impossible if the mass of uneducated negroes are allowed to vote." Thus, the real problem in the South was the lack of education of a majority of black voters and "the danger which arises from ignorance of the voter can not be denied."[10]

Garfield's solution to this problem centered on the importance of education. "For the North and South alike there is but one remedy. All the constitutional power of the nation and of the States and all the volunteer forces of the people should be surrendered to meet this danger by the savory influence of universal education." However, Garfield also indicated a willingness to protect the franchise rights of blacks in the South through the use of federal authority. He concluded that "it will be the purpose of my Administration to maintain the authority of the nation in all places within its jurisdiction; [and] to enforce obedience to all the laws of the Union in the interests of the people."[11]

Garfield appointed Isaac Wayne MacVeagh of Pennsylvania as his attorney general. During the Civil War, MacVeagh had served as district attorney for Chester County, Pennsylvania, and was known primarily as a "champion of reform." During his brief tenure as attorney general, MacVeagh's energies were primarily directed toward the prosecution and investigation of the Post Office Department scandals and the prosecution of Garfield's assassin. The attorney general did keep some personal direction over the prosecution of election cases in South Carolina and Florida.[12]

MacVeagh's biggest problem in South Carolina was the inactivity of District Attorney Lucius Northrup. Attorney General Devens had, as discussed above, often found it necessary to encourage Northrup to be more active and less eloquent in the prosecution of election cases. This state of affairs continued, and was recognized not only by Attorney General MacVeagh but by Republican Circuit Court Judge Hugh Lennox Bond as well. The situation came to a head in April 1881. Judge Bond refused to hold court with Northrup as district attorney, and even postponed the pending election cases to a time when he hoped Northrup would no longer be in office. Despite pleas by Northrup that he was the victim of "attempts to disgrace and starve me and my little ones," the attorney general asked for, and received, Northrup's resignation. In his place MacVeagh appointed former United States Marshal Samuel Melton.[13]

In Florida, the Justice Department was involved in a number of prosecutions growing out of the recent presidential election. The most important of these was a murder case involving Charles Savage, "colored man and active politician." On February 8, 1881, a young Madison County attorney, Frank

Patterson, was shot and killed in the county courthouse. Savage admitted shooting Patterson, but maintained that it had been done entirely in self-defense. Savage had given some supposedly damaging testimony about Patterson to a recent local grand jury investigating election frauds, "and because of this testimony as well as that which he was supposed to have given before the Grand Jury of the U.S. Court, as well as his well known influence as an active republican, he was attacked by Patterson who would have murdered him had he got the first shot."[14]

The trial of Savage, along with several others who were indicted for conspiracy in the crime, aroused political passions in northern Florida. Savage himself sent agonizing letters to the attorney general expressing concern for his own personal safety and the possibility of becoming the victim of a lynch mob. Eventually the venue of the trial was changed from Madison to Hamilton County, where a jury found Savage guilty of first-degree murder. On the grounds that Savage had been denied "the equal protection of the law" because of his race, under the provisions of the Fourteenth Amendment and the Revised Statutes the Justice Department entered the case to attempt to secure Savage's freedom. U.S. Assistant District Attorney Alva A. Knight was given charge of the case, and an appeal was taken to the state supreme court. Knight's appeal was successful; the Florida Supreme Court reversed the conviction of first-degree murder and ordered a new trial. According to a local Republican paper, the *Madison Times*, the outcome of such a new trial was very promising owing to the deaths of a number of the prosecution's witnesses. The paper also concluded that "a revival of the former excitement in relation to the case is not anticipated."[15]

On September 19, 1881, Garfield died, and the following day Chester A. Arthur took the presidential oath of office. In the past, Arthur had "demonstrated that he was not greatly concerned with affairs in the South." His address to Congress soon after taking office was the first such speech since the Civil War that did not mention the race question at all. But Arthur did not intend to abandon the South to the Democratic party any more than had Presidents Hayes or Garfield. Whereas Hayes had emphasized support for Republican alliances with conservative

Bourbon Democrats in the South, Arthur decided to concentrate on the various Independent movements that were springing up throughout the South during these years. Independents were for the most part former Democrats who had become disgruntled with their party, usually because of economic issues. By supporting these dissident Democrats, who would hopefully turn to southern Republicans for votes and assistance, Arthur felt he could not only break up the Democratic hegemony of southern politics but also spark a resurgence of southern Republicanism at the same time.[16]

A key component of this attempted alliance between Independents and Republicans in the South was the protection of the ballot box. "Corruption of the ballot box and the forthright stealing of elections were also grievances of the Independents. Since the same tactics of fraud and violence were employed against the Independents that had been and continued to be used against the Republicans, the two minority parties, though usually standing on opposite poles on economic issues, were drawn into co-operation against a common foe by this common grievance."[17]

This "new movement" in the South, as one Justice Department official called it, had the "full sympathy" of many southern Republicans. While such an effort "must be outside of and independent of the republican party," only "the well-directed blows of a vigorous, compact and well-organized republican phalanx in full and harmonious co-operation with this independent movement" could achieve the defeat of the Democratic party in that section. In addition to Republican support for Independents, it was also hoped that the movement would receive the cooperation "of law-abiding liberal anti-bourbons who are ready to make common cause for the full recognition of an honest ballot fairly counted."[18]

To direct Republican efforts in the South, President Arthur chose two members of his cabinet: Secretary of the Navy William E. Chandler and Attorney General Benjamin Brewster. Chandler was selected because "he was on the best and friendliest terms with the old-line party managers in the South, to the extent that they regarded him as their particular representative in the Cabinet and as their main refuge in the administration." The choice of Brewster was due less to his experience with southern politics than to his position as attorney general, and the responsibility invested in that position for enforcing federal election laws.[19]

After his initial appointment as attorney general, Brewster continued personal direction of the Star Route cases and the final stages of the trial of Garfield's assassin. However, Brewster began to devote more attention to other matters, including pending election cases in the South. He sent letters to district attorneys in Mississippi, Georgia, Florida, Arkansas, Texas, and Louisiana requesting full reports on the status of election cases brought after the election of 1880. Initially, the attorney general's chief concern was with the prosecution of election cases in South Carolina.[20]

Since replacing the controversial Northrup in South Carolina, District Attorney Samuel Melton had attempted to revitalize the various government prosecutions involving violation of the election laws. In a letter written soon after his appointment, Melton explained his position and his plans for his office. He concluded that "under the administration of W. [sic] Northrup the federal service in this state has been most inefficient—I want to say contemptible. It is a reproach." However, Melton was certain that he had "the sympathy of a large portion of the white people in denouncing outrages upon the suffrage: and I am not so sanguine in believing that I can do something of material reform in checking, if not wholly preventing, them. This it is my duty to do if called upon. But it is certainly not my duty to seek such an occasion."[21]

Melton did not have to seek such an occasion. Upon assuming office he was faced with "several hundred cases" for violation of the election laws. Of these cases, he noted, a few had been placed on the court docket, while "the others are in an undigested mass. In most instances the Commissioners before whom the complaints were made, did not take the testimony of the witnesses; and there is nothing to indicate the character of the case except the mere formal statement of the complaint."[22]

The district attorney was aware of the many obstacles to successful prosecution of these cases. "Nevertheless, this effort must be made, and with the sympathy and cooperation of the Department of Justice, I am ready to make it; with an energy and singleness of purpose commensurate with the great issues involved." Melton then summed up the importance of these election cases for the Republican party and the freedman in the South. "If we are to have a 'free vote and a fair count' in the South, these cases must be prosecuted with exceptional vigor and ability. The State of South Carolina has become distinguished as the locality where such crimes are the most flagrant. The question to be solved is familiarly designated as the 'South Carolina problem.' If it may be solved consistently with the integrity of the ballot, the solution must be found there."[23]

Melton asked the department to appoint an additional United States attorney for the state for one year in order to aid in the prosecution of the election cases. He suggested that such a person be a Republican, as well as a "liberal-minded, conservative" lawyer from the state. On February 17, 1881, Brewster appointed Dallas Saunders as a special U.S. attorney to assist Melton, and Brewster instructed the district attorney to treat Saunders "with the utmost consideration."[24]

Saunders's duties in South Carolina were defined at length by the attorney general a month later. Brewster instructed Saunders to make sure that Melton "prosecuted forthwith" all those accused of violating the election laws in the state. He expressed complete confidence in Saunders's ability to do this, acknowledging that Saunders's own "pronounced position as a Democrat would prevent the community . . . from questioning the motives of your actions." Brewster also instructed Saunders to direct his prosecutions toward "those who stand high in the community and have thus ventured to violate the law and encourage others to do it" as well. The conviction of a "few insignificant and obscure persons" would make little impact on those contemplating similar actions in the future. "The abuse of the right of suffrage such as charged to have been perpetrated in South Carolina is a practical treason against the dignity of the people" and such a right must be protected "no matter who suffers."[25]

Brewster concluded his instructions with what he felt was his nonpartisan rationale in desiring these prosecutions to be vigorously pursued:

> I wish to express my Republican convictions upon this subject, but irrespective of my Republican convictions I intend most emphatically to indicate how important all of this is to both sides that there should be fair play all around. There is no just judgment of popular will in any election that is controlled or biased by force or fraud, and I do insist that both Democrats and Republicans should have their faces set as flint against any abuses against the free and fair use of the ballot box.[26]

The district attorney and his special counsel began preparation of the election cases. Throughout February and March 1882, they gathered evidence, interviewed witnesses, and selected those cases that seemed to have the best chance for successful prosecution. Finding sufficient evidence and corroborating testimony was particularly difficult in many places. As Saunders reported, "I found that the defendants were all white men, that the witnesses were all colored men and that the witnesses were not disposed to testify and did not desire to have the cases tried. I could not obtain any white testimony in corroboration of the colored testimony."[27]

Despite such difficulties, cases were put together from five South Carolina counties. In addition to indictments being drawn against party managers and other individuals, prosecutions were also instituted against several boards of county canvassers. These boards, Saunders indicated, "had taken upon themselves judicial powers and had refused to count the votes of many voting precincts in their respective counties." Saunders contended that these boards had in fact only "ministerial powers" and that their duty "was merely to count the vote and make the proper return to the State Board of Canvassers who had the power to hear and determine" the validity of such ballots.[28]

During the preparation and trials of the election cases, the attorney general kept in constant communication with both Saunders and Melton. Brewster sent long letters of detailed instructions to each man, emphasizing above all his desire for convictions in these cases. Brewster was also at pains to remind the two "that these are not political prosecutions" and that "it is not a question of Democrat or Republican, it is a question of enforcing the law." The attorney general stressed the importance of "fair play" on the part of the government. He wanted the defendants in these cases to be as vigorously defended as they would be prosecuted. "I want no verdict against any man that is not the result of a thorough investigation of the case upon both sides. Every man should be vigorously defended." Brewster maintained that only by such a course of action could "party strife" be avoided and obedience to the law enforced.[29]

The election trials began in early April 1882, and continued for the rest of that month. In addition to Saunders and the regular Assistant U.S. Attorney Warren Marshall, Brewster sent W. W. Ker, another Philadelphia attorney, to aid in the preparation of the legal pleadings and indictments. The necessity for this lay in the fact that the original indictments, drawn up by former District Attorney Northrup, had been found by the court to be defective in that they were insufficient in law to present any case for trial. Or, in other words, they did not sufficiently specify what, if any, crime had been committed. This was remedied by Ker and Saunders with a new set of pleadings, and these were sustained by Judge Hugh Bond. In all, twenty cases were brought to trial during the April term of federal court.[30]

The majority of cases tried involved acts of election managers and their acceptance of ballot boxes that had been stuffed with the kinds of tissue ballots used in prior southern elections. In these cases the evidence was fairly conclusive, since the number of ballots found in the boxes at the end of election day were always in excess of the total number of registered voters in the precinct. In several instances the difference was several hundred votes. As indicated in the previous chapter, at the end of an election day, the ballot boxes were vigorously shaken, causing the bundles of tissue ballots to fall loose and mingle with the regular ballots honestly cast. Since these actions were not particularly concealed, the connivance of the election managers was necessary to the fraud. The managers had the duty of opening and inspecting the ballot boxes in the morning and again at the end of the day. They were also responsible for directing the counting of the ballots. The use of tissue ballots was therefore impossible without their help or knowledge.[31]

Along with the cases against the election managers and the members of the boards of county canvassers, there were several trials involving persons accused of placing the packets of tissue ballots in the boxes, of other forms of ballot box stuffing, and of intimidation of blacks attempting to vote. Despite the efforts of Melton, Marshall, Ker, and Saunders, the results of the election trials were far less successful than either they or the attorney general had anticipated. In one case, two members of the Sumter County Board of Canvassers pleaded guilty to charges of illegally rejecting vote counts from several precincts in the county. However, with the approval of the district attorney, judgment was suspended against both defendants since it was understood that they had only "accidentally committed technical violations of the law." The rest of the cases were either continued until the following November term of court or resulted in not guilty verdicts for the defendants. In some of the cases a guilty verdict was indeed reached, but the jury informed the judge that the verdict had been reached despite the fact the jury itself was not unanimous in its views. In one instance this situation followed upon Judge Bond's refusal to discharge the jury until it had rendered a guilty verdict. Ultimately, on the motion of the district attorney, all those cases were declared mistrials and also continued to a future date.[32]

In his lengthy and detailed report, Melton could offer no reason for the government's failure in these elections cases. Saunders, however, was convinced that the juries had been tampered with and that "strong influences were brought to bear upon certain members of the panel." He noted that in one instance a defendant found guilty in one of the early cases was subsequently acquitted in a later trial on similar charges—"on the ground of mistaken identity." Saunders felt that "to my mind every case tried by the District Attorney and in which he pressed for conviction would have been followed by a conviction if tried before an impartial, unprejudiced jury."[33]

With the completion of the April trials, Saunders returned to

Philadelphia. Melton continued to work on further preparation of those cases in anticipation of the coming November term of federal court. In July 1882 he requested the appointment of another special counsel to assist in the election cases. The attorney general explained that department funds were very limited at that time and "the necessities of the Department" obliged Brewster to refuse the district attorney's request. In particular, the attorney general was not looking toward the coming congressional elections and the added expenses and problems to the Justice Department that these elections would entail.[34]

The congressional elections of 1882 offered Republicans the first major opportunity to implement their strategy of giving support to Independent movements in the South. According to William Chandler:

> It is important to carry the House, for the next presidential election depends on it. We cannot carry as many seats in the North as two years ago. We must increase our Southern representation by ten to twenty. That depends upon Republican support of the Democratic revolt in the South and the overthrow of the Bourbons there. . . . Every independent Democrat in the South pledges himself to a free vote, an honest count, the obliteration of race distinctions and popular education by the common school system. Shall we fail to follow our principles when they are vital? Our straight Republican and carpetbag and Negro governments cannot be revived. Without the aid of Independent Democrats in the South we cannot carry enough seats there to save the next presidential fight. Beyond that, the safety of the colored race at the polls depends upon it.[35]

It was thus recognized that a crucial element of this Republican strategy was the protection of the "free ballot and a fair count." The Department of Justice and the attorney general reflected the Republican-Independent concern for honest elections and the franchise rights of black voters in the South. Following the 1882 elections, department officials in the South actively attempted to prosecute cases involving the violation of the election laws. As will be discussed, the involvement and activity of the department during this time was generally greater in those states where the Republican-Independent alliance was itself more viable and successful. This was the case in North Carolina, South Carolina, Georgia, Virginia, Mississippi, and to a lesser extent Texas, Alabama, and Louisiana.

In October 1882, Attorney General Brewster issued a Circular Letter of instructions to all United States attorneys, and a similar Circular Letter to all federal marshals. Both letters discussed the purposes behind the federal election laws and the duties and responsibilities of federal officials at the congressional elections to be held the following month. In addition, both letters were the most detailed and comprehensive set of instructions to date for department officials regarding the enforcement of the federal election statutes.

According to the attorney general, there were three main purposes behind the election laws relating to congressional elections, which the Justice Department had the duty to protect. The first purpose was simply to "secure perfect freedom to voters in exercising their right" to vote. This could be accomplished "by manifest preparation for enforcement followed by vigorous prosecutions of every offender, since facts are more impressive than words." A second reason for enforcing the election laws was to "prevent unlawful voting." In this respect, the activities of the supervisors, the marshals, and the general and special deputies were the most relevant. The district attorney was to keep accurate lists of all these officials and make sure all of them were legally qualified to hold their positions. Finally, the district attorney was to be certain "that . . . all offenses coming within their knowledge and not prosecuted by some other authorized officer must be forthwith reported to you." The third purpose for enforcing the election laws was to protect suffrage rights of voters from injury by local or national officers charged with duties involving the process of voting. "Such offenses as tampering with the registry or poll lists, stuffing the ballot boxes, making a false count, return or certificate of the result, and the like, can hardly be committed unless by some of these officials, or with their connivance."[36]

To make sure these purposes were carried out properly Brewster gave district attorneys careful instructions on how to go about enforcing the laws and prosecuting those who disobey them. District attorneys were to devote their full time to election matters and were to be thorough and vigorous in their prosecutions, taking care to "dispel any such illusions as that the proceedings are taken for temporary effect and will be suffered to die out." Prosecutions should not be "rashly begun," but when instituted "they must be pushed to the end." Brewster also demanded constant and complete reports from local federal officers on conditions in their respective districts and the disposition of prosecutions that were brought.[37]

Expectations of trouble were borne out by reports of fraud and intimidation from almost every southern state at the 1882 elections. Such conditions, in most instances, were particularly widespread in those states where Independent party movements attempted political fusion with regular Republicans. District Attorney Melton reported that in South Carolina "fraud and intimidation prevailed in every District to such an extent that prosecutions can and will be instituted sufficient to occupy all the available time of the Court for two years." Melton explained that such crimes had been directed not only at blacks and Republicans, but at supporters of the state Greenback-Labor party as well. This party had been organized by dissident South Carolina Democrats, and their slate of candidates for state office in the 1882 canvass had been endorsed by the Republican party. The district attorney was positive that they could and would give valuable testimony with respect to the outrages committed. "I have put myself in official correspondence with the Committee of the Greenback Party, and I now have the assurance of their thorough co-operation with me in these prosecutions."[38]

An important factor in the South Carolina elections of 1882 had been the recently passed state election law. Known as the "Eight Box Law," the act provided for separate ballot boxes for the various national, state, and local offices. Although the explicit purpose of the law was to provide a form of literacy test in which the voter was required to choose the correctly labeled ballot box, "it would be simple for election managers to help those illiterates who would vote 'right' and let others void their ballots through ignorance." The state election law also provided for a complicated system of registering to vote, in which election supervisors were given wide discretionary powers in determining those who might be qualified to vote. This too provided an effective means for screening out blacks and other "undesirable voters."[39]

The use of the separate ballot boxes in South Carolina affected the federal government's attempts at prosecuting those accused of election fraud and intimidation in that state. In 1880 only one ballot box had been used, so that investigation of the presidential and congressional vote had involved the investigation of the state elections as well. This fact had been used by the defense in a number of subsequent election trials, in which they argued that federal control of elections did not extend to state elections even when the two coincided. Furthermore, because the state was involved, the defendants had the opportunity of being represented in court by the state attorney general, with no expense to themselves. In 1882 the use of separate ballot boxes did not allow such a defense to be used. However, the South Carolina legislature did appropriate over four thousand dollars to pay for the defense of those accused of election law violations in the 1882 election.[40]

Soon after the elections, the November term of the federal circuit court began. At this term the cases from the previous April were due to be retried. Melton felt that it would be more beneficial to forget these cases and begin prosecution of those cases arising from the more recent election. The attorney general agreed and instructed Melton to "select a small number of the most clearly established cases" to prosecute. Brewster maintained that a few immediate convictions would be the most effective way of preventing future crimes of a similar nature in the district.[41]

During the next several months the district attorney continued with his investigations into the election cases. At various times during these months he was assisted by special United States attorneys appointed by Brewster. The first two attorneys, W. P. Snyder and Benjamin Butterworth, proved unsatisfactory to Melton, and both eventually resigned. During the April 1883 term of the circuit court, the first of the election cases was presented, but was continued until the following November. Thus, it was not until a year after the election that the first of the election cases was tried.[42]

To aid Melton in the conduct of the trials, the attorney general sent District Attorney Emory Speer from Georgia. Speer was a leader of the Independent movement in that state. Melton felt the "utmost confidence" in the successful outcome of the trials because of Speer's help and because for the first time a majority of the panel of jurors selected were reckoned to be either Republicans or Independents. The election trials lasted through December, and every one resulted in a mistrial due to the inability of the jury to reach a unanimous verdict. Despite this, Melton was satisfied. "The friends of a free ballot and free speech are greatly uplifted and encouraged, not only by the real success of the prosecution, but by the fact of the presence and excellent conduct of the distinguished Counsel who represented the government.... The presence of Mr. Speer is recognized as a direct expression of the determined purpose of the government to suppress crimes against the elective franchise."[43]

South Carolina Independents were also satisfied with the outcome of the trials. The chairman of the state Independent party, W. Walker Russell, sent a letter of appreciation to the attorney general for the department's efforts in "the cause of thoroughly free speech and honest ballot in this State." Although no convictions had been secured, the trials had a "tremendous moral effect" on the "recuperation" of the political rights of South Carolina Republicans. Russell also expressed pleasure with the "courageous and able assistance" of Emory Speer, and asked the attorney general to reappoint Speer to aid in future election cases. "His visit here has inspired new hope and courage in the hearts of men both white and colored who have for these many years been patiently waiting for the clouds of worry and fear to roll away."[44]

The elections of 1882 in North Carolina proved an "excellent example" of Republican policies in the South. The state had an active Independent party which was based primarily on opposition to Democratic support of prohibition. Although

Republicans suffered losses in the 1882 canvass, especially in the Black Belt counties, these losses were more than offset by Independent victories. During the election, at which "the freedom of the ballot was one of the issues," instances of fraud and intimidation against Republicans and Independents were reported in many North Carolina counties. J. J. Mott, chairman of the Republican State Executive Committee, wrote to the attorney general directly asking for the Justice Department's assistance in prosecuting those who had broken the law.[45]

The district attorney for the Eastern District of North Carolina, W. S. O'B. Robinson, began investigations into the election cases. During the November 1882 term of the circuit court, Robinson had been able to secure indictments and convictions in several election cases from the previous June. A local newspaper described it as the "first case of this kind which has come to judicial notice." During the November term of court, the defendants convicted were fined five hundred dollars each. Such a light penalty prompted the attorney general to reprimand the district attorney. According to Brewster, "Imprisonment is the most effective punishment of such grave offenses and in view of the milder judgment in the case of Bell and Bryant and the views of the Court as shown in the slip enclosed by you, it is not likely that these parties, if convicted, would be more severely punished." Thus, the district attorney was directed that in all future election cases where a conviction is obtained, "urge a sentence of imprisonment."[46]

In the Western District of the state, District Attorney John E. Boyd reported various instances of fraud at the recent elections but was satisfied that sufficient evidence existed for prosecutions. However, it would "help matters," he felt, if he could be given the assistance of a special prosecuting attorney to aid in the investigation and preparation of the election cases. Brewster agreed on the usefulness of such a move, and sent H. J. Haywood, a Republican lawyer from Indiana, "to be used by you [Boyd] in detecting and prosecuting violations of the election laws at the late Congressional election."[47]

After receiving detailed instructions from Boyd on conditions in North Carolina, Haywood began his investigations. From the moment of his arrival, Haywood had a difficult time carrying out his responsibilities. The local papers had described him as an assistant attorney general, and this apparently caused additional animosity among Democrats in the district, who were already angered at what they believed to be a campaign of political persecution against them by the government. Local Democratic papers also described Haywood as being from Philadelphia, and not Indiana, and they objected to the government using what they derogatorily referred to as a "Philadelphia lawyer" to act as a "paid agent" of the Republican party. During the next five months Haywood continued his investigations. In early April 1883, he submitted his report to the department, noting that although there had been frauds at the recent elections he had been unable to secure sufficient evidence; it might yet be assembled, but he would need at least four additional men to help him. "If I get sufficient evidence and have the ability I will make it hot for some of these good, proud and honest Democrats."[48]

Not only was Haywood's request for additional men refused, but in May the attorney general informed Haywood that because of a lack of department funds Haywood's services were no longer necessary. District Attorney Boyd concurred in this suspension, though he did not "think that these prosecutions should finally stop here." Boyd felt that it was important to continue the cases until at least the beginning of the next fiscal year when there would be sufficient funds to rehire a special prosecutor. Boyd characterized Haywood's services as "useful" and hoped that his present assistant attorney could continue with the material gathered by Haywood.[49]

It appears, however, that the district attorney was not pleased with Haywood's work. The federal marshal for the district, Thomas B. Keough, wrote the attorney general in late July saying the district attorney had asked Keough "to join him in submitting to [the attorney general] a plan to properly investigate the charges of violations of the election laws in this district." Soon after this, two attorneys were appointed to assist the Assistant District Attorney William S. Ball in the election cases. The two men appointed were John T. Wallace of Washington,

D.C., and Eugene Eckel of Greensboro, North Carolina. Boyd and Keough expressed satisfaction that the investigations were now "in the hands of discreet men—men who will not force the Department into wild and untenable positions."[50]

Both Wallace and Eckel continued the investigations during the rest of 1883 and well into 1884. The final report on the election cases was not made until April 1884. In that report, District Attorney Boyd indicated that the slowness in the completion of the election investigations was due "to the many obstacles to be met in the prosecution of this class of criminals in the South," noting, for example, the reticence of grand juries to indict and the problems of trial juries "composed of men in political sympathy with defendants and ready on the smallest pretext to acquit." Most important, the district attorney reported, was the fact that even "local Republicans of position and influence evinced little disposition in most instances to aid us in procuring evidence of fraud in the election." Boyd cited the example of one unsuccessful Republican congressional candidate, Col. D. H. Dockery, who had actively "discouraged" such prosecutions.[51]

Despite all these obstacles, Boyd still believed that cases could be worked up and successfully prosecuted. He cited a number of instances where evidence had been obtained showing fraud against Republicans and Independent voters at the 1882 election; such cases "should be prosecuted and the guilty parties punished." The attorney general agreed and urged that they be "vigorously prosecuted." However, Brewster was not convinced that all the cases outlined by Boyd were under the department's jurisdiction. "A large part of the statement of facts [presented by Boyd] is taken up with alleged violations of election rights as to which the complainants seem to have been unable to connect their allegations specifically with the elections for members of congress. This Department has no right or disposition to interfere with violations of the law which it is not bound to prosecute."[52]

The district attorney was instructed to prosecute those cases involving obvious instances of fraud at the congressional elections of 1882. For example, in one county the votes were cast into tin buckets and other unlawful receptacles, and then taken into the woods and disposed of. But before Boyd could bring these cases before a grand jury, he was informed that once again the department had run out of funds to pay for witnesses, and prosecution of elections cases should therefore be discontinued.[53]

In the Eastern District of North Carolina, prosecutions for election law violations were more successful. District Attorney Robinson reported that although frauds were evident during the 1882 canvass in his district, "the actual voting at the polls was in most cases concluded with reasonable fairness." He noted, however, that "the similarity of the offenses occurring in different places, indicates system and previously concerted action." Pressure "by the friends of a fair ballot" forced Robinson to begin his investigations. In his request for additional help from the Justice Department, Robinson boasted defensively, "You will see that there is no intimation of any unwillingness on my part to prosecute this class of offenses for in view of this fact, that this is the only district in the State in which there has been a conviction for violation of the election laws, any intimation of this sort would be unwarranted." Robinson was not given the additional counsel requested, but over the next several years seven election cases were brought in the district and convictions were obtained in two of them.[54]

Independent movements in Virginia, Mississippi, and Georgia were particularly active, and in 1882 political fusion between Republicans and these Independent movements was generally successful. The Virginia Readjuster party was the model for other Independent movements in the South. Basically, the Readjusters were in favor of scaling down the huge state debt built up from Civil War days in Virginia. Blacks in the state supported the Readjusters not only for economic reasons, but because the party was relatively liberal on the race question and supported equal political rights for the freedman. The Readjusters, for their part, endorsed the "free ballot and a fair count" because they recognized that "if the ruling Bourbons were to be defeated, the black vote would have to be won over."[55]

The high tide of the Readjuster movement in Virginia came during the years 1879 to 1883. During this time a majority of the state legislature and Governor William Cameron were Readjusters; and in 1881, the acknowledged leader of the party, William Mahone, was elected to the U.S. Senate. The election of Mahone was particularly important because it was the first real test of President Arthur's attempts at a Republican alliance with southern Independents—and it worked. As one historian has concluded, "Arthur had gambled heavily on a Readjuster victory, because he felt that if Mahone could swing Virginia out of the Democratic column, other Independents might duplicate his feat in their states . . . [and] then the Republicans might well be on their way to redeeming the South."[56]

In the congressional elections of 1882 the Readjusters were again successful, electing six of their candidates to the House of Representatives. Probably the success of the Readjusters and their support of the political rights of the freedman explain why there were actually few instances of fraud and intimidation of voters reported by Justice Department officials in the state. However, a number of prosecutions were begun by District Attorney John S. Wise. Even after Wise was replaced by S. Waddill as district attorney, Wise continued to serve as special counsel in the prosecution of the election cases. By far the most important of these cases was the prosecution of a Virginia tax commissioner, Robert Mumford, for preventing a large number of Virginia citizens from being allowed to vote.[57]

The basis of the Mumford case was the state constitutional amendment of 1876, which had provided for a poll tax as a prerequisite for voting in Virginia elections. The Readjusters had pledged to get rid of the tax, especially since it disfranchised poor whites as well as blacks. In fact, the Readjuster-dominated state legislature did repeal the tax after the November 1882 elections. However, before and during the election, the tax was used as a means of disfranchising voters. Mumford, a Democratic tax commissioner, was accused of conspiracy to prevent voters in the Third Congressional District of Virginia from voting by failing to assess the poll tax.[58]

Mumford was convicted and his appeal was decided in April

1883 by Circuit Court Judges Hugh Bond and Robert Hughes. Bond and Hughes were both Republican appointees, and both supported the enforcement of federal election laws. The basis of defendant Mumford's claim was that Section 5506 of the Revised Statutes was unconstitutional. In his decision in the Mumford case, Judge Bond went into the legislative background of Section 5506, explaining how Congress had essentially taken the same statute declared unconstitutional by the Supreme Court in *Reese* and merely eliminated reference to the Fifteenth Amendment and race and color as the basis for prohibiting interference with franchise rights at elections for any federal officials.[59]

Instead, Congress based Section 5506 on the fourth section of the first article of the Constitution, which gave Congress the power to regulate "the time, places, and manner of holding elections for senators and representatives." In upholding the constitutionality of the section, as well as Mumford's conviction, Bond drew this distinction between his decision and that of the Supreme Court in *Reese*:

> The Court in the *Reese Case* decided that Sect. 5506 was not appropriate legislation to enforce the Fifteenth Amendment. That section said nothing of race, color, or previous condition. It was at a municipal election, and therefore was not within the power of Congress under Article 1, sec. 4 of the Constitution, which gives Congress power over federal elections. Had the same crime been committed at a federal election the court would, we think, have found authority for section 5506.[60]

In a concurring opinion, Judge Hughes also analyzed the Supreme Court's decision in the *Reese* case, emphasizing that the Court there had limited the Scope of the Enforcement Act of 1870 insofar as it related to Congress's power to enforce the Fifteenth Amendment. Nothing was said about Article 1, sec. 4 of the Constitution. Thus, Hughes concluded, Section 5506 of the Revised Statutes is constitutional because "Congress must be presumed to have passed a constitutional law, unless it otherwise palpably appears; and because, therefore, it is necessary implication that the object of the section is the constitutional one of protecting voters in federal elections."[61]

The circuit court's decision in *Mumford* was another in a series of Supreme Court and lower federal court rulings after 1878, which upheld the constitutionality of the federal election laws and the power of Congress to pass legislation protecting voters and voting rights at federal elections. These decisions culminated the following year in the Supreme Court's strong affirmation of these principles in its decision in *ex parte Yarbrough*. The effect of the *Mumford* decision on conditions in Virginia was unfortunately minimal. During the state elections in 1883, Virginia Democrats resorted to extensive use of intimidation and outright force against their political opponents. These tactics proved successful: large numbers of black voters stayed away from the polls, the Democratic party regained its majority in the state legislature, and the "Readjuster era" in Virginia government came to an end.[62]

Another successful Independent movement in the 1882 elections appeared in Mississippi. The leader was James R. Chalmers, a former Confederate general and three-time Democratic congressman from Mississippi. Chalmers broke with the Democrats in 1882 and ran for Congress on a platform attacking national banks, advocating the free coinage of silver, and supporting "a free ballot and a fair count." Although Chalmers's defection caused a split in the Republican as well as the Democratic ranks, he was able to emerge victorious at the polls.[63]

Chalmers's support from the national Republican administration came primarily through the Justice Department. In response to possible Democratic frauds, "Chalmers was reported to have personally led United States marshals who took possession of the polls in Marshall County, 'dictated the conduct of the election,' and attempted to 'awe and intimidate' [the voters] with threats of Federal prosecution." Other instances were reported of federal marshals actively helping the Chalmers campaign. As one historian of Mississippi concluded, "The incongruity of Republican federal officials using such tactics to elect a man whom their party had recently turned out of Congress" because of his own use of fraud and intimidation "did not pass unnoticed. Now it was said, the Republican party had turned to

Chalmers 'on his promise to use the same means in its favor.'"[64]

Republicans, for their part, continued to use Chalmers after the election. At the request of District Attorney Green Chandler of the Northern District of Mississippi, Chalmers was appointed special assistant attorney for the prosecution of the election cases stemming from the 1882 elections. With Chalmers in charge, the prosecutions were immediately begun and indictments secured against thirty-four persons charged with election law violations. The major problem in securing convictions was, as was true elsewhere in the South, the difficulty in getting the juries in such cases to convict. As a result of the inability to get impartial juries, the early cases tried resulted in mistrials. By the summer of 1883, few of those indicted had been brought to trial, and Chalmers resigned because the department refused his request for an increase in his salary. As the attorney general put it: "Gentlemen who are employed, as I have you, for these high duties should remember that there is connected with the employment a dignity and an honor which will exclude the idea of converting the employment into an opportunity for gain."[65]

Although a large number of the cases brought by the department in Mississippi were dismissed, the overall record of prosecutions of election cases was the best of any southern state during the years 1882–84. This included the Southern District of the state where the district attorney was Luke Lea. After the 1882 elections, the department appointed a special prosecutor to investigate and try the election cases in the Southern District. In 1883, fourteen cases were prosecuted; there were three convictions. After 1882 the national administration continued to support Chalmers and his fellow Independents, primarily through the Justice Department. As Green Chandler, district attorney for Mississippi's Northern District, concluded in a letter to Secretary of the Navy William Chandler, the Independent movement was the "first ray of light Mississippi Republicans have seen since 1875," and it had been entirely due to "the President's policy of promoting liberalism in our Bourbon-ridden State."[66]

In Georgia the involvement of the Justice Department with the Independent movement was even more direct than in Mississippi. The leader of the Independent party in Georgia was

District Attorney Emory Speer. Soon after the 1882 election, Speer was sent to South Carolina by the attorney general, where he aided District Attorney Melton in the prosecutions of the election cases in that state. However, in the spring of 1883, Speer returned to Georgia where he took charge of the government's prosecution of the Ku Klux Klan members of Banks County, Georgia. In response to the Independent movement and that movement's support by Republicans and blacks, the Klan had once again become active in Georgia. The center of that activity was Banks County.[67]

In October 1883 a number of parties were indicted by a federal grand jury for the "most cruel outrages on colored people ... principally on account of their votes in the late congressional election." According to Speer, "The people of the neighborhood have held a mass meeting in which without regard to party they have demanded the perpetrators of these outrages, and it will give me the greatest possible pleasure to prosecute the offenders with all the zeal and energy which I can bring to the discharge of that duty."[68]

Among those indicted in the Banks County cases were members of the family of Jasper Yarbrough. The Yarbrough family was part of a Democratic organization known as the "Pop and Go Club." Although at the trial a weak attempt was made to present the club as a baseball club, it was obvious that the group was organized for the purpose of wreaking vengeance on those blacks who "had voted the Independent ticket." During the summer of 1883, the "Club" had made numerous night excursions through the countryside, dragging blacks out of their homes and beating and whipping them, and in one instance shooting and killing a black man.[69]

The prosecution of the Banks County Klan was pushed "with great earnestness" by the district attorney. According to a local paper, this was particularly so as it gave Speer, himself a defeated Independent candidate in the 1882 canvass, on opportunity of "getting even with old adversaries." The prosecutions were successful: all eight men indicted were convicted and sentenced to two years imprisonment. Speer was obviously pleased with the results. "I am persuaded that these convictions will be of decided effect in the advancement of social order and the protection of all classes of our people in the exercise of the rights guaranteed by the Constitution of the United States, and I believe their conviction has been received with approval by the best class of our people.[70]

In Texas, Alabama, and Louisiana, Independent movements from the regular Democratic ranks took the form of Greenback parties. In these states the Republican-Independent alliance was reflected in the attempts by local Justice Department officials to enforce the federal election statutes. In Texas, the district attorney for the Eastern District, Edward Guthridge, reported on instances of fraud and intimidation of voters at the 1882 congressional elections and how this affected the outcome of the elections. According to Guthridge, "all the outrages were perpetrated in counties where the opposition to the Democratic candidates had a chance of success, and no matter how people *vote* if their votes are not counted and outlaws and ruffians can steal ballot boxes, and stuff them, of course [the] election is a farce."[71]

Guthridge noted that because of the Greenback campaign the Democratic majority in Texas was reduced by eighty thousand votes. He also indicated that had there not been extensive fraud, that majority would have been reduced even more. "I mention this . . . not for political reasons, but in order to show that should the trial come in the future when the political complexion of Texas will be liable to change, such actions as herein reported will be perpetrated upon a more extended scale, and no matter how many votes any candidate may receive at the polls, they will do him no good if they are not counted for him." Thus, Guthridge felt that immediate and vigorous prosecution of election cases was necessary in order to insure future Republican and Independent gains.[72]

The attorney general agreed with Guthridge's analysis and appointed I. Morris Chester to assist the district attorney in the preparation of the election cases. "As you will see he [Chester] is a colored gentleman and has been selected because of special facilities, which it is thought he would have, for detecting the crimes in question, through his relation with those of his own race and color, against whose rights it is presumed the crime was specifically directed. You will find that he has been properly instructed as to the nature of his duties and his subordination to yourself in their discharge." Guthridge was "satisfied that he will be of great service not only to me but to all courts of justice in investigating and bringing to justice the violators of the law."[73]

Chester began his investigations, interviewing "the active political workers in the interest of the Republican and Independent parties," all of whom Chester described as being of "African descent." According to the special prosecutor, "My progress was necessarily slow, because I had to rely upon my own resources and such limited means as circumstances might suggest." He was able, however, to discover evidence of election law violations, including several persons "who were in the pay of the democracy, and the individuals from whom they received money, to deceive the Republican voters, by the imposition of Democratic tickets."[74]

The prosecution of the Texas election cases was hampered by several problems. The first involved charges of bribery made against the district attorney. Guthridge was accused of accepting money in exchange for allowing defendants in the election cases in Jefferson County, Texas, to plead guilty and accept a nominal fine of five dollars plus costs. The investigation of these charges was placed under the direction of the Justice Department's examiner general, Brewster Cameron. Cameron sent Deputy Examiner J. Wiegand to Texas to look into the charges and report to the attorney general.[75] Wiegand's report, and a corroborating statement by special prosecutor Chester, cleared Guthridge of the bribery charges.

In the Jefferson County cases it appeared that the defendants, in order to secure the best possible counsel to defend themselves, pooled their funds, which were then placed in the hands of a Democratic lawyer and state representative, W. T. Armistead. The sum of money collected was alleged to have been quite considerable. However, on the advice of Armistead the defendants pleaded guilty and were each fined one dollar and the costs of the prosecution. "And because they were not sent to prison, they seem to assume that one thousand dollars of the amount [collected] was given to Mr. Guthridge, for the exercise of his good offices, to enable them to escape confinement. That is how they reached a conclusion for not having received a more severe sentence."[76]

Although Guthridge was cleared of the bribery charges, the report of Examiner General Brewster Cameron did not reflect favorably on the activities of the district attorney. "It does appear," Cameron concluded, "that the failure of these cases was due to the fact that they were improperly brought." According to Cameron, the district attorney subpoenaed all of the Republicans voters in the precinct where the fraud was alleged to have occurred, instead of summoning just a few of them as witnesses.

> The defence also subpoenaed a large number, which, together with the defendants and their friends, brought an immense crowd of people to the town during the holding of the court; the result naturally was great excitement and demonstrations bordering on a riot. The fear of an outbreak influenced the court to accept pleas of guilty, imposing a nominal fine and waiving imprisonment. This gave rise to an unfounded suspicion that the District Attorney had been bribed in connection with these cases.[77]

In addition to the February cases in which the defendants pleaded guilty, a large number of other election cases were postponed. Brewster was not pleased with this decision and hoped the district attorney's judgment in asking for a continuance would "not prejudice the status of the cases." In April 1883 the election cases were again continued until the following July. However, in July another event took place which prevented the prosecution of the Texas election cases. This event was the assassination of Judge Charles Haughn, one of the "main witnesses" for the government in the election cases still pending.[78]

The attorney general ordered Examiner Wiegand and A. J. Evans, district attorney for the Western District of Texas, to investigate the matter. The assassination of Judge Haughn touched off a wave of anti-Republican violence and attacks on blacks in the district by bands of "white men Democrats." By

August, Guthridge was thoroughly discouraged. The department's investigators had been unable to find Haughn's murderer or murderers, and the intimidation of blacks continued. In addition, the attorney general had once again begun an investigation into new charges of corruption in Guthridge's office. The district attorney's marshals and their deputies were accused of rendering fraudulent expense accounts. All were finally convicted, and though not directly implicated himself, Guthridge tendered his resignation on August 25, 1883.[79]

With the resignation of the district court judge soon after, the Eastern District of Texas was left without a district attorney or any federal judge. The feeling of Texas Republicans at this time was summed up by W. E. Singleton, who served as chief clerk for the United States district and circuit courts in Texas. Singleton indicated, "We rather feel that the Government has deserted us and its enemies have taken courage to more fully carry out their heinous purposes." Singleton detailed the various instances of intimidation and murder that had been going on in the district since the resignation of Guthridge and the murder of Judge Haughn, and concluded that the prosecution of election cases in east Texas had for all practical purposes been abandoned."[80]

In Alabama, Republican support through the activities of the Justice Department was acknowledged by Independents. According to one Alabama Greenbacker:

> In prosecuting crimes against fair elections and indeed all crimes against the United States you do give us much valuable assistance and encouragement. I am glad to assure you that today a much more hopeful feeling exists in my state among the law abiding, union loving men than for years past and this condition of affairs is traceable largely to your open vigorous prosecution of all offenders whether for civil or political offenses against existing law.[81]

After the 1882 elections, the attorney general received reports from all three districts in Alabama indicating that although the election in that state was "generally peaceful," it was "not generally honest." Brewster ordered all district attorneys to investigate and prosecute those accused of violations of the election laws. To W. H. Smith, U.S. attorney in Montgomery, Brewster wrote: "I wish it understood that these offenses [against the election laws] are among the most serious that can be committed and that the officers of the law are determined to enforce it. I therefore desire that your personal attention may be given to these cases and that they shall have preference except where there is other public business which cannot be postponed without more serious injury to the public interests."[82]

District Attorney Smith instituted prosecutions but was able to secure only two indictments. He concluded that "under the operation of the present jury law it is impossible in this state to punish election frauds. As soon as an election case is prosecuted, the jury decides according to their politics; that division necessarily under the law being about equal, no indictment is found." Smith was equally pessimistic about the trials of those indicated. "It is well understood that no convictions can be had in such cases, that the people laugh at the trials as farces, and farces they are; I have tried quite a number of election cases, knowing that the jury before which I was compelled to try, would not convict." Furthermore, he determined, "Public sentiment justifies these acquittals on the ground that they are necessary for the supremacy of the white race, and the juries who thus acquit, instead of being condemned, are sustained by public opinion." Smith's pessimism was born out by the fact that in May 1883 the election cases on the two indictments secured were tried and, despite the obvious evidence of guilt, the jury rendered a verdict of not guilty after deliberating for only ten minutes.[83]

In the Middle District of Alabama, the prosecution of election cases was completely eclipsed by the investigation and prosecution of U.S. Marshal Paul Strobach and several of his deputies for rendering false accounts to the department. In the Southern District, a number of indictments for federal election law violations were obtained, but were ultimately dismissed by District Attorney Duskin. Several election cases still pending from 1880 were also dismissed inasmuch as all the candidates for Congress from which these cases had derived had since died, and "the animosities engendered by that struggle have almost died out, and as these cases alone remain to revive them, at the expense of the government as well as the annoyance of all concerned."[84]

Republican support for Independent movements in 1882 was not universal throughout the South. In Louisiana, the president did not lend support to the Greenback party in that state, but "turned his back on them and gave his blessing to the regular [Republican] organization candidates." However, fraud and intimidation in Louisiana during the 1882 congressional elections was as common as it had been in elections in that state since 1876. To aid in the prosecution of election cases in southern Louisiana, Brewster sent attorney Charles E. Woods to New Orleans as special assistant to District Attorney Leonard. Woods, the son of Supreme Court Justice William B. Woods, was instructed to "take these matters in hand, make a thorough investigation as to the facts, employing deputies to assist ... if necessary, and devote for the present ... [your] entire time to the subject."[85]

In January 1883, Woods and Leonard submitted a report of their work to the attorney general. The district attorney indicated that the Justice Department's investigations were being supplemented by a "Committee" of New Orleans Republicans. The result of their efforts was the handing down of twenty indictments by the federal grand jury based on evidence that showed "a preconceived plan to prevent the expression of the popular will" at the 1882 elections. Leonard was confident that more indictments would be secured and that the trial of those already indicted should be postponed until all possible indictments were secured. Leonard felt that such a postponement would give him more time to prepare the cases, and "because if the arch conspirators can be found, it would be better to try them than the tools through whom they acted."[86]

In February all the indictments were quashed by District Court Judge Billings, on the grounds that the grand jury had been improperly drawn and that the indictments themselves were defective. The defects in the indictments that Judge Billings found to be "serious" were that the documents were not "tested" or signed in the name of the Chief Justice of the United

States, and that they were addressed to the "Marshal of Louisiana" instead of the "Marshal for the Eastern District of Louisiana." According to Will Haight, a department examiner, Special Prosecutor Woods began immediate preparation of new indictments. Haight also informed the attorney general that Woods did not seem "to receive the proper support from the District Attorney, who is absent from the District upon private business, for, although I presume Mr. Leonard has your permission to be absent from his district at this time, still it would appear that his absence at this critical period in the election cases might do great harm to the government's interests."[87]

Although ignored by Republicans in the election campaign, Louisiana Independents strongly supported the Justice Department's efforts at prosecuting violators of the election laws. A New Orleans newspaper noted, "The Independent Party and every honest citizen is vitally interested in having the swindlers punished. If they escape this time the ring will not scruple to work still more disgraceful outrages on the people of New Orleans in the future. . . . Already the State courts are impotent against them, and if the United States authorities suffer their rascalities to continue, every vestige of liberty, right and honest government will vanish."[88]

During March 1883, the new indictments were secured and the election cases brought to trial. It had become clear that the district attorney was not particularly interested in the prosecution of these cases, as he continued to remain absent from New Orleans for various periods of time during the trials. Under Special Attorney Woods, several of the first cases tried resulted in "not guilty" verdicts for the defendants. Despite the conclusion of Examiner Brewster Cameron that the rest of the cases would still be tried, the district attorney felt that it was probably fruitless to continue. In addition, District Court Judge Billings refused to try any more election cases on the grounds that "other important cases required his attention." After the judge's refusal to hear any more cases, Woods resigned and asked to come to Washington to talk with Brewster about the events in New Orleans. The election cases still to be tried were postponed indefinitely, and in the following months the district attorney spent most of his time in the investigation of alleged expeditions gathering in New Orleans to aid insurrectionaries in Cuba.[89]

In the Western District of the state, District Attorney M. C. Elstner reported that he had uncovered "flagrant violations of the federal election laws" at the 1882 canvass. A number of indictments were brought and the cases set for trial in Monroe, Louisiana. Because of the volatile conditions there, Elstner received permission to have the trials moved elsewhere. However, this proved of little value as all the district attorney's cases involving election law violations resulted in acquittals for the defendants.[90]

Until reaction set in, the Independent insurgency in the South and the Republican-Independent alliance had achieved some electoral success and some measure of economic reform. That such reform was insufficient would be demonstrated a decade later. "Future Populist leaders began their political education in the Independent campaigns of the seventies . . . and it was then that the seeds of later revolt were planted."[91]

However, just as important as the political and economic aspects of the Independent movement was the fact that it again focused attention on the question of voting rights and free and honest elections in the South. Whatever their other differences, and there were many, Republicans, blacks, and Independents agreed on the need for "a free ballot and a fair count." Between 1880 and 1884, the Justice Department reflected this shared need, and attempted to make it a reality through the enforcement of the federal election laws.

Notes

1. Kirk H. Porter and Donald B. Johnson, eds., *National Party Platforms, 1840–1956* (Urbana, Ill., 1956), 64. The use of the "bloody shirt" tactics was not approved of by all Republicans. Some northern businessmen opposed its use because they felt their business interests in the South would be adversely affected. Stanley Hirshson, *Farewell to the Bloody Shirt: Northern Republicans and the Negro, 1877–1893* (Chicago, 1968), 79–86.

2. Devens to U.S. Attorneys, Nov. 17, 1880, *Letters Sent by the*

Department of Justice: Instructions to U.S. Attorneys and Marshals, RG 60, National Archives (Hereafter cited as *Instructions*.); Devens to Durkee, Nov. 10, 1880, *Instructions*; Devens to Osborn, Oct. 29, 1880, *Instructions*.

3. Devens to U.S. Marshals, Nov. 1, 1880, *Instructions*; Devens to MacKey, Oct. 29, 1880, *Instructions*; Devens to Osborn, Oct. 30, 1880, *Instructions*. At one point Devens suggested the possible use of a presidential order to enforce the election laws, but nothing appears to have come of this idea at the time.

4. Devens to Albertson, Nov. 11, 1880, *Instructions*.

5. Devens to Stickney, Nov. 20, 1880, *Instructions*; similar letters were sent to district attorneys in South Carolina, Mississippi, Louisiana, and Alabama.

6. Ibid.; Devens to Thomas Hunt, Nov. 24, 1880, *Instructions*; Devens to Chandler, Jan. 25, 1881, *Instructions*; Devens to Northrup, Nov. 11, 1880, *Instructions*; Devens to Marshall, Jan. 27, 1881, *Instructions*.

7. Theodore C. Smith, *The Life and Letters of James A. Garfield* (New Haven, Conn.,1925), 470; James G. Blaine et al., "Ought the Negro to be Disfranchised? Ought He to Have Been Enfranchised?" *North American Review*, 128 (March 1879), 225–83.

8. Ibid., 244–50.

9. Ibid.

10. U.S. Congress, *Inaugural Addresses of the Presidents of the United States from Washington to Kennedy* (Washington, D.C., 1961), 143–47.

11. Ibid.

12. Arthur Robb, *Biographical Sketches of the Attorneys General* (Washington, D.C., 1946), 83; Robert Sobel, ed., *Biographical Directory of the United States Executive Branch, 1774–1971* (Westport, Conn., 1971), 229; John M. Taylor, *Garfield of Ohio* (New York, 1970), 232. For MacVeagh's activities in the Star Route and Guiteau cases, see chap. 7 below.

13. For details of the Bond-Northrup conflict, see *Source-Chronological Files*, RG 60, Box 652, National Archives (Hereafter cited as *Source Files*). Judge Bond had been a "staunch Unionist" during the Civil War and had been rewarded by Grant with the federal judgeship. Until the 1890s, Bond supported the strong enforcement of the election laws and upheld the constitutionality of these laws on a number of occasions. Everette Swinney, "Enforcing the Fifteenth Amendment, 1870–1877," *Journal of Southern History*, 28 (May 1962): 213. Northrup to MacVeagh, April 8, 1881, *Source Files*; MacVeagh to Northrup, March

26, 1881, March 28, 1881, April 7, 1881 (2 letters), *Instructions*.

14. Sworn statement of D. Egan to Stickney, May 30, 1881, *Source Files*; A. A. Knight to MacVeagh, April 9, 1881, Feb. 3, 1882, *Source Files*.

15. Knight to MacVeagh, Feb. 3, 1882, April 9, 1881, *Source Files*; Knight to Savage, Sept. 2, 1881, *Source Files*; Savage to MacVeagh, May 15, 1881, July 2, 1881, *Source Files*. See also Stickney to Brewster, July 27, 1882, *Source Files*.

16. Hirshson, *Bloody Shirt*, 99–106; Vincent P. DeSantis, *Republicans Face the Southern Question: the New Departure Years, 1877–1897* (Baltimore, 1959), 156; Carl N. Degler, *The Other South* (New York, 1974), chap. 9.

17. C. Vann Woodward, *Origins of the New South, 1877–1913* (Baton Rouge, La., 1951), 81.

18. I. Heyman to Brewster, April 28, 1882, *Source Files*.

19. DeSantis, *Republicans Face the Southern Question*, 151–52; Hirshson, *Bloody Shirt*, 109–10; Woodward, *Origins*, 101–3.

20. Brewster to Leonard, May 20, 1882, *Instructions*; Brewster to Luke Lea, Feb. 2, 1882, *Instructions*; Brewster to Green Chandler, Feb. 2, 1882, *Instructions*; Brewster to Stickney, May 25, 1882, *Instructions*; Brewster to C. C. Waters, March 18, 1882, *Instructions*; Brewster to J. S. Bigby, May 26, 1882, *Instructions*; Brewster to Guthridge, April 13, 1882, *Instructions*.

21. Melton to Col. Wallace, March 11, 1881, *Source Files*. Melton's appointment was approved by South Carolina Republicans. The *Greenville Daily News*, April 7, 1881, described Melton as a liberal who had always received as large a share of confidence and popularity as is possible for a member of his party (*Source Files*).

22. Melton to Brewster, Jan. 20, 1882, *Source Files*.

23. Ibid.; Melton to MacVeagh, July 4, 1881, *Source Files*.

24. Ibid.; Brewster to Melton, Feb. 16, 1882, *Instructions*; Brewster to Saunders, Feb. 17, 1882, *Instructions*. Despite Melton's earlier suggestion that the special counsel be a Republican from the state, he was glad that Saunders was a Democrat and from Philadelphia. Melton felt that having a Democratic special counsel from out of the state would show the seriousness with which the government viewed the election cases. Melton to Brewster, Feb. 18, 1882, *Source Files*.

25. Brewster to Saunders, March 18, 1882, *Instructions*.

26. Ibid.

27. Saunders to Brewster, *Source Files* for February and March 1882, generally; Saunders to Brewster ("Report of Election Cases"), May 11, 1882, *Source Files*.

28. Ibid.

29. Brewster to Melton, March 29, 1882, March 31, 1882, *Instructions*; Brewster to Saunders, April 4, 1882, April 10, 1882, *Instructions*.

30. Melton to Brewster, May 12, 1882, *Source Files*; Saunders to Brewster, May 11, 1882, *Source Files*.

31. Ibid.

32. Ibid.; The *Annual Report* of the Attorney General for 1882 indicates thirty-two total cases brought in South Carolina under the election laws during 1882. Of these, one conviction, one acquittal, and thirty nol. pros. or continued are listed. (Washington, D. C., 1882).

33. Melton to Brewster, May 21, 1882, *Source Files*.

34. Brewster to Melton, July 8, 1882, *Instructions*.

35. Chandler to James A. Blaine, Oct. 2, 1882, quoted in Leon B. Richardson,*William Chandler: A Republican* (New York, 1940), 346.

36. Brewster to U.S. Attorneys, Oct. 31, 1882, *Instructions*.

37. Ibid.

38. Melton to Brewster, Nov. 18, 1882, Dec. 20, 1882, *Instructions*; George B. Tindall, *South Carolina Negroes, 1877–1900* (Columbia, S.C., 1952), 50–51.

39. Ibid., 69–71.

40. Ibid., 72; Melton to Brewster, Nov. 18, 1882, Dec. 20, 1882, *Source Files*.

41. Brewster to Melton, Dec. 1, 1882, Nov. 21, 1882, *Instructions*.

42. Brewster to W. P. Snyder, Feb. 9, 1883, *Instructions*; Melton to Brewster, March 8, 1883. *Source Files*; Butterworth to Brewster, April 11, 1883, *Source Files*; S. Phillips to Melton, April 16, 1883, *Instructions*; Melton to Phillips, April 17, 1883, *Source Files*; Snyder to Brewster, May 4, 1883, *Source Files*.

43. Melton to Brewster, Sept. 29, 1883, *Source Files*; Melton to BrewsterCameron, Nov. 28, 1883, *Source Files*; Melton to Brewster, Dec. 30, 1883, Dec. 21, 1883, *Source Files*.

44. Russell to Brewster, Dec. 13, 1883, *Source Files*. For a contrasting view of Speer, see Hirshson, *Bloody Shirt*, 118. According to Hirshson, Speer was among a number of "chronic Negro Haters" in the South who received support from northern Republicans; Hirshson's characterization is taken from an editorial by the black journalist T. Thomas Fortune.

45. DeSantis, *Republicans Face the Southern Question*, 161 and 180–81; Robinson to Brewster, April 28, 1883, *Source Files*; Mott to Brewster, Nov. 13, 1882, *Source Files*.

46. Robinson to Brewster, Nov. 24, 1882, *Source Files*; Brewster to

Robinson, Nov. 27, 1882, *Instructions*.

47. Boyd to Brewster, Dec. 21, 1882, *Source Files*; Brewster to Haywood, Dec. 27, 1882, *Instructions*.

48. Boyd to Haywood, Jan. 9, 1883, *Source Files*; Haywood to Brewster, Feb. 28, 1883, *Source Files*; Haywood to Brewster Cameron, April 1, 1883, April 10, 1883, *Source Files*; Haywood to Hon. W. W. Dudley, April 11, 1883, *Source Files*.

49. Brewster to Haywood, May 1, 1883, *Instructions*; Boyd to Brewster, April 28, 1883, July 9, 1883, *Source Files*; Haywood to Brewster, April 30, 1883, *Source Files*.

50. Keough to Brewster, July 15, 1883, *Source Files*; Boyd to Brewster, July 26, 1883, *Source Files*; Keough to Brewster, July 26, 1883, *Source Files*; Boyd to Brewster Cameron, Oct. 20, 1883, *Source Files*.

51. Boyd to Brewster, April 14, 1884, *Source Files*. However, see the letter from Dockery to Robinson in January 1883, asking that prosecutions be immediately instituted against violators, and stating that Dockery wanted "every son of a bitch of them punished."

52. Boyd to Brewster, April 14, 1881, *Source Files*; Brewster to Boyd, April 30, 1884, May 3, 1884, *Instructions*.

53. Ibid.

54. Robinson to Brewster, April 28, 1883, Feb. 12, 1883, March 15, 1883, *Source Files*; Brewster to Robinson, March 19, 1883, *Instructions*.

55. DeSantis, *Republicans Face the Southern Question*, 153–55. Charles E. Wynes, *Race Relations in Virginia, 1870–1902* (Charlottesville, Va., 1961), 16–18; Degler, *Other South*, 277. Degler's chapter on the Independent movements, "Southern Dissenters On Their Own," focuses on Mahone and the Readjusters. According to Degler, the Readjusters "were the most successful political coalition of whites and blacks organized in the South between Reconstruction and the 1960's." (270).

56. DeSantis, *Republicans Face the Southern Question*, 153–55.

57. Wise to Brewster, Feb. 6, 1883, *Source Files*; Brewster to Wise, March 5, 1883, *Instructions*; Wise to Brewster, March 22, 1883, March 26, 1883, *Source Files*; Waddill to Brewster, March 3, 1883, *Source Files*; Judge Hughes to Brewster, Feb. 14, 1883, *Source Files*.

58. Wynes, *Race Relations*, 23–25; Wise to Brewster, March 22, 1883, *Source Files*; *U.S. v. Mumford*, 16 Fed. 223 (1883).

59. Ibid.; *U.S. v. Reese*, 92 U. S. 214 (1876).

60. *U.S. v. Mumford*, 228–29.

61. Ibid., 233.

62. For a complete discussion of these decisions, see chap. 5 below.

Wynes, *Race Relations*, 30–32; Teackle Brown to Brewster, Nov. 19, 1883, *Source Files*; Degler, *Other South*, 292–300.

63. DeSantis, *Republicans Face the Southern Question*, 160–61; Willie D. Halsell, "James R. Chalmers and Mahonism in Mississippi," *Journal of Southern History*, 10 (1944): 37–58. For a discussion and relevant documents regarding the split in the Republican party caused by Chalmers's candidacy, see Willie D. Halsell, ed., "Republican Factionalism in Mississippi, 1882–1884," *Journal of Southern History*, 7 (1941): 84–101.

64. Albert D. Kirwan, *Revolt of the Rednecks: Mississippi Politics, 1876–1925* (Lexington, Ky., 1951), 13–14; Brewster to Morphes, Nov. 3, 1882, *Instructions*.

65. Chandler to Brewster, Dec. 4, 1882, *Source Files*; Brewster to Chandler, Dec. 9, 1882, *Instructions*; Chandler to Brewster, Dec. 22, 1882, July 9, 1883, Nov. 3, 1883, *Source Files*.

66. Lea to Brewster, *Source Files*, Box 498, generally; Halsell, "Republican Factionalism," 97. According to the annual reports of the attorney general, between 1882 and 1884 a total of 117 election cases were brought in Mississippi, in which there were 35 convictions obtained.

67. Brewster to Speer, Nov. 9, 1883, *Instructions*.

68. Samuel Dunlop to Speer, Aug. 1, 1883, *Source Files*; Speer to Brewster, Aug. 6, 1883, Aug. 21, 1883, Oct. 13, 1883, *Source Files*.

69. Speer to Brewster, Oct. 27, 1883, *Source Files*; Dunlop to Speer, Aug. 1, 1883, *Source Files*.

70. Speer to Brewster, Oct. 27, 1883, Oct. 30, 1883, Dec. 18, 1883 (newspaper accounts from the *Atlanta Constitution*), *Source Files*. Because of the political significance of the case, the conviction of the Banks County Klan members was appealed to the U.S. Supreme Court. Speer continued his involvement in the case and requested that he be allowed to participate along with the solicitor general in the oral arguments of the case before the Court. The Supreme Court's decision, discussed in detail below, upheld the convictions and congressional regulation of federal elections and voting rights. *Ex parte Yarbrough*, 110 U.S. 650 (1884); Speer to Brewster, Jan. 4, 1884, *Source Files*.

71. Guthridge to Brewster, Nov. 29, 1882, *Source Files*.

72. Ibid.

73. Brewster to Guthridge, Nov. 21, 1882, Dec. 27, 1882, *Instructions*; Guthridge to Brewster, Feb. 17, 1883, *Source Files*. From all the evidence examined, it appears that Chester was the first and only instance in which the Justice Department used a black man in the prosecution of

election cases in the South. In March 1883, Chester filed a confidential report with Brewster Cameron in which he indicated that among Texas Republicans and Independents there was a "manifest inclination and growing sentiment towards the head of the Department of Justice" as a possible presidential candidate in 1884, "because of the prosecution of the election cases in the south, which is bringing him into prominence. A free ballot and a fair count is likely to be the paramount issue next year; and that statesman who has the best record in this respect will be sure to receive the support of the South in the National Convention." *Source Files,* March 19, 1883.

74. Chester to Brewster, Feb. 17, 1883, *Source Files.*

75. Wiegand to Brewster, Sept. 1, 1883, *Source Files;* Chester to Brewster, undated report, *Source Files.*

76. H. Hodges to Brewster, May 9, 1883, *Source Files;* Wiegand to Brewster, Sept. 1, 1883, *Source Files;* Brewster Cameron to Brewster, Sept. 5, 1883, *Source Files;* Brewster to Guthridge, Feb. 2, 1883, *Instructions.*

77. Cameron to Brewster, Sept. 5, 1883, *Source Files.*

78. Brewster to Guthridge, April 12, 1883, *Instructions;* Deputy Marshal J. North to Brewster, July 3, 1883, *Source Files.*

79. North to Brewster, July 3, 1883, *Source Files;* Brewster to Evans, July 21, 1883, *Source Files;* Guthridge to Brewster Cameron, Aug. 1, 1883, *Source Files;* Petition of Republicans of Marion County, Texas to President Arthur, July 3, 1883, *Source Files;* Guthridge to Brewster, Aug. 25, 1883, *Source Files.*

80. Singleton to Brewster, Oct. 2, 1883, *Source Files.* The election cases were resumed under Attorney General Garland, along with new cases in the district. See chap. 5 below.

81. Heyman to Brewster, April 28, 1882, *Source Files.*

82. Ibid.; Brewster to Smith, Nov. 11, 1882, *Instructions.*

83. Ibid.; Brewster to Osborn, Nov. 21, 1882, *Instructions;* Smith to Brewster, Dec. 9, 1882, *Source Files;* Brewster to Smith, Jan. 23, 1883, *Instructions;* Smith to Brewster, May 8, 1882, *Source Files.*

84. For details of the Strobach case, see chap. 7 below; Duskin to Brewster, Dec. 7, 1881, *Source Files;* Groom and Lewis to Brewster, Oct. 23, 1883, *Source Files;* Brewster to Duskin, Dec. 10, 1883, *Instructions.*

85. DeSantis, *Republicans Face the Southern Question,* 164–65; Brewster to Leonard, Dec. 21, 1882, *Instructions.*

86. Leonard to Brewster, Jan. 25, 1883, *Source Files.* Brewster had asked for this report because of public criticism of the government's "sincerity" in the prosecution of election cases in New Orleans.

Brewster to Leonard, Jan. 20, 1883, *Instructions*.

87. Leonard to Brewster, Feb. 15, 1883, *Source Files*; Haight to Brewster, March 10, 1883, Mar. 12, 1883, *Source Files*; Woods to Brewster, March 7, 1883, *Source Files*.

88. Ibid.

89. Woods to Brewster, March 20, 1883, *Source Files*; Leonard to Brewster, March 25, 1883, *Source Files*; Brewster Cameron to Brewster, April 2, 1883, *Source Files*; Leonard to Brewster, March 29, 1883, April 14, 1883. *Source Files*; Woods to Brewster, April 21, 1883, May 1, 1883, *Source Files*.

90. Elstner to Brewster, Dec. 12, 1882, March 18, 1883, *Source Files*; Brewster to Elstner, Feb. 19, 1883, *Instructions*.

91. Woodward, *Origins*, 106.

5

Voting Rights and the Democratic Interregnum, 1884–1888

THE DEMOCRATIC VICTORY in the presidential election of 1884 did not mark the end of the enforcement of voting rights in the South by the federal government. On the contrary, with respect to the franchise protection for southern blacks the years 1885 to 1888 were marked by a number of elements of continuity between the earlier Republican administrations of Hayes and Arthur and the recapturing of the presidency by the Republicans in 1888 under Benjamin Harrison. Probably the most important factor in this continuity was the series of federal court decisions, culminating in 1884 with the Supreme Court's ruling in *ex parte Yarbrough*, which upheld the federal election statutes and the responsibility of the federal government to protect voters at elections in which officials for national office were chosen.

The revised election laws passed by Congress after the Supreme Court's decision in 1876 in the *Reese* case were consistently upheld by the federal courts after 1878. In a Louisiana Circuit Court decision in 1878, Justice William B. Woods upheld the power of the federal government to punish anyone intimidating a voter at a federal election. According to Woods, Article 1, sec. 2 of the Constitution gave Congress the "ultimate power" of protecting a voter at an election for a member of congress "in making his choice, and afterwards expressing that choice at the polls."[1] Woods also concluded that a voter qualified by state laws "derives his right to vote for members of Congress from the Constitution of the United States" and that "Congress has the power to protect him in that right."[2]

A year after Justice Woods's decision, the Supreme Court confronted the constitutionality of the revised election laws in the companion cases of *ex parte Siebold* and *ex parte Clarke*. In affirming the conviction of Maryland and Ohio state election officials at the 1878 congressional elections, Justice Bradley upheld the constitutionality of all the sections of the revised election statutes, particularly those sections involving the appointment of special federal election supervisors and deputy marshals. Of special concern to the Court was the question of federal versus state jurisdiction over the regulation and supervision of elections in general. Counsel for the defendants had argued that since the basic qualifications for voting came from the states, then any conflicts arising out of attempts by Congress to regulate elections and voting should be decided in favor of the states. Bradley rejected this argument, noting that "the regulations made by Congress are paramount to those made by the State legislature; and if they conflict therewith, the latter, so far as the conflict extends, ceases to be operative."[3]

In respect to elections where federal officeholders were selected, Bradley maintained that there existed a "concurrent authority" between the federal and state governments. The justice used this principle drawn from the Supreme Court's decision in 1837 in *Cooley v. Board of Wardens* relating to regulation of interstate commerce. In *Cooley* it was held that where no federal regulations existed for some area of commerce, the states were free to regulate on their own. However, when the federal government chose to act, then such laws or regulations would become "paramount" and necessarily supersede those of the states. This principle applied to the area of voting and elections as well, or at least to those elections where there was a "national interest," as in the case of elections for members of Congress.[4]

Not only were private individuals subject to federal regulations, but state officials were also covered by the provisions of the federal election laws. "A violation of duty is an offence against the United States for which the offender is justly amenable to that government. No official position can shelter him from this responsibility." On this basis the Supreme Court upheld the conviction of the Maryland and Ohio election officials convicted of ballot-box stuffing, failing to convey the ballot boxes to the county clerk, and allowing ballot boxes to be open and the ballots inside destroyed.[5]

Between 1880 and 1883 a number of decisions were handed down by lower federal courts that applied the principles enunciated in *Siebold* and *Clarke* and that reaffirmed the use of federal power, as well as federal officials, in protecting suffrage rights at federal elections. In *ex parte Geissler*, for example, the circuit court of the Northern District of Illinois affirmed the power and use of federal supervisors of elections. The court concluded that "under the authority of the acts of Congress a duly qualified supervisor of elections has the rights, in the absence of the United States marshal and his deputies, to preserve order, and to arrest without warrant or process, any person who interferes with him in the discharge of his duties as such supervisor."[6]

But the most important statement of federal control over congressional elections was the Supreme Court's decision in 1884 in *ex parte Yarbrough*. The Yarbrough brothers had been convicted by a federal district court in Georgia for intimidating black voters at the 1882 congressional elections in that state. Their convictions were appealed to the Supreme Court on the grounds that the sections of the revised election laws under which they were convicted were unconstitutional.[7]

In a unanimous decision the Supreme Court affirmed the conviction of Jasper Yarbrough and his brothers. The opinion, written by Justice Miller, dealt less with the specific laws in question than with the general power of Congress to pass such laws. This power, concluded Miller, was both necessary and considerable. "If this government is anything more than a mere aggregation of delegated agents of other States and governments, each of which is superior to the General Government, it must have the power to protect the elections on which its existence depends from violence and corruption." Miller went on to discuss the various measures passed by Congress during the first three quarters of the nineteenth century "to remedy more than one evil arising from the election of members of Congress occurring at different times in the different States." While the justice conceded that most of this legislation dealt with the times and places of holding such elections, "will it be denied that it is in the power of [Congress] . . . to provide laws for the proper conduct of those elections?" Miller thought it could not be denied, and that any doubts on the issue were due simply to the fact that Congress "through long habit and long years of forbearance . . . in deference and respect to the states" had refrained from passing such laws.[8]

Having upheld the power of Congress to regulate the "conduct" of federal elections, Miller went on to discuss the various objections made to the revised franchise laws. The first issue raised was that the parties assaulted were private citizens and not public officials, and that Congress's power to control the conduct of elections could only extend to the latter. The Court found in fact no distinction between the two, and Congress's power to protect one included the power to protect both. It was the duty of Congress to make sure that such elections "shall be free from the adverse influence of force and fraud practiced on its agents, and that the votes by which its members of Congress and its President are elected shall be the free votes of the electors, and the officers thus chosen the free and uncorrupted choice of those who have the right to take part in that choice."[9]

A related issue confronted by the Court was whether the right to vote was dependent on Congress or on the states. Counsel for the defendants had argued that since the qualifications of voters were determined by the states, then it must of necessity follow that the right to vote in itself came from the source that determined who might vote, namely, the states. They noted that the Supreme Court in *Minor v. Happersett* had declared that "the Constitution of the United States does not confer the right of suffrage on anyone."[10] Justice Miller rejected this contention, saying "it is not true . . . that electors for members of Congress owe their right to vote to the state in any sense which makes the exercise of the right to depend exclusively on the law of the State." According to Miller, the Fifteenth Amendment clearly showed "that the right of suffrage was considered to be of supreme importance to the National Government, and was not intended to be left within the exclusive control of the States."[11]

At this point, Justice Miller came to the crucial issue in the case, the relationship of the Fifteenth Amendment to the voting rights of the freedman. In *Reese* the Supreme Court had said that the Fifteenth Amendment gave no affirmative right to vote to blacks, it merely was designed to prevent discrimination against blacks. In *Yarbrough* the Court, in effect, seriously qualified this prior ruling, claiming that "under some circumstances" the amendment was the source of an immediate right to vote on the part of black citizens. What were these circumstances? "In all cases where the former slaveholding States had not removed from their Constitutions the words 'white man' as a qualification for voting," the Fifteenth Amendment and any subsequent congressional legislation did confer a positive grant of suffrage. Such laws "being paramount to the state law, and a part of the state law," annulled the discriminating word "white" and left the freedman "[i]n the enjoyment of the same rights as white persons." Miller then concluded that "in such cases this 15th Amendment does, *propio vigore*, substantially confer in the negro the right to vote, and Congress has the power to protect and enforce that right."[12]

In light of the Supreme Court's 1876 ruling in *Reese* and the Court's decision in 1883 in the Civil Rights Cases, the strong support for national power and black political rights shown in the *Yarbrough* case is not easily explained. One commentator, who characterized the *Yarbrough* decision as an example of "judicial statesmanship," maintained that the shift from *Reese* to *Yarbrough* was due to a change in personnel of the Supreme Court in the eight years between the two decisions. During that time, five new justices took their place on the Court, and all of them were Republican appointees. This explanation is fairly persuasive, but leaves unanswered the question of why these same justices a year prior to *Yarbrough* struck down the Civil Rights Act of 1875. The explanation for this can be found in the *Yarbrough* decision itself, and is very relevant to the question of voting rights enforcement after 1876.[13]

At the end of his opinion in the *Yarbrough* decision, Justice

Miller made an implicit reference to the Supreme Court's decision in the Civil Rights Cases in 1883. He stated that "the reference to cases in this court in which the power of Congress under the first section of the 14th Amendment has been held to relate alone to acts done under state authority, can afford petitioners no aid in the present case." Miller drew a distinction between protection of private rights and the protection of those rights "conferred by the Constitution of the United States essential to the healthy organization of the government itself." The latter, he claimed, were so important to the maintenance of republican government that they admitted of no limitation. In other words, *ex parte Yarbrough* represented the judicial acceptance of the political concept of the "free ballot and a fair count." Although Republican politicians, and now Republican judges, were willing to concede to southern states the handling of the question of the social and civil relations between the races, they were determined to maintain at least a minimum basis of political equality for the freedman. Congress could not protect blacks from "Jim Crow," but Congress could protect black voters at elections where federal officials were to be chosen.[14]

In terms of the protection of basic political rights, *Yarbrough* is surely a landmark decision. As one historian of federalism has noted, the Supreme Court's decisions in the *Siebold* and *Yarbrough* cases "were destined to play important roles in the twentieth century unfolding of the constitutional law governing . . . elections. Moreover, in these decisions the Waite court sustained important extensions of congressional authority into areas of election regulation which had hitherto been left largely to the states." Still another writer has said of Justice Miller's opinion in *Yarbrough* that "the opinion he wrote for voting rights accomplished in a minor way what Harlan, in his brilliant dissents, did for civil rights in a major way. Both began to build the judicial foundation of the civil rights revolution, which began in earnest in the 1940's and bore fruit in the constitutionality of the Civil Rights Acts of 1964 and 1965."[15]

In fact, the *Yarbrough* decision bore more immediate fruit. As discussed below, it explains why even the Democratic President Grover Cleveland and his attorney general felt obligated to enforce the federal election statutes. In addition, subsequent court decisions over the next fifteen years gave further affirmation to the concept of federal control of congressional elections. In a circuit court decision in 1887, Justice John M. Harlan stated that Congress's authority to enact statutes regulating such elections was "no longer an open question in the courts of the Union." According to Harlan, the congressional election laws "are sustained by the elaborate judgments of the United States Supreme Court in which the power of Congress . . . is placed upon grounds which can't be shaken. Those cases cover the whole field of argument."[16] And in *Logan v. U.S.*, Justice Horace Gray concluded:

> The whole scope and effect of this series of decisions is that, while certain fundamental rights, recognized and declared, but not granted or created, in some of the amendments to the Constitution, are thereby guaranteed only against violation or abridgement by the U.S., or by the states, as the case may be, and cannot therefore be affirmatively enforced by Congress against unlawful acts of individuals; yet that every right, created by, arising under, or dependent upon the Constitution of the United States, may be protected and enforced by Congress by such means and in such manner as Congress . . . may in its discretion deem most eligible and best adapted to attain the object.[17]

Yet, at the same time that the courts were upholding congressional power over federal elections, violence and intimidation of blacks and Republicans in the South was reaching new highs. The electoral successes achieved by Independents and Republicans in the South in the congressional elections of 1882 were short-lived. Elections for state officials in 1883 marked the return to power of Democratic-controlled state legislatures and Democratic governors in a number of states in the South where the Independent-Republican alliance had been effective. A major reason for these Democratic victories was the resort by Democrats to widespread use of force and intimidation against their political opponents. This situation was particularly evident in Virginia and Mississippi. According to one Virginia Readjuster:

> The election was carried as I predicted by intimidation and worse, if you please, the threats of ostracism and being turned outdoors by every voter who might even attempt to defend or vote the [Readjuster] machine tickets; and even the few rich men in my locality who did vote for Mahone have been subjected to all manner of disrespect.... In my neighborhood ... 2 years ago there were a number of prominent citizens who voted the Readjuster ticket; but during the late canvass they were bulldozed and socially terrorized into stultifying themselves by voting the opposite way.[18]

The most outrageous instance of violence in Virginia took place a week before the election in 1883 in Danville. During the election campaign, Democrats vociferously pointed out that not only did blacks constitute a majority of the town's population but controlled a good part of its government as well. These scare tactics, aimed basically at the white citizens of the community, made the normally peaceful relationship between the races in Danville extremely tense. On November 4, 1883, a brawl erupted; when it was over, one white man was dead and four wounded, and four blacks had been killed and six wounded. It was claimed by some Republicans that the riot was planned by the Democrats. Whatever the case, the Danville Riots, as they were called, proved a decisive blow to the Readjuster-Republican campaign in Virginia. "Thoroughly intimidated, large numbers of Negroes stayed away from the polls in a quiet election with an otherwise heavy turnout. The Democrats won a two-thirds majority in both houses of the legislature, partly due to the perpetration of election frauds on an even grander scale than usual."[19]

A comparable outbreak of violence during the 1883 state elections occurred in Copiah County, Mississippi. Intimidation of blacks by groups of "night riders" during the campaign there culminated with the murder of J. P. Mathews, the white chairman of the Republican Executive Committee of Copiah County. Mathews was murdered as he was going to the polls on election day to cast his ballot. The effect of the intimidation and violence in Mississippi was the same as that in Virginia: large numbers of blacks stayed away from the polls and "Mississippi fell more deeply than ever under Bourbon control."[20]

As a result of these incidents a special Senate committee was formed on January 25, 1884, to investigate the elections in Mississippi and Virginia. The committee consisted of five Republicans and four Democrats. After several months of investigations, the majority report, signed by the five Republican members, concluded that the outcomes of the elections in Mississippi and Virginia were a direct result of the intimidation, fraud, and violence used by Democrats in those states against their opponents.[21] A further result of these incidents was their effect on President Arthur and the Republican party. "The Independent defeats in 1883 had the same effect upon Arthur as the Republican failures in Louisiana and South Carolina in 1878 had had upon Hayes. Arthur now became convinced that his Southern program had failed." So did his fellow Republicans. The failure of his southern policy coupled with the failure of the Star Route trials contributed to Arthur's failure to receive the Republican presidential nomination at that party's June 1884 convention in Chicago. Despite Arthur's position as an incumbent, the convention instead nominated James G. Blaine of Maine as its presidential candidate. The Democrats, meeting in Chicago later that summer, selected Grover Cleveland, governor of New York, as their presidential choice.[22]

On the question of voting rights, both major parties in the election of 1884 were similar. The platforms of each made explicit reference to the protection of a "free ballot and a fair count." At the same time, Democrats and Republicans accused each other of being responsible for the fraud and violence taking place in the South, and both promised to uphold the political rights of all citizens. Although Blaine polled almost 400,000 votes more than Garfield had in 1800, Cleveland was victorious as the Democrats captured the electoral votes of New York, New Jersey, Connecticut, and Indiana, along with those of the eleven southern states of the Old Confederacy.[23]

As president, Cleveland began implementation of what one of his biographers has characterized as a "Bourbon-Mugwump program," based on concern for good government, laissez-faire economics, and friendship with businessmen and conservatives, particularly those in the South. While blacks were not essential, they were not to be ignored either. In this regard, Cleveland and Democrats generally were careful to avoid giving the impression that Democratic rule meant a return to antebellum conditions. In his inaugural address Cleveland stated that concerning the freedman in the South, "the fact that they are citizens entitles them to all the rights due to that relation, and charges them with all its duties, obligations, and responsibilities." And according to Speaker of the House John G. Carlisle, "The Democratic party is as competent and as willing to punish these crimes against the purity and independence of the ballot as the Republican party is, notwithstanding the latter's boast of superiority in morality and patriotism."[24]

As cabinet members, Cleveland appointed two southerners, both of whom were conservatives and of the Bourbon class. The president chose Lucius Q. C. Lamar as secretary of the interior and Augustus Garland of Arkansas as attorney general. Garland had a long career of public service which included membership in the Confederate Congress and the U.S. Senate, and a term as governor of Arkansas during Reconstruction. One of the reasons behind Garland's appointment was his familiarity with southern conditions and problems. According to one historian, "an examination of Cleveland's correspondence for the period reveals that many contemporaries looked upon the inclusion of Garland in the Cabinet as a move to conciliate blacks and calm their fears. There were those who felt that Garland had given blacks a fair deal when he was Reconstruction governor from 1875 to 1877, and that he had their confidence."[25]

Although the enforcement of the federal election statutes in the South was never a major part of the Cleveland administration's program, the president and the attorney general did recognize and accept the responsibility for the protection of voters at post-1884 elections for members of Congress. This responsibility was no doubt underlined by the Supreme Court's unambiguous affirmation of that duty in the *Siebold* and *Yarbrough* decisions. On October 5, 1886, just prior to the congressional contests of that year, the president ordered Attorney General

Garland "to take general charge of the execution of the Statutes of the United States touching the appointment of Supervisors of Election and special deputy marshals, and the performance of their duties and their compensation, so far as these subjects are by the Constitution and laws under the supervision and control of the Executive branch of the Government."[26]

Several days later the attorney general sent out a short letter of instructions to federal marshals relating to their duties at the upcoming congressional elections. The marshals were directed to make themselves "familiar with the Statutes referred to, and see that they are understood by your deputies, who should be discreet men, impressed with the importance of an honest franchise." Marshals were given a wide degree of authority with a minimum of interference promised by the attorney general and his department in Washington.

> The manner of discharging these duties by yourself and your deputies is largely left to your discretion. In matters involving questions of law, you are directed to consult the attorney of the United States for your district, for needed information and advice. It is assumed that the duties can be performed without infringing upon the rights of any citizen, in a manner that shall be firm and at the same time free from an unnecessary display of authority.[27]

There was only one major series of prosecutions for violation of the election laws growing out of the elections of 1886. While these prosecutions do not indicate a vigorous policy of election law enforcement on the part of the Cleveland administration, they are illustrative of the acceptance by Cleveland and Garland of federal control over congressional elections and a willingness to enforce federal laws where possible, even if against fellow Democrats. The cases resulted from the 1886 congressional canvass in Washington County, Texas. According to one recent historian of Texas blacks after Reconstruction, "racial dissension that had been brewing in Washington County since Reconstruction erupted in 1886." The election campaign was marked by intimidation and violence, culminating on election day with the alleged murder by blacks of the son of a Democratic candidate.

The son was killed as he was in the process of stealing a ballot box. Three blacks accused of the crime were taken from the local jail and lynched. Republicans in Washington County complained not only of such violence, but of widespread fraud at the polls costing their party thousands of votes. Not only was another congressional investigation begun by Republicans, but action was also initiated by local Justice Department officials.[28]

In February 1887, a federal grand jury was called in Austin to investigate the various charges of fraud and intimidation that had occurred at the 1886 election. District Attorney Rudolph Kleberg reported that "there is no question that great irregularities have occurred in said election and the situation calls for thorough investigation by the Court now in session. The evidence so far adduced shows that boxes were violently taken from the hands of the Supervisors of election and destroyed and also instances of threats and intimidation at the polls."[29]

One of the problems the district attorney had during the meeting of the grand jury was having all the necessary witnesses appear. Many of these witnesses were testifying in Washington, D.C., before the Senate committee investigating the elections in Washington County. Kleberg suggested that the committee "instruct" the witnesses before it to return home by way of Austin so they could appear before the grand jury without any additional expense to the government. While the district attorney had intended his suggestion as a means of cooperating with the Senate investigation and facilitating the work of both bodies investigating the elections, he was accused of attempting to "obstruct" the committee's work, and his suggestion was apparently ignored.[30]

The grand jury completed its work in March 1887. Indictments were handed down "against various persons" for intimidation of voters and interference with election officials, as well as conspiracy to commit these various crimes. Most of the witnesses for the government were blacks, and Kleberg noted that they were "very much frightened" about appearing in court and giving testimony. However, the district attorney "assured them that the Government will use every legitimate means to protect them, and if we can, secure their attendance upon the trial of the cases, in full confidence of a successful prosecution in most of the cases."[31]

Kleberg promised the attorney general to present a "strong case" upon each of the indictments, though he pointed out that every case would be "bitterly contested," and the "the best talent in the state will represent the defendants, and all that can be done with money and influence to overthrow the Government's case, will be done." Despite this the district attorney was confident of an outcome favorable to the government. He held that the people of Washington County generally supported the enforcement of the laws and "desire nothing but a fair trial and a vigorous prosecution of these cases."[32]

The first of the election cases was tried in the summer of 1887. In each of these cases tried the jury was unable to reach any verdict; the jury members were dismissed and the cases continued. The district attorney felt that the mistrials had not weakened the prosecutions but in fact had "strengthened" them. This interpretation of the results was not universally accepted. Senator Richard Coke of Texas attended the first of the Washington County trials and concluded: "[T]he trial convinced all who gave attention to the proceedings of the utter futility of the effort to convict the parties. . . . I cannot believe it is in the interests of the Court to continue the prosecutions of those people under such circumstances, promising nothing in the end but heavy cost bills to be footed by the Government and unnecessary expense and loss of time by the people of Washington County."[33]

Based on Coke's letter and others like it, the attorney general instructed Kleberg to make a full report on the "propriety of continuing [the] proceedings in [the] so-called Washington County election cases." The district attorney defended the prosecutions and his intentions of giving the defendants "a fair hearing and a vigorous prosecution." Kleberg also maintained that he was conducting the prosecutions as impartially as possible. "We have not allowed the Republicans of Washington County to give any political coloring to the prosecution, nor have we permitted our attachment to the Democratic party to sway us from the full performance of our duty as sworn officers of the government in the prosecution of the defendants."[34]

Despite the district attorney's report, Attorney General Garland was under constant pressure from Democrats in Texas and Washington to have the cases dismissed. Garland forwarded Kleberg's report to President Cleveland, and asked the president for instructions as to how to handle the prosecutions. The attorney general included with the report his own opinion that "it would not be wisdom, but the contrary, to advise dismissal." The president returned the report to Garland with the notation on the bottom: "I return your letter and the statement relating to the prosecutions in Texas under the Federal election laws and have only to say that I agree with you fully in the conclusions you have reached." On this basis, Garland informed District Attorney Kleberg that the department would not interfere in the prosecution of the election cases in any way and that the district attorney should "proceed with them according to [his] . . . best judgment." Garland also added that the applications made to him for the dismissal of the cases would be "denied."[35]

Although hampered by the continuing congressional investigations and the lack of sufficient funds for witnesses, the district attorney went on with the prosecution of the election cases. In April 1888, the cases were once again brought to trial; after a "closely contested trial," a "not guilty" verdict was rendered in favor of all the defendants. Kleberg reported:

> [W]e preferred this course as we are satisfied that a conviction could not be obtained, or at least was not likely as we had selected the strongest cases for trial. In that case we insisted and had a right to expect a verdict of guilty, however, it resulted in a mistrial the first time and an acquittal after the second trial. While we still believe that all of the defendants in these cases have violated the law, we do not think that a continuation of these prosecutions will subserve public justice but will simply result in a useless expense to the Government.[36]

Kleberg concluded, however, that the prosecutions had not been entirely devoid of some good as they may have the effect of deterring persons "from committing like offenses" in the future.[37]

Kleberg's optimism was misplaced, as "the Washington

County episode of 1886 was . . . the signal for repression of the Negro [vote] in the Black Belt" counties of Texas. Indeed, repression of the Republican and the freedman voter continued in almost all the southern states during the years 1885 to 1888. Yet, the actions of the president, Attorney General Garland, and District Attorney Kleberg in Washington County, Texas, indicated that as a result of the judicial affirmation of federal power over national elections the federal election statutes were not yet "dead letters." Nor was southern Republicanism. Although many Republican politicians during the middle years of the 1880s began turning toward economic issues, such as the tariff question, as the key to recapturing the presidency in 1888, a number of important GOP leaders, like William Chandler, continued to stress franchise protection as the only way to insure the existence of the Republican party in the South.[38]

Another element of continuity during the middle 1880s was the response of blacks themselves to the erosion of their political and civil rights in the South. Black politicians, educators, and writers, and conventions of black organizations, all spoke out against the emergence of segregation and the growing violence and intimidation against black voters. Nor, it must be added, was such protest directed only at the Democrats. A special black Civil Rights Congress, held in Washington, D.C., in 1883, denounced the Supreme Court's ruling in the Civil Rights Cases and indicted both the Democrats and Republicans for their failure to live up to their promises of safeguarding the liberties and rights of black citizens in the South. And during the years 1882 to 1884 there was considerable dissatisfaction on the part of blacks in the South with Arthur's attempts at alliance with Independent movements there. While supporting political rights and the "free ballot and a fair count" for the freedman, such movements sometimes contained men who were described as among "the colored man's worst enemies."[39]

However, despite occasional misgivings and dissatisfaction with Republicans, southern blacks continued to remain within the ranks of the Republican party. Acceptance of black participation by Democrats never materialized. While Cleveland accepted the responsibility of attempting to protect voters at federal elections, and even appointed several black men to positions in his administration, blacks continued to look to the party of Lincoln and Reconstruction for their political salvation. The approach of the presidential election of 1888 was marked by stirrings of interest among Republican politicians for a renewed attempt at revitalizing the southern wing of the party. Such feelings were reciprocated by blacks themselves. According to the influential black journalist T. Thomas Fortune of New York, "The South is good missionary ground. Let the Republican party contest it, and stop standing afar off and yelling, 'Stop Thief'"[40] And once again a key to that revitalization would be the protection of the "free ballot and a fair count" and the enforcement of the federal election statutes.

Notes

1. *U.S. v. Goldman*, Fed. Case No. 15,225 (1878), 1350–54. Inasmuch as no mention was made in any of the revised statutes as to their applicability to congressional elections, it is perhaps worthwhile to speculate on the origin of the judicial rationale based on Article 1, sec. 2 of the Constitution. It appears that in this instance the courts followed the lead of the Justice Department. In response to requests from district attorneys and marshals as to their duties at the congressional elections of 1878, Attorney General Charles Devens had based his instructions on that particular section of the Constitution. Though no judicial determination had as yet been made as to the constitutionality of the revised election laws, Devens assured local federal officials that Congress had the power to regulate elections for its own members. The case from which Justice Woods's decision in *U.S. v. Goldman* was drawn came out of the 1878 congressional elections in Louisiana. Thus, the specific use of Article 1, sec. 2 to support the federal election laws by the courts appears to have followed its use by the executive department. See also chap. 3 above.

2. *U.S. v. Goldman*, 1354.

3. *ex parte Siebold*, 100 U.S. 399 (1879); *ex parte Clarke*, 100 U.S. 399 (1879).

4. Ibid. Cf. *U.S. v. Amsden*, 6 Fed. 819 (1881).

5. Ibid. In *U.S. v. Bader*, 16 Fed. 116 (1883), the Circuit Court in

Louisiana held that the state officers and state laws at congressional elections become *pro tanto* officers and laws of Congress, and their violation subject to federal punishment.

6. *ex parte Geissler*, 4 Fed. 188 (1881).
7. *ex parte Yarbrough*, 110 U.S. 651 (1884).
8. Ibid., 660–64.
9. Ibid.
10. *Minor v. Happersett*, 88 U.S. 631 (1874).
11. *ex parte Yarbrough*, 657.
12. Ibid., 658.
13. Richard Claude, "Constitutional Voting Rights and Early U.S. Supreme Court Doctrine," *Journal of Negro History*, 51 (April 1966): 114–24. The five new justices were Samuel Blatchford, Horace Gray, William B. Woods, Stanley Mathews, and John M. Harlan. It should be noted that Claude maintained that by the time *Yarbrough* was decided, the question of federal enforcement of black voting rights had become "ironically moot" inasmuch as Attorney General Brewster, involved in the Star Route trials, had "virtually abandoned the enforcement of federal election law in the South." (123)
14. *ex parte Yarbrough*, 664.
15. John R. Schmidhauser, *The Supreme Court as Final Arbiter in Federal-State Relations, 1789–1957* (Chapel Hill, N.C., 1958), 112; William Gillette, "Samuel Miller," in Fred Israel and Leon Friedman, eds., *The Justices of the United States Supreme Court, 1789–1966: Their Lives and Major Opinions*, 2:1011–24.
16. *In re Coy*, 31 Fed. 803–4. However, see *ex parte Perkins*, 29 Fed. 900 (1887).
17. *Logan v. U.S.*, 144 U.S. 263 (1892). See also *U.S. v. Belvin*, 46 Fed. Rep. 381 (1891); *In re Quarles*, 158 U.S. 535 (1898); and U.S. v. Lackey, 99 Fed. Rep. 952 (1900).
18. Teackle Eliot to Brewster, Nov. 19, 1883, *Source-Chronological Files*, RG 60, National Archives.
19. Stanley Hirshson, *Farewell to the Bloody Shirt: Northern Republicans and the Negro, 1877–1893* (Chicago, 1968), 119–20; Charles E. Wynes, *Race Relations in Virginia, 1870–1902* (Charlottesville, Va., 1961), 29–34; *Congressional Record*, 48th Cong., 1st sess., Senate, pp. 588–89.
20. Ibid.; Harrison C. Thomas , "The Return of the Democratic Party to Power in 1884," *Studies in History, Economics and Public Law: Columbia University*, 89, no. 2 (New York, 1919): 130.
21. U.S. Senate, *Report of Committee on Elections in Virginia and*

Mississippi, 48th Cong., 1st sess., 1884, S. Repts. 521 and 579, 36–69. The majority report also called for the publication and distribution of the testimony taken before the committee, and reserved for future consideration "the question of submitting to the Senate further legislation and of conferring new powers on Congress by an amendment to the Constitution to afford further protection to the rights of citizens." On the other hand, a minority report put out by the four Democratic members of the committee blamed Republicans for the Danville and Copiah County outrages and for attempting to use the incidents for their own political purposes. The minority also accused the Republicans of caring more about the outcome of future elections in the South than about the rights of citizens there. (21–22)

22. Hirshson, *Bloody Shirt*, 120–22; Homer Cummings and Carl McFarland, *Federal Justice: Chapters in the History of Justice and the Federal Executive* (New York, 1937), 260; Thomas, "Return of Democratic Party to Power," chap. 8.

23. Kirk H. Porter and Donald B. Johnson, eds., *National Party Platforms* (Urbana, Ill., 1956), 66–67, and 74. For an analysis of Cleveland's victory, see Lee Benson, "Research Problems in American Political Historiography," *Common Research Frontiers in the Social Sciences*, ed. Mirra Kommarovsky (New York, 1965), 113–46. Using election data, Benson attacks the traditional and "impressionistic" interpretation of the Democrats' victory in 1884 as being due to the issues of "Rum, Romanism, and Rebellion." Rather, Benson sees the victory in light of the general decline of the Republican party, which began in 1872, and gains made by the Democrats in the elections of 1882–83. It might also be noted that of the eighteen states in which Republicans in 1894 actually improved on their percentage of the vote over their totals in 1880, eight of the states were in the South. In fact, only two southern states, Georgia and South Carolina, showed a constant decline in Republican percentages of the vote during the period 1880 to 1888 (134–37). This is additional confirmation of the proposition that southern Republicanism was still viable during the 1880s, and that Republican leaders were not wrong in attempting to maintain that viability through protection of franchise rights.

24. Horace Merrill, *Bourbon Leader: Grover Cleveland and the Democratic Party* (New York, 1957); U.S. Congress, *Inaugural Addresses of the Presidents of the United States from Washington to Kennedy* (Washington, D.C., 1961), 152; John G. Carlisle, "The Continuance of Democratic Rule," *The Forum*, 4 (October 1887): 120.

25. Robert Sobel, ed., *Biographical Directory of the United States*

Executive Branch, 1774–1941 (Westport, Conn., 1971), 124–25; Cummings and McFarland, *Federal Justice,* pp. 355–56; George Sinkler, *Racial Attitudes of American Presidents from Lincoln to Roosevelt* (New York, 1971), 259.

26. Cleveland to Garland, Oct. 5, 1886, *Letters Sent by the Department of Justice: Instructions to U.S. Attorneys and Marshals,* National Archives. (Hereafter cited as *Instructions.*)

27. Garland to U.S. Marshals, Oct. 15, 1886, *Instructions.*

28. Lawrence D. Rice, *The Negro in Texas, 1874–1900* (Baton Rouge, La., 1971), 119.

29. Kleberg to Garland, Feb. 11, 1887, *Case Files,* RG 60, National Archives (hereafter cited as *Case Files*). After 1884, correspondence from local department officials to Washington was filed by a case number and the source. For example, all communications involving election matters had a single case number under which any future letters, etc. would be filed from any one particular district. Within each case from each district, communications were then filed according to the date received.

30. Ibid.; Garland to Kleberg, March 4, 1887, *Instructions*; Kleberg to Garland, Feb. 16, 1887, *Case Files.*

31. Kleberg and Thomas Franklin (assistant U.S. attorney) to Garland, March 15, 1887, *Case Files.*

32. Ibid.

33. Kleberg to Garland, Aug. 27, 1887, *Case Files*; Coke to Garland, Dec. 12, 1887, *Case Files.*

34. Garland to Kleberg, Dec. 14, 1887, *Instructions*; Kleberg to Garland, Dec. 21, 1887, *Case Files.*

35. Garland to Cleveland, Dec. 30, 1887, *Case Files*; Cleveland to Garland, Jan. 5, 1888, *Case Files*; Garland to Kleberg, Jan. 6, 1888, *Instructions.*

36. Garland to Kleberg, Jan. 12, 1888, *Instructions*; Senate Committee on Privileges and Elections to Garland, March 24, 1888, *Case Files* ; Kleberg to Garland, April 25, 1888, *Case Files.*

37. Kleberg to Garland, April 25, 1888, *Case Files.*

38. Rice, *Negro in Texas,* 120; Hirshson, *Bloody Shirt,* 152–56.

39. C. Vann Woodward, *The Strange Career of Jim Crow,* 3d ed. (New York, 1975), 31–65; August Meier, *Negro Thought in America, 1880–1915* (Ann Arbor, Mich., 1966), chaps. 2 and 5; Hirshson, *Bloody Shirt,* 115; Vincent P. DeSantis, "Negro Dissatisfaction with Republican Policy in the South, 1882–1884, *Journal of Negro History,* 36 (April, 1951): 148–59; "Proceedings of the Civil Rights Mass Meeting Held at Lincoln Hall,

October 22, 1883" (Washington, D.C., 1883), reprinted in Herbert Aptheker, ed., *A Documentary History of the Negro People of the U.S.* (New York, 1951), 2:658–59.

40. Quoted in Vincent P. DeSantis, *Republicans Face the Southern Question: the New Departure Years, 1877–1897* (Baltimore, 1959), 193.

6

Revitalization Again: Harrison and Voting Rights Enforcement, 1888–1893

THE RETURN TO POWER by Republicans in 1888 did bring a renewed concern for the protection of voting rights in the South and the enforcement of the election statutes. Between 1889 and 1892 the Justice Department and its officials in the South were active in the prosecution of election law violations and the attempt to bring about a "free ballot and a fair count." These years marked the final attempt by Republican leaders to prevent the rise of a solid Democratic South and rejuvenate southern Republicanism through the protection of the ballot box. Despite the failure of Congress to pass the election bill of 1890, the Department of Justice continued to enforce those election statutes still on the books, until the repeal of the laws by Congress in 1893.

The activity by the Justice Department was a reflection of a number of political factors and developments during this time. One such factor was a growing concern in Congress about voting rights and their violation in the South, thereby prompting consideration of additional legislation enforcing the Fifteenth Amendment. As a result of the 1888 elections, Republicans captured control of both houses of Congress, and almost immediately leading Republican members, including the prestigious Henry Cabot Lodge and George Frisbie Hoar, "began to study . . . proposals for federal supervision of elections for national officeholders."[1]

Another factor that influenced enforcement activity by the Justice Department was the attitudes and concerns of the new president, Benjamin Harrison. During the campaign of 1888, Harrison ignored the admonitions of the "manufacturers, mugwumps, and merchants" within his own party that he campaign entirely on economic issues and appeal to southern Democratic protectionists in order to split the Democratic vote in the South. Harrison was consistent and explicit in his support for the plank of the Republican party platform, which called for "the supreme and sovereign right of every lawful citizen ... white or black, to cast one free ballot in public elections, and to have the ballot duly counted."[2]

The results of the 1888 presidential canvass gave further hope to Republicans committed to revitalizing the Republican party in the South. Harrison received more votes from the South than any Republican presidential candidate since the end of Reconstruction, and he lost the electoral votes of North Carolina, Virginia, and Tennessee by narrow margins. Along with other northern Republicans, the new president concluded "that enough Republican voters lived in the South to give the party some victories, but that their votes had either been suppressed or not counted." The strategy should therefore be to "have this vote counted instead of devising a policy to drum up Republican sentiment among southern Democrats where it did not exist or could not be cultivated."[3]

In a speech in Indianapolis shortly after the election, Harrison asserted this theme by claiming that "the only fear we should now have is a corruption or suppression of the free ballot, and your utmost exertions should be to prevent it." In his first address to Congress, Harrison promised that "the colored man should be protected in all his relations to the federal government, whether as litigant, juror, or witness in our courts ... [or] as an elector of members of Congress."[4]

While the president believed that part of the answer to the problem of protecting black voters and promoting Republican voters in the South was additional congressional legislation, he also was aware of the responsibility of the executive branch, and specifically the Justice Department, for enforcing existing federal election laws. In 1885 Harrison had been pessimistic about the possibility of federal election law enforcement. He deplored that "we may place the U.S. Marshals at the polls, if we ever recover the Presidency again; but it has been demonstrated that local sentiment is such that convictions for any violations of election laws is impossible." However, as president, Harrison by 1889 was willing to commit the resources of the executive branch, in cooperation with Congress, to insure franchise rights. "The freedom of the ballot is a condition of our national life, and no power vested in Congress or in the Executive to secure and perpetuate it should remain unused."[5]

The importance of election law enforcement by the Justice Department was also expressed by the president's supporters in the South. According to Emory Speer of Georgia, now a federal judge, the election laws could be enforced in the South; the key to such enforcement was the appointment of "good" district attorneys and marshals. Such men, Speer maintained, should be of "fearless character." Judge Speer also advised Harrison "to let it be known that the Department will regularly, firmly and unflinchingly, prosecute every intentional violation of the election laws. To let the law breaker, and his political manager, know that his prosecution with its costs will certainly follow his crime. Let the voter have the encouraging assurance that a strong, vigilant and just government is at his back."[6]

In his cabinet appointments Harrison was "determined to appoint one genuine friend from his own state, one whose fidelity and qualifications he could not doubt." The position the president chose to fill with such a person was the attorney generalship, and the man he chose to fill that position was his former law partner, William Henry Harrison Miller. Although Miller had had no previous political experience, he soon became one of Harrison's most "trusted advisors," particularly in matters involving the administration and the South.[7]

Upon assuming the duties of attorney general, Miller, as well as the president, was swamped by letters and telegrams from Republicans throughout the South putting forward their particular candidates for district attorney and marshal. Running through these communications were the themes expressed by

Judge Speer: the importance of able Republicans in the enforcement of the federal laws, and the importance of the enforcement of the federal laws to the future of the Republican party in the South. According to one Republican leader in South Carolina, "We want in the District Attorney's office men of commanding position at the bar; such men have the respect and admiration of the masses of the people, and will win confidence and respect for the administration." The editor of the *Southern Industrial Record* thus advised the attorney general: "Occupying the position you do, you can greatly aid in this work [building up southern Republicanism] by recommending republicans for federal positions in the South that have the acceptance and confidence of the people and with whom they would be willing to co-operate without hesitation."[8]

Shortly after taking office, the attorney general turned his attention to the enforcement of the federal election laws. He directed district attorneys in the South to report on possible violations of the federal election statutes at the 1888 election, and to begin prosecution of such cases in their respective districts as soon as possible. Such prosecutions were begun in North Carolina, South Carolina, Alabama, Arkansas, Virginia, Tennessee, and Florida.[9]

The prosecutions in North Carolina, South Carolina, Alabama, and Virginia were not extensive, nor were they particularly successful. However, they do illustrate the concern by the Harrison administration to begin as soon as possible the enforcement of the election law. These cases are also indicative of the increased difficulties facing local federal officials in attempting to prosecute successfully violations of the election laws. Whereas prior to this time district attorneys had trouble securing guilty verdicts in election cases, now the federal attorneys had similar problems in securing indictments from grand juries in these cases. In at least one instance the inability to secure grand jury indictments resulted in a district attorney's attempting an alternate means of bringing charges—what was known as the filing of an information. In other instances the refusal of local federal grand juries to indict those accused of election law violations simply ended the prosecution of such cases.

Republican electoral successes after four years of Democratic rule in Washington sparked renewed interest among North Carolina Republicans in the enforcement of the election statutes. According to one Republican in that state, "The public interest as well as public virtue in this state has . . . suffered from the neglect to prosecute election frauds. This has especially been the case for the last four years or more." Although petty revenue cases had been prosecuted with sufficient vigor in the past, "the greatly more important offence of interference with a free ballot and a fair count, which is sapping the foundation of free government, has been so often overlooked or condoned that offenders have scarcely any regard for the majesty of the law."[10]

On the basis of other such reports from North Carolina, the attorney general instructed the United States attorneys in that state to investigate possible violations of the election laws, and to prosecute such cases vigorously. Charles Price, district attorney for the Western District, reported that he had already begun preparation of several election cases and would "spare no effort" to find evidence for additional cases. While indictments were secured in these cases, their trial was constantly put off, and the cases were never heard. This did not particularly bother Price, since he felt that a "pending indictment untried will go far to prevent any similar disturbances."[11]

Charles Cook, district attorney for the Eastern District of North Carolina, also indicated that he would readily comply with the attorney general's instructions regarding election cases. "Unless vigorous action is taken and the guilty strongly prosecuted, elections in this state will degenerate into a farce and the election law brought into contempt." Cook drew up six bills of indictment aimed at members of the Warren County Canvassing Board for failure to count the properly returned votes from several eastern townships. However, the grand jury refused to indict the six board members. Cook reported that "a number of the grand jury consisted of political friends of the defendants; and one of them as I am informed, is himself charged with violations of the election law, by parties in his own township."[12]

The attorney general then directed Cook to find "if possible by legal means" a grand jury that would "decide according to law upon the facts and return indictments where the laws have been violated." Miller told the district attorney to present such violations to "every grand jury until the statute of limitations intervenes." In addition, the attorney general authorized the appointment of Judge D. L. Russell as special counsel in the prosecution of the election cases. In June of 1890, bills of indictment against the Warren County Board of Canvassers were re-presented to a federal grand jury by Russell and Cook, and again the bills were ignored. Two indictments were handed down in "comparatively unimportant" election cases. The district attorney was "becoming satisfied that the Grand Jury would not return a true bill in any case of much importance."[13]

Unable even to secure indictments and anxious to "close matters of this character as soon as possible," the attorney general suggested that the services of Judge Russell be "discontinued." However, in December of 1890, Judge Russell reported "with much surprise and exquisite pleasure" that the grand jury in Wilmington, North Carolina, had at last handed down indictments against those charged with election law violations at the 1888 elections. The following June these cases were tried, and after a three-day trial all the defendants were acquitted. The district attorney concluded that "the jury rendered a partisan verdict (being composed almost entirely of Democrats—unavoidable on the part of the government). In fact the draft for this term was the worst we have ever had."[14]

In South Carolina the initiation of prosecutions of election cases was largely a result of the hesitancy of the Senate to confirm President Harrison's nominee for district attorney in that state, Abial Lathrop. The attorney general informed Lathrop that the Senate's reluctance to confirm him was due to their belief that Lathrop had "not made any vigorous attempts to punish parties who were guilty of election frauds in the election of 1888" and that his "personal affiliations, associations, and sympathies, are rather with the men who have committed and sanctioned these wrongs upon the ballot box, than with those who suffered by them." Miller expressed his own support of Lathrop, but thought it imperative that the acting district attorney show he had been "standing firmly and earnestly for the maintenance and vindication of the law and the rights of all citizens."[15]

In a lengthy reply, Lathrop defended his Republican principles and affiliations and his conviction that "a fraud upon the ballot [was] one of the worst of all crimes." Lathrop explained that he had not taken any action with regard to election law violations stemming from the 1888 elections because he had no personal knowledge of such violations. He felt that part of the reason for this was that for the 1888 elections, in most of the precincts there had been no Republican candidates running for office other than the president. Lathrop did claim that he had possible evidence for two cases, and he promised to attempt to secure indictments in these cases.[16]

At the July term of the grand jury in 1890, Lathrop was unsuccessful in securing the promised indictments. Despite what he felt was "clear and positive evidence," the grand jury refused to hand down indictments, and the district attorney concluded that "a true bill could not be obtained from that Grand Jury in election cases." Lathrop blamed the grand jury's failure to indict on its composition, which had been "drawn from boxes prepared several years ago." This indicated that all members of the jury were probably Democrats. Although Lathrop again promised to bring the cases before the next meeting of the grand jury, no further action on his part in prosecuting election cases appears to have been taken.[17]

In Virginia, where Harrison had lost by only fifteen hundred votes, fraud was perhaps less of a factor in the outcome than apathy and dissention among Republicans and Readjusters. However, under District Attorneys Craig and Borland, prosecutions for election law violations were instituted. In the Western District of the state, U.S. Attorney William E. Craig attempted to prosecute violations of the election statutes by filing informations against persons suspected of violating these laws. Informations were similar to indictments except that they were presented by a competent legal official under oath instead of being presented by a grand jury. Craig believed that, given the political climate in his district, he would have a hard time getting a grand jury to indict any Democrat, so it might be more effective to proceed by informations. There were, however, problems with this approach. Bringing criminal charges by information had been confined to state criminal proceedings. It had not been used before in federal courts. Moreover, the Enforcement Acts specifically required that charges be brought by indictment. Thus, any alternative procedure would have necessitated congressional action.[18]

The use of informations filed by Craig was appealed by counsel for the defendants in the election cases. In June of 1890, District Court Judge Paul upheld the use of this procedure on the part of the district attorney. According to Craig, "This is a very strong opinion and determines the question squarely and will, I believe, be sustained by the Supreme Court, should the question be carried to that Court." At the same time, the district attorney took the opportunity to file informations against other individuals for election law violations. In a report to the attorney general, Craig noted the general effect of Judge Paul's decision. "Instead of the defiant manner by which I was first met, these parties are now begging for a compromise. The cases are exciting wide attention and are having a beneficial effect."[19]

The trial of the election cases in Craig's district were not completed until October 1891. The district attorney then reported that "we have been very successful in our prosecutions, having secured convictions in all important cases." One of the cases in which a guilty verdict was obtained had been based on the filing of an information by the district attorney. Craig pointed out that "it is the first conviction of the kind in our state, and its effect is expected to be very beneficial."[20]

In the Eastern District in Virginia, U.S. Attorney Thomas R. Borland was not as successful as his Western District counterpart. Borland was able to obtain indictments against six persons in his district for hindering and intimidating voters at the 1888 elections. During the grand jury's deliberations it was discovered that the foreman of the jury, Dr. William H. Taylor, had earlier acted as a United States commissioner and had been responsible for issuing the warrants for the arrests of several of the men being indicted. The presiding judge, Robert Hughes, thereupon replaced Taylor with a new foreman and the grand jury handed down its indictments. The defendants then attempted to have the indictments quashed on the grounds that the grand jury had been improperly impaneled because of Judge Hughes's actions.[21]

The indictments and the motions to have them quashed were presented April 1890. By January of 1891 nothing more had been done in the matter and the attorney general instructed Borland to report on the status of the election case prosecutions. "I have not heard from you in regard to them in a long time. I want to know just what indictments are pending, for what offenses, against what persons, what is the prospect for trials, in short, the status of the whole business." Miller concluded his instructions by stating, "It is my desire that if there have been intentional violations of the election laws, that they shall be prosecuted vigorously."[22]

In his report to the attorney general, Borland acknowledged that there appeared to be "a lack of activity on the prosecution" of the election cases, but indicated there had been "several causes of delay" with respect to the advancement of the prosecutions. The most important cause was, he believed, that the jury summoned for the trial of the cases the previous October "was so strongly partisan, as to forbid any hope of a fair and impartial trial, that would have resulted in an acquittal of all the parties concerned." Thus, Borland had even delayed the court arguments on the motions by the defendants to quash the indictments. "If the motion to quash had been decided in our favor, counsel for the defendants would have clamored for an immediate trial before the jury then summoned." Borland was now, however, forced to concede that this course of action had been of "doubtful utility," since the next April term jury "will probably be as much biased as the October jury."[23]

The attorney general accepted Borland's explanations and directed him to "have the validity of the indictments disposed of, and then arrange for trial.... It is not so much that many may be convicted as that it shall be shown that the law can be enforced, and is enforced against intentional wrongdoers."[24] The election cases never reached trial, for on April 22, 1891,

Judge Robert Hughes quashed all the indictments against the defendants. Repeating his own earlier arguments from *U.S. v. Mumford* [25] that the statutes under which the defendants had been indicted were constitutional, Hughes based his decision on the fact the indictments themselves were "in vague, general terms, without such special averments as are required by the rules of criminal proceeding."[26]

Judge Hughes concluded that challenging a voter, if such challenging was done lawfully, was not a crime under the federal election statutes. However, "To hinder a voter from voting in a federal election is. Therefore, when an indictment charges too generally that the accused hindered a voter from voting, it does not and cannot cure the defect of that charge to specify that the hindering was by means of challenging voters." What Hughes was doing was simply going back to the Supreme Court's 1876 decision in *U.S. v. Cruikshank*. In that decision the Supreme Court dismissed indictments against persons accused of similar crimes on the same grounds. Indeed, the language of the two decisions, quashing the indictments on the grounds that they were too vague and general, is strikingly similar. In any case, the decision of Judge Hughes in the *Belvin* case ended the prosecution of further election cases in Virginia until after the presidential election of 1892.[27]

Despite reports of widespread election law violations in Alabama in 1888, only two convictions resulted from prosecutions in these cases. District Attorneys M. D. Wikersham and Lewis Parsons had been instructed by the attorney general to investigate and prosecute all such violations. In June 1890 both attorneys were themselves charged by Republican Congressman J. V. McDufee of Alabama and C. Daniels of being "incompetent or something else." Daniel's letter claimed that fifty election cases had been brought in Mobile by District Attorney Wikersham and that in these cases there were only two convictions. According to Daniels, the cases were not brought to enforce the election laws; rather, "the game has been to defraud and draw from the department all fees and for every case they can."[28]

The attorney general instructed both Wikersham and Parsons

to answer these charges and explain why more was not being done to achieve successful prosecution of the election cases. Both attorneys replied, defending their prosecutions and explaining their apparent lack of success. According to Parsons, it was impossible to secure indictments in these kinds of cases "because the Grand Jury had a majority of Democrats on it.... Until the jury laws are changed or the Clerk of the Court puts Republicans on the juries it will hardly be possible to indict in these cases." Wikersham also defended his lack of success by complaining about Democratic juries and the impossibility of securing convictions and indictments in election cases from such juries. Despite promises by both district attorneys to vigorously enforce the election laws, no further action was taken by either man to prosecute election cases in Alabama.[29]

The prosecutions in these four states show that although the attorney general was actively interested in enforcing the election laws, it was difficult for southern district attorneys to even secure indictments from grand juries in such cases. One possible solution in this problem was prosecution by informations, as was done in the Virginia cases. The attorney general acknowledged this possibility, and hoped that he could get legislative approval of this method of prosecution by Congress, which was then considering the revision of the federal election statutes. In reply to District Attorney Wikersham's suggestion that legislative provision should be made for the use of informations in election cases, Miller wrote "that other District Attorneys have brought this to my attention, and I have urged legislation to this end upon the Judiciary Committee of both the House and the Senate." Miller also directed Wikersham's attention to Judge Paul's decision in Virginia, apparently giving judicial support to this procedure. However, the defeat of the elections bill in Congress ended hopes for the possibility of legislative sanction for this method of getting around recalcitrant southern grand juries.[30]

In Tennessee and Arkansas, prosecutions for violation of the election laws were more extensive than in the states discussed above, and the number of actual convictions obtained in these cases was impressive. Under District Attorney C. C. Waters, prosecutions for election law violations were begun and indictments handed down in cases from five Arkansas counties. Waters asked for, and received, permission to appoint Judge John C. McClure as a special prosecuting attorney to assist him in the handling of the election cases. These cases were tried in April of 1889 and March of 1890, and out of nineteen persons indicted and tried, the government was successful in convicting twelve. However, despite the number of guilty verdicts, the possible effects of the convictions were offset by the light sentences given the defendants.[31]

In cases from Union and Cleveland counties in Arkansas, two men were tried for interfering with federal election supervisors. Reuben W. Darden, described as "the old man," was convicted of interference with election officials and driving a voter away from the polls in Union County. Darden was sentenced to two years imprisonment. Thomas Dansby, described in reports as "a young man," was convicted of interfering with a federal supervisor in Cleveland County. He was fined five hundred dollars. In sentencing Dansby, the court justified the imposition of only a fine because evidence presented indicated that Dansby's offense "appeared to be more the result of drunken recklessness than of any preconceived design to keep the supervisor away from the polls."[32]

In other election cases, persons from several counties charged with interference with election supervisors were fined only ten dollars after pleading guilty. According to presiding Judge Caldwell, the fines in these cases were "nominal" because "no intention to commit a criminal violation of the law was shown . . . and that this case with others had been brought in order that all might be more forcibly impressed with the duties devolving on officers of election."[33]

A year later the rest of the Arkansas election cases were tried, and once again the defendants pleaded guilty and were fined ten dollars each and court costs. This time the court's actions were defended by Judge McClure, who admitted:

> It is true the fines imposed are not great, but they are the same fines that were imposed, where pleas of guilty were entered at

Little Rock, in like cases [the year before].... Judge Caldwell admonished all present that the law fine imposed must not be regarded as a precedent in future cases; that he was now satisfied the public was familiar with the law governing Congressional and presidential elections, and in the future persons contemplating the violations of the laws, must be prepared to accept the full penalty of the law.[34]

The prosecutions for election law violations in Tennessee were centered in the Western District of the state.[35] In June of 1889, District Attorney Samuel W. Hawkins reported that the grand jury meeting in Memphis had returned seventy-three indictments against persons in that district for election law violations involving "various offenses." A number of election judges were indicted for failure to return poll books, and others were charged with preventing large numbers of black citizens from voting through use of the state law requiring voters to cast their ballots in their own districts or wards.

> At the November election in many wards in Memphis this statute was enforced against the negroes, but the white men were allowed to vote wherever they choose.... At the polling place two alleys are made, one for the negroes the other for whites. Now to illustrate: at 3rd ward one hundred negroes are not allowed to vote, estensibly [sic] for want of time, nearly all of them being challenged and delayed until they can show that they reside in that ward. White men from other wards come there and vote, thus adding to the detention.[36]

To help prosecute these cases, Hawkins requested the appointment of W. W. Murray, the former U.S. attorney for the Western District, as "he is well and favorably known throughout the State, and by all parties conceded to be a man of great ability." The district attorney also confessed to Miller that because of the large number of indictments handed down, there was a good amount of criticism of the department in that district for attempting to "put fat fees in the pockets of the federal court officials." Hawkins denied this emphatically. Rather, "the question of the power of the Government to punish violations of the election laws ... is to be determined in these cases. Unless some of these parties are brought to justice all elections hereafter in this state will simply be a farce."[37]

The attorney general agreed to the appointment of Murray and instructed Hawkins to prosecute the election cases with "the utmost care and vigor." In respect to the criticism of the department bringing these cases simply to obtain fees, the attorney general concluded, "I trust that we shall be able to show these gentlemen that the purpose of these prosecutions is somewhat entirely different from making fees."[38]

The election cases were set for trial in December of 1889. Hawkins believed that there was "ample testimony to sustain these indictments. . . . I think the proof is ample to convict if the jury will do their duty." The attorney general gave Hawkins a free hand in the prosecutions and explained to him that "I have no suggestions to make except as I have always said with reference to violations of the law, whether relative to the elective franchise or other matters, the policy of the Department is vigorous prosecution."[39]

The first of the cases tried resulted in a mistrial. The most important of these was the case against E. E. Carpenter and others of Fayette County for ballot-box stuffing. Special prosecuting attorney Murray reported that "the defendant's counsel made a desperate effort to carry the jury for acquittal as by doing so they hoped to break the back of the prosecution. Every possible effort was made by counsel to stir up the prejudice of the white man against the negro." However, the defendants and their attorneys were in fact greatly "disheartened and disappointed" at the outcome of the trial, as "two of the six jurors voting for conviction were Democrats." Murray concluded that the guilt of those accused had been established beyond doubt, but "prejudice against the negro alone prevented a verdict of guilty"[40]

The Carpenter case was tried again in January of 1890, and again resulted in a mistrial. The district attorney reported that this time nine jurors were for outright acquittal and three were in favor of conviction. The defendants themselves urged that the case be continued at some future time, claiming that they were being financially ruined by the prosecutions and their attorneys "constantly engaged in this suit to the exclusion of all other business." Hawkins had high praise for the efforts of special attorney Murray, particularly since Murray had been seriously ill during the latter part of the trial. However, "I gave him [Murray] the privilege of closing the argument, and although he was unable to stand, and was urged by friends and physicians not to attempt an argument, and if he did so he did so at the risk of his life, yet he made one of the finest arguments I have ever heard in a court house . . . sitting in a chair while he delivered it."[41]

Despite the lack of convictions up to that point, Attorney General Miller expressed satisfaction with the "vigor and determination" with which the election cases had been prosecuted by Hawkins and Murray. Miller instructed both men, if they felt the evidence was sufficiently strong to ultimately insure a guilty verdict, to continue with these cases and to bring the cases to trial once more. The election cases were then set by the district attorney for the coming November term of the district court in Memphis, although Hawkins was by now somewhat pessimistic about the outcome of these trials: "While some of the remaining cases are important ones, I do not believe that we can ever make out a stronger case than we have, and, while I would like to have the assistance of General Murray in trying these cases, I can hardly say that even with his assistance that I will be able to secure convictions." The district attorney noted that in addition to the Carpenter case awaiting trial, there were three other similiar cases: two cases involving illegal voting and one for intimidating voters.[42]

By December, Hawkins was completely convinced of the impossibility of securing convictions, and asked permission to have the election cases dismissed. He felt that in these cases a not guilty verdict would be much worse than no trial at all. However, Hawkins was sure that the prosecutions had been of some value. "The vigorous prosecution of these election frauds has had a good effect, and the conviction had for the minor offenses, together with the great publicity given to these cases . . . has brought the matter to the attention of the people." The district attorney also concluded that there was little need for the continued attempts at enforcement of the federal election laws in

Tennessee, since the newly passed state election law was proving effective in disfranchising black voters without resort to violating federal laws.⁴³

The most important enforcement activity by the Justice Department in the years 1889 to 1892 took place in the Northern District of Florida. The resistance to the prosecution of election cases by local federal officials in that district was closely followed not only by the attorney general, but by President Harrison as well. Indeed, conditions became so critical in four of the northern counties of the state that the attorney general and the president took preliminary steps toward what might have become the first use of federal troops in the South since the end of Reconstruction—to help enforce the Civil War amendments to the Constitution. The events in Florida clearly illustrate Harrison's policy of active executive department action in the protection of the elective franchise. Also important was the fact that the president and the attorney general were contemplating the use of martial law and troops in the South at the very time Congress was considering the Lodge bill, aimed at strengthening the federal election statutes.

In response to the attorney general's request for a report on possible violations of the election laws, District Attorney J. N. Stripling of the Northern District of Florida reported that at the 1888 congressional and presidential contest in the state there had been many "flagrant" and "gross" violations of the franchise statutes. Stripling promised to have the cases "promptly and vigorously prosecuted" and to submit a more detailed report of such cases after additional investigation. The district attorney was well aware of the obstacles facing a successful prosecution of the cases in his district. For one thing, the "political prejudices" engendered by the last election were still running high, and this could have its "influence in the jury box & in all probability defeat the ends of justice." For another thing, Stripling felt that "the successful prosecution of these cases will require an almost extravagant amount of money, as in many instances, whole communities are in sympathy with the persons accused and it would be dangerous to attempt an arrest without a strong posse."⁴⁴

The most flagrant violations of the election laws took place in Madison County. According to Stripling, at the 1888 election a mob of some two hundred persons went undisguised to several polling places in that county and destroyed the ballot boxes and the votes in them. In addition, the mob drove the various officers of election from the polling places. Stripling indicated that a majority of the persons who participated were "well-known" and that "their conduct on the occasion referred to could easily be established by reliable witnesses, provided they could have responsible assurance of protection from violence from these parties." The district attorney also had "good reason to believe that a conspiracy has been formed by these parties to resist, forcibly if necessary, the execution of any process for their arrest, and, by the same means, to rescue any one or more of their class that should happen to be arrested."[45]

Stripling's fear that these parties would resort to violence and assassination "whenever they deem it necessary to shield themselves from punishment" was realized the following month. John Bird, a government witness in the election cases, was "called out of his house after he had retired, and was shot down." In response to the murder of Bird, the attorney general directed Stripling to find "a first-rate local lawyer" to assist in the Madison County election cases. In addition, Miller also stated that "I can say here that it is the purpose of the President, as well as myself, to stand by you, and stand by the Marshal, and protect the officers of the Court, and the witnesses, and to raise whatever force may be necessary to that purpose."[46]

The response by the citizens of Madison County to the indications of the district attorney of his intent to vigorously enforce the federal laws was to begin a systematic resistance to the execution of any federal process in that county. Two deputies, sent by U.S. Marshal John R. Mizell to Madison County to arrest certain persons in connection with the election cases, were halted by an armed group of men. The men claimed that they would prevent any witness from leaving the county and "also declared that they would resist any attempt to arrest anyone in that county . . . that they were thoroughly armed and organized and could muster five hundred winchester rifles on short notice."[47]

Mizell suggested to the attorney general that since it had become impossible to enforce the laws by the "ordinary course of judicial proceedings," resort might be had to Section 5298 of the Revised Statutes, which provided for the use of federal troops by the president in cases of internal "insurrection." The attorney general, however, felt at that point that every effort should be made by the marshal and the district attorney to avoid resorting to such an extreme measure. Miller did direct the marshal to organize a posse "of sufficient force" to go into Madison County to bring out the witnesses and those accused of violating the election laws. "Whether this force would be ten or twenty or fifty men, is of course, a matter largely in your discretion. It would probably be better that they should be white men, and while there should be no hesitation and vacillation in the premises, yet at the same time there should always be the utmost care to avoid conflict and trouble if possible."[48]

Despite the attorney general's reluctance to "resort to extraordinary measures without exhausting ordinary measures," he instructed the district attorney to secure from the local federal district court judge a statement that "in his judgment the laws cannot be enforced in the matter by the ordinary course of judicial proceedings." The same day District Court Judge Charles Swayne submitted such a statement to the Justice Department, and Miller commented that "it is the purpose of the President and the Department to enforce the law, and see that the process of the court is respected and executed."[49]

At the end of October, 1889, the federal grand jury convened in Jacksonville to consider indictments in the election cases. Ten indictments, covering thirty-one persons, were handed down by the grand jury as well as "a number of other true bills in election cases which will be presented as soon as they can be prepared." A good deal of the court's time during the October session was involved with defense motions to have the venue of both future grand juries and the election case trials moved to Tallahassee. The district attorney strongly opposed these attempts, believing that Tallahassee "is the center of the district in which a great majority of frauds are committed & in which excitement, as we expected, is now running so high." Stripling also indicated that he had been unable to find a Democratic lawyer in the district to aid in the prosecution of the election cases, not "because of any disapproval of these prosecutions or of anything that has been done by the Court. Their objections are based purely on antagonisms which they would expect to incur & result in injury to their practice."[50]

Having secured indictments against a good number of persons for violation of the election laws, the district attorney and marshal were faced with the task of arresting those persons, mostly in Madison County, for whom warrants had not been issued, as well as protecting witnesses in these cases. This, it was accepted, would not be easy. "The combination in that county is formidable that they have succeeded in terrorizing and intimidating the whole population of the County, so that it is next to an impossibility to obtain any information as to the identity or whereabouts of the parties for whom warrants have been issued." Finding and protecting witnesses was also problematical. The murder of the witness John Bird "has . . . completely terrorized witnesses that they are about as hard to find as the criminals."[51]

In addition, resistance to federal enforcement was beginning in counties other than Madison. In Alachua County a mob one evening called "a prominent republican," L. A. Barnes, out of his home and warned him that he would be murdered if further attempts were made to prosecute election cases in that county. Several days after this the registrar of elections for Alachua County pleaded guilty in federal court to two indictments charging him with failure to register persons in that county entitled to vote. District Attorney Stripling reported:

> [I]n consideration of his confession of his guilt coupled with his assurance and the assurance of his political friends, who are among the most prominent citizens of that County, that there shall not be a repetition of this offense in the future . . . I have been importuned by some of the most prominent republicans of this county not to pray judgment against him . . . until December, '90. . . . The purpose of this, of course, is to have judgment finally suspended."[52]

The attorney general strongly rebuked Stripling for considering taking this course of action with regard to the registrar. "This program does not commend itself to my judgment. If this man has deliberately and flagrantly violated the law I think he ought to be punished. He undoubtably [sic] would not have confessed and plead [sic] guilty except that he saw himself inextricably in the toils, and it does not comport with my views of the administration of the law that one so evidently guilty of a grave crime should entirely escape punishment."[53]

The attorney general was becoming even more dissatisfied with the manner in which Marshal Mizell was attempting, or not attempting, to arrest those persons indicted in the Madison County election cases. Mizell reported sending into the county a "corps" of sixteen deputy marshals, who were unable to locate any of the defendants or witnesses. According to Mizell, "it is a fixed policy of the State authorities as well as offenders, that no U.S. Court mandate, shall be executed in Madison County. The Telegraphs & Railroads are in full accord and sympathy with them, hence I find myself hampered on every hand; and it is useless to further disguise the fact that the Court and its Officials, are completely unable to enforce its mandate in this County."[54]

The attorney general informed Mizell that President Harrison had been following the activities of the marshal and that "he is not pleased with the manner in which attempts have been made to serve process in Madison and Gadsden Counties." Miller instructed the marshal to personally accompany any force sent to the counties to make arrests, since the deputies sent "do not seem to have been armed with any evidence of their official character, nor do they seem to have gone about the execution of their work with any degree of resolution." The attorney general authorized the posting of a $250 reward for the "arrest and delivery" of four of the most prominent men indicted. He also indicated that the use of federal troops, which Mizell had again suggested, could not be called until the issuance of a proclamation by the president ordering those persons resisting lawful court process to disperse to their homes. "The President does not like to issue a proclamation of this kind without some evidence of some actual resistance."[55]

By January of 1890 the marshal had still made no arrests in Madison County. He did report that he was in the process of organizing a force of forty to fifty men to "operate" in Madison, Leon, Jefferson, and Gadsden counties, and that such a force "will require considerable time to select and organize." This did nothing to satisfy the attorney general who again repeated his belief that "no earnest and determined effort has been made to execute these rights." Miller directed the marshal to "go quietly" into the county "without any display of arms" to make arrests, and to take with him only a small force of deputies. "If you meet with actual resistance or have prisoners arrested who are rescued, the President and the Department will take prompt action." In addition, Miller increased the reward offered for the capture of the four "ringleaders" to $500 for each person.[56]

On February 5, 1890, Mizell went to Madison County with a posse of six deputy marshals, but was unable to find anyone for whom warrants had been issued. At his hotel that night a mob appeared outside and demanded entrance. The landlord of the establishment went out and refused entrance to any members of the mob, saying that he would kill anyone who tried to enter. Mizell was at the top of the stairs with a "pistol in each hand" waiting and listening. The men did not enter the hotel, but did patrol outside of it all night, and in the morning finally dispersed. Mizell returned to Jacksonville, again not having made any arrests. In addition, two of his deputies, "having caught very severe chills and fever whilst lying out in the woods," had to recuperate.[57]

Nine days later conditions in northern Florida became even more critical when Deputy Marshal W. B. Saunders was assassinated during the convening of the grand jury in Tallahassee. Stripling and Mizell were instructed to come immediately to Washington to discuss matters with Miller and the president, though only Mizell went. Then on April 10, 1890, the attorney general complained that since Mizell's return from Washington "nothing has been done by him toward the execution of the warrants in his hands for the arrest of parties in the counties of Madison, Jefferson, Leon, and Gadsden, charged with violations of the election laws." Stripling stated that conditions in his district were critical and the people there "depressed" and "discouraged," particularly when seeing "indicted parties quietly pursuing their daily avocations, apparently, without any fear of molestation."[58]

The district attorney also expressed some bitterness about the lack of support he felt he was getting from the department, and that in spite of the "energy and zeal" he had displayed in bringing the parties involved to justice, the only result had been "that I am now in a position that renders it unsafe for me to leave Jacksonville, except under the greatest precautions." Stripling concluded that "after having been encouraged to undertake these prosecutions, it would not only be a mockery of justice, but very unfair to me now to abandon them, and leave me at the mercy of the offenders."[59]

On April 17, 1890, Mizell resigned, and Harrison appointed former Lieutenant Governor Edmund C. Weeks to succeed him as marshal for the Northern District. A week later, the president wrote a letter to the attorney general on the situation in Florida. Because of the widespread interest in the resistance to federal law enforcement that was taking place in northern Florida, the letter was published in papers throughout the state as well as in the *New York Times*. Harrison began by reminding the attorney general of their frequent conferences within the past six months with regard to the situation in Leon, Gadsden, Jefferson, and Madison counties. "It is not necessary to say more of the situation than that the officers of the United States are not suffered freely to exercise their lawful functions. This condition of things cannot be longer tolerated." The attorney general was told to instruct Marshal Weeks to execute the rights of arrest for persons charged with violation of the election laws, and to do it "at once." Furthermore, the president ordered Miller to instruct the marshal that if the latter should encounter any sort of resistance in his attempts to execute federal processes he should "employ such civil posse as may seem adequate to discourage resistance or to overcome it."[60]

The president concluded his letter with a strong statement of his determination to make sure that the federal statutes would be enforced in Florida. He stated: "You will assure the officers of the law, and those who have foolishly and wickedly thought to set the law at defiance, that every resource, lodged with the Executive by the Constitution and the laws, will as the necessity arises be employed to make it safe and feasible to hold a federal commission and to execute the duties it imposes."[61]

Along with the president's letter was published a letter from the attorney general to the newly appointed Marshal Weeks. Miller instructed Weeks to "proceed upon the lines indicated in [the President's] letter, and . . . report promptly any attempts to interfere with you in the discharge of your duties." The attorney general also wondered about reports of "great inconvenience" to federal officers in civil matters in that district who were being refused "the ordinary accommodations such as house hire, hotel entertainment, etc." Miller indicated that if such reports were true, "means can and will be found for transporting and subsisting the government officers wherever it is necessary for them to go in order to arrest and bring into court offenders against the law.[62]

Marshal Weeks reported that he had had no problems in moving around "freely" and that he was of course prepared to meet "force with force," should the need arise. During the month of May 1890, Weeks made numerous trips to Leon County, where he was successful in arresting a total of six persons charged with violation of the election laws. The attorney general was pleased that arrests were at last being made, but indicated that he would also like to see arrests made "in some of the other counties as well as in Leon."[63]

During the following month, Weeks continued to remain in Leon County, which he felt was the center "from which issues most of the opposition I have to contend with." The marshal reported that he had made nine more arrests, including a leader of the "young democracy of Middle Florida," a leading planter, and the secretary of the Leon County Democratic Committee. In addition, Weeks felt sure that he had been successful in "disabusing" the minds of most of the defendants that opposition to the mandates of the court would be tolerated, and he promised to "push the work as fast as practicable and will keep you informed from time to time."[64]

By this time, the attorney general was again becoming dissatisfied with the prosecution of the election cases in northern Florida by the marshal and the district attorney there. In response to the marshal's request to come to Washington before making a "determined" effort to make arrests in Madison and Gadsden counties, the attorney general sent a sharp letter of admonition to Weeks. "I am surprised that a '<u>determined</u>' effort has not been made before this time. Why has it not? . . . I do not see any reason for a further consultation with me about it before making a '<u>determined</u>' effort. If you can make these arrests, I want it done; and I want it done at once; if you cannot, say so, and why."[65]

The district attorney was also instructed to explain why the prosecution of the election cases of those already arrested had not been more vigorous. Stripling admitted that "the results have been less satisfactory to me than anyone else." He explained that it was difficult to bring to trial persons who had not yet been arrested, and in the election cases, this condition was generally true. However, based on the arrests made by Weeks in Leon County, the district attorney was able to bring to trial the case of E. M. Gregg for violation of the election laws. Because of various delaying motions by the defendant, reports of bribery of some of the jurors, and the district attorney's inactivity, the Gregg case dragged on until February 1891. To help prosecute this and other election cases, the attorney general appointed Henry Bisbee to act as a special prosecuting attorney. In addition, Miller sent a department examiner, Samuel Kercheval, to investigate the prosecution of election cases in northern Florida.[66]

Two other election cases were finally brought to trial along with the Gregg case, and in all three the department was able to secure convictions. However, that was the last attempt made to prosecute the persons originally indicted in the northern district. In May 1891, Marshal Weeks reported that he had been ready to take a force into Madison County to make arrests, but that there had been a fire in the courthouse and all the warrants had been destroyed. No order was sent to have the warrants reissued, and no further attempt was made by the marshal to make arrests, or by the district attorney to indict or try election cases in the district.⁶⁷

While the Justice Department was involved in the prosecution of election cases in Florida and other southern states during the last half of 1890, Congress was considering a new federal elections bill. The attorney general was fairly active in the preparation of the bill and closely followed its progress in the House and then in the Senate. In July of 1889, Miller had issued a Circular Letter to all federal officials in the country asking for suggestions as to possible changes in the federal election statutes. Among the responses he received were several from southern district attorneys and judges. Miller passed on these recommendations to George Edmunds, chairman of the Senate Judiciary Committee, and Ezra Taylor, chairman of the House Judiciary Committee.⁶⁸

The federal elections law, or the Lodge bill, as it came to be known, was basically a supplement to the revised statutes of 1876. It was neither the cure-all that its supporters claimed it to be, nor the abomination that its opponents believed it might be. As Professor Richard Welch accurately concluded, "The measure did not . . . embody a provision for the use of federal troops or marshals, and it did not affect directly the election of any state or local officials. It was hardly a nonpartisan measure, but only by the most strained etymology was it a force bill. But such it was labeled by its opponents, and these opponents by means of relentless repetition made the label stick.⁶⁹

Historians have examined in great detail the congressional struggle over the Lodge bill and its subsequent failure. In general, it is agreed that the failure of the bill can be ascribed to the defection in the Senate of the Silver Republicans, who were more interested in silver legislation, and by some northern Republicans like Senators Quay and Cameron of Pennsylvania, who "undoubtedly dislike the prospect of sectional controversy on the score that it would be poor for business." Symbolically, it may be true that the Lodge bill was the "last explosion of sectional anger and bitterness in the post-Civil War generation and the last significant effort in behalf of equal political rights for the American Negro." However, to say this, ignores the fact that at the same time Congress was considering a so-called force bill, the attorney general and the president already had the option of using federal troops in the South to enforce the election laws in Florida. It also overlooks the fact that the failure of the Lodge bill did not automatically repeal those statutes already in existence.[70]

That the federal election statutes were still viable was recognized by the attorney general during the presidential election of 1892. Prior to the election, Miller issued a three-page letter of instructions to federal marshals and district attorneys. The letter dealt with the appointment of special deputy marshals and supervisors of elections, and the enforcement of the election laws. Miller indicated that the ultimate responsibility for the enforcement of the federal laws rested with the attorney general and the Justice Department and its officials, and such authority "has, I believe, never been revoked."[71]

After discussing the various specific duties and responsibilities of the election officials, Miller reminded all federal officials "that they are officers of the peace, as well as officers of the election, and never forgetting that where State Statute conflicts with the Statute of the United States touching these elections, the National Statute is paramount and must be obeyed." In addition, "these officers should go forward quietly, but resolutely, in the discharge of their duties, without fear or favor, but with firm determination, so far as in them lies under the law, to see that there is an honest, free, and fair election and a fair return and canvass of the votes."[72]

The attorney general also issued a further set of instructions in response to "certain alleged instructions to the police and State officers in Alabama, Arkansas, and New York with reference to their conduct towards deputy marshals as may be in attendance at the polling places." Miller strongly warned that interferences with federal officers by state officials and police would not be tolerated. "An honest ballot and a fair count is what the law was designed to provide, and its constitutionality has been strongly upheld by the Supreme Court, and the paramount power of the Federal Government so clearly asserted by the Supreme Court, that it would be idle to discuss the matter."

Miller concluded that the possibility of interference by state authorities was not a "partisan question." No party, he claimed, can "justly hope to deserve or win success by defiance or violation of the law of the land. However that may be, our duty is plain. The laws must be enforced. The marshals are warned under the penalties of the law against any interference with the rights of citizens and at the same time they will guard and protect such rights at whatever cost."[73]

Reports of fraud and intimidation of voters at the 1892 elections were received by the attorney general from several southern states. In Birmingham, Alabama, a mob attacked federal election supervisors, and in Virginia election supervisors and federal marshals were arrested by local police and "Democratic Bulldozers," put into jail, and refused bail. Despite these reports and Miller's strong statements in his earlier letters of instructions, the attorney general made no apparent attempt to press the prosecution of such possible election cases. Part of the reason for this may have been, as in 1884, the anticipation of a Democratic administration soon to take office and the futility of beginning cases that would in all likelihood be discontinued at some future time.[74]

However, in Virginia, several election law prosecutions were instituted under U.S. Attorney Thomas Borland. Indictments were secured and the trials set for April of 1893. By that time the Democratic Cleveland administration had taken office. In October 1893, the new district attorney, James Lyons, reported to Attorney General Richard Olney that the indictments in the election cases brought by Borland had been quashed by District Court Judge Robert Hughes, and that no attempt would be made to have the cases further prosecuted.[75]

After the dismissal of the Virginia cases, there were only a few scattered attempts by the Justice Department to prosecute cases arising out of the 1892 election. Four months after Judge Hughes quashed the Virginia indictments, Congress repealed all the sections of the revised statutes of 1873 dealing with federal control of elections for members of Congress and the protection of voters at these elections. Debate on the repeal measure lasted for about a month, and centered mainly in the Senate. The fiercest opponents of repeal were Senators Hoar, Chandler, and Lodge, all of whom two years earlier had been behind the federal elections bill. The final vote on repeal was thirty-nine to twenty-eight; as was also true with the 1890 elections bill, the margin for repeal was partly made up of western Silver Republicans like Stewart of Nevada. The repeal of the election laws ended what for more than half a century had been the active involvement of the federal government and the Justice Department in the regulation and protection of the elective franchise in the South. There were simply no more laws for the Department to enforce.[76]

NOTES

1. Richard E. Welch Jr., "The Federal Elections Bill of 1890: Postscripts and Prelude," *Journal of American History*, 52 (December 1966): 512.

2. Stanley Hirshson, *Farewell to the Bloody Shirt: Northern Republicans and the Negro, 1877–1893* (Chicago, 1968), chaps. 6 and 7; Kirk H. Porter and Donald B. Johnson, eds., *National Party Platforms, 1840–1956* (Urbana, Ill., 1956), 80.

3. Vincent P. DeSantis, *Republicans Face the Southern Question: The New Departure Years, 1877–1897* (Baltimore, 1959), 196.

4. Charles Hedges, ed., *Speeches of Benjamin Harris* (New York, 1892), 190.

5. Harry J. Sievers, ed., *Benjamin Harrison, 1833–1901: Chronology, Documents, Bibliographic Aids* (Dobbs Ferry, N.Y., 1969), 37; U.S. Congress, *Inaugural Addresses of the Presidents of the United States from Washington to Kennedy* (Washington, D.C., 1961), 160.

6. Quoted in George Sinkler, *Racial Attitudes of American Presidents from Lincoln to Roosevelt* (New York, 1971), 298–99.

7. Harry J. Sievers, *Benjamin Harrison, Hoosier President: The White House and After* (Indianapolis, Ind., 1968), 19–20; Arthur Robb, *Biographical Sketches of the Attorneys General* (Washington, D.C., 1946); Robert Sobel, ed., *Biographical Directory of the United States Executive Branch, 1774–1971* (Westport, Conn., 1971), 242–243.

8. Thomas Keough to Miller, April 5, 1889, *Appointment Files*, RG 60, National Archives (hereafter cited as *Appointment Files*); A. L. Harris to Miller, May 16, 1889, *Appointment Files*; M. L. Sterns to Miller, Feb. 18, 1889, *Appointment Files*; Joseph H. Durkee to Harrison, March 15, 1889, *Appointment Files*; T. S. Wimarth et al. to Miller, March 12, 1889, *Year Files* (hereafter cited as *Year Files*); Harrison Reed to Harrison, March

1889 RG–60, National Archives, *Appointment Files*; Thomas Cavender to Harrison, March 8, 1889, *Appointment Files*; L. C. Hawk to Harrison, April 20, 1889, *Appointment Files*; "Arkansas State Republicans" to Harrison (telegrams), May 20 and 21, 1889, *Appointment Files*; Logan Roots to Miller, April 23, 1889, *Appointment Files*; A. C. Widdicome to Harrison, May 19, 1890, *Appointment Files*; "Resolution of Mobile County Republican Executive Committee" to Harrison, March 1889, *Appointment Files*; J. B. Hyde to Gen. W. W. Russell, March 4, 1889, *Appointment Files*; "Petition of Greenville County, South Carolina Republicans" to Harrison, Jan. 1889, *Appointment Files*.

9. U.S. Congress, *Annual Report* of the Attorney General, 1889, section on "Lawlessness." Miller also called for congressional revision and strengthening of the election laws.

10. Eugene Grissom to Miller, Dec. 3, 1889, *Year Files*.

11. Miller to Cook, Dec. 4, 1889, *Letters Sent by the Department of Justice: Instructions to U.S. Attorneys and Marshals*, RG 60, National Archives (Hereafter cited as *Instructions*); Charles Price to Miner, Dec. 6, 1889, *Year Files*; Price to Miller, June 10, 1890, *Year Files*.

12. Cook to Miller, Dec. 11, 1889, *Year Files*.

13. Miller to Cook, Dec. 16, 1889, *Instructions*; Cook to Miller, June 9, 1890, *Year Files*; Miller to Cook, June 11, 1890, *Instructions*.

14. Miller to Cook, Aug. 27, 1890, *Instructions*; Russell to Miller, Dec. 6, 1890, *Year Files*; Cook to Miller, June 9, 1891, *Year Files*. After this, the only concern with election cases in North Carolina was related to the controversy over the payment of fees in these cases to Judge Russell. That fee was finally set at $1,500. Miller to Cook, June 17, 1891, *Instructions*; Miller to Russell, Aug. 8, 1891, Nov. 21, 1891, *Instructions*.

15. Miller to Lathrop, Feb. 6, 1890, June 10, 1890, *Instructions*.

16. Lathrop to Miller, June 18, 1890, *Year Files*.

17. Lathrop to Miller, July 25, 1890, *Year Files*; Miller to Lathrop, July 28, 1890, *Instructions*.

18. Charles E Wynes, *Race Relations in Virginia, 1870–1902* (Charlottesville, Va., 1961), 42–43; Craig to Miller, Dec. 9, 1889, *Year Files*. The use of informations was a permissible, if not often used, method of common law criminal procedure. The major drawback was that the official who swore out the information left himself personally open to possible charges of perjury. As to election prosecutions in Virginia, it should also be noted that right after the election in 1888, several election law prosecutions were begun under Democratic District Attorney J. C. Gibson. Gibson to Garland, Nov. 14 and 17, 1888, *Year Files*.

19. Craig to Miller, June 28, 1890, *Year Files*; Miller to Craig, May 26, 1891, *Instructions*.

20. Craig to Miller, Oct. 10, 1891, *Year Files*.

21. Borland to Miller, April 14, 1889, *Year Files*.

22. Miller to Borland, Jan. 23, 1890, *Instructions*.

23. Borland to Miller, Jan. 28, 1891, *Year Files*.

24. Miller to Borland, Feb. 7, 1891, *Instructions*; Borland to Miller, April 24, 1891, *Year Files*.

25. *U.S. v. Mumford*, 16 Fed. 223 (1883).

26. *U.S. v. Belvin*, 46 Fed. 382 (1891).

27. Ibid., 386–87.

28. J. V. McDufee to Miller, June 13, 1890, *Year Files*; C. Daniels to Miller, Feb. 24, 1890, *Year Files*. Earlier, Miller had written a letter of strong praise to Wikersham for the district attorney's efforts at "using your office to encourage legitimate and discourage illegitimate prosecutions." Miller to Wikersham, Aug. 2, 1889, *Instructions*.

29. Miller to Parsons, June 14, 1890, *Instructions*; Miller to Wikersham, June 18, 1890, *Instructions*; Parsons to Miller, June 18, 1890, *Year Files*; Wikersham to Miller, Feb. 20, 1890, *Year Files*.

30. Miller to Wikersham, July 5, 1890, *Instructions*. See also Miller to Cook, June 11, 1890, *Instructions*.

31. C. C. Waters to Miller, April 1889 (various dates), *Year Files*; Miller to Waters, April 6, 1889, *Instructions*.

32. Ibid.

33. Ibid.

34. McClure to Miller, March 22, 1890, *Year Files*.

35. In the Middle District of the state, U.S. Attorney John Ruhn reported that as a result of his investigations he had discovered large numbers of voting irregularities at the 1888 elections. However, all these violations involved illegal voting by students from various universities in the Nashville area. With the attorney general's approval, Ruhn did not attempt to prosecute these cases, but instead sent a circular letter to all the "numerous institutions of learning" in the area. In this letter the district attorney informed the heads of these institutions of this "abuse" by the students. He indicated that some students had voted even though they were not of age, and quite a large number voted although they were neither residents of the county nor of the state. Ruhn asked the school authorities to "cheerfully lend their aid" in stopping these practices in the future and told them that he would not prosecute those students whose identities had already been ascertained. Ruhn enclosed with the circular letter a copy of the election

statutes "which, I suggest, should be made known and fully explained to the students of your institutions to the end that they may avoid offenses against the law which would surely bring upon them severe punishment." Ruhn to Miller, Aug. 9, 1889, *Year Files*; Miller to Ruhn, Sept. 5, 1889, *Instructions*; C. W. Chapman (acting attorney general) to Ruhn, Aug. 17, 1889, *Instructions*; Ruhn to Miller, Sept. 16, 1889, *Year Files*.

36. Hawkins to Miller, June 18, 1889, *Year Files*.

37. Ibid. Hawkins also indicated to the attorney general that "I am advised the National Republican Executive Committee will assist the Department in these prosecutions with money, if desired." Hawkins asked Miller to talk to Senator Quay, chairman of the committee, about this, "if you think proper."

38. Miller to Hawkins, June 25, 1889, *Instructions*.

39. Hawkins to Miller, Nov. 22, 1889, *Year Files*; Miller to Hawkins, Nov. 29, 1889, *Instructions*.

40. Murray to Miller, Dec. 15, 1889, *Year Files*; Evans to Miller, Jan. 21, 1889, *Year Files*.

41. Hawkins to Miller, Jan. 21, 1890, *Year Files*.

42. Miller to Hawkins, Jan. 29, 1890, *Instructions*; Hawkins to Miller, Aug. 28, 1890, Sept. 4, 1890, *Year Files*.

43. Hawkins to Miller, Dec. 22, 1890, June 1, 1891, *Year Files*. The new state elections laws were a comprehensive series of measures providing numerous ways of harassing and preventing qualified voters from registering and casting their ballots. For details of the laws and their effect on voting in Tennessee, see J. Morgan Kousser, "Post-Reconstruction Suffrage Restriction in Tennessee: A New Look at the V. O. Key Thesis," *Political Science Quarterly*, 88 (December 1971): 655–83.

44. Stripling to Miller, June 5, 1889, June 28, 1889, *Case Files*.

45. Stripling to Miller, Sept. 5, 1889, *Case Files*.

46. Ibid.; J. R. Mizell to Miller, Oct. 15, 1889, *Case Files*; Miller to Stripling, Oct. 16, 1889, Oct. 17, 1889, *Instructions*.

47. Mizell to Miller, Oct. 18, 1889, *Case Files*.

48. Ibid.; Miller to Mizell, Oct. 22, 1889, *Instructions*. The federal Revised Statute states:

Whenever, by reason of unlawful obstruction, combinations, or assemblages of persons, or rebellion against the authority of the Government of the United States, it shall become impracticable, in the judgment of the President, to enforce, by the ordinary course of judicial proceedings, the laws of the United States within any State or Territory, it shall be lawful for the President to call forth the militia of any or all the States, and to employ such parts of the land and naval forces of the United States as he may deem necessary to enforce the faithful execution of the laws of the United States, or to suppress such rebellion, in whatever State or Territory thereof the laws of the United States may be forcibly opposed, or the execution thereof forcibly obstructed. (*Rev. Stat.* 1034, sec. 5298)

Section 5299 of the Statutes also gave the president similar powers in the use of federal troops to suppress insurrections in violation of the civil rights of any citizen because of the failure of the "constitutional authorities" of any state to protect "the rights, privileges, and immunities . . . named in the Constitution."

49. Miller to Stripling, Oct. 22, 1889, *Instructions*; Swayne to Miller, Oct. 22, 1889, *Case Files*; Miller to Stripling, Oct. 26, 1889, *Instructions*.

50. Stripling to Miller, Oct. 30, 1889, *Case Files*.

51. Miller to Mizell, Oct. 31, 1889, Nov. 7, 1889, *Instructions*; Stripling to Miller, Nov. 9, 1889, *Case Files*.

52. Stripling to Miller, Nov. 9, 1889, *Case Files*; Mizell to Miller, Nov. 9, 1889, *Case Files*; Stripling to Miller, Nov. 13, 1889, *Case Files*.

53. Miller to Stripling, Nov. 21, 1889, *Instructions*.

54. Mizell to Miller, Nov. 9, 1889, *Case Files*. See also the letter from the foreman of the grand jury, John Talbot, to Miller, Dec. 11, 1889, *Case Files*.

55. Miller to Mizell, Dec. 9, 1889, Dec. 11, 1889, Dec. 21, 1889 (2), Dec. 24, 1889, Dec. 26, 1889, Dec. 27, 1889, *Instructions*.

56. Mizell to Miller, Jan. 17, 1890, Jan. 18, 1890, *Case Files*; Miller to Mizell, Jan. 23, 1890, *Instructions*; Miller to Stripling, Jan. 29, 1890, Jan. 7, 1890, *Instructions*. Miller directed Mizell to handle the increase in the reward money by not making a public offer of it, "but quietly to promise the payment . . . to any party or parties willing to undertake the task." Miller to Mizell, Jan. 7, 1890, *Instructions*.

57. Miller to Mizell, Feb. 5, 1890, Feb. 6, 1890, *Instructions*; Miller to Stripling, Feb. 6, 1890, *Instructions*; Mizell to Miller, Feb. 5–7, 1890 (series of telegrams), *Case Files*.

58. Mizell to Miller, Feb. 10, 1890, Feb. 14, 1890, *Case Files*. The assassination of Deputy Marshal Saunders was deplored on the floor of the Senate by William Chandler in an impassioned speech during the debate on the federal elections bill. Leon Richardson, *William E. Chandler: Republican* (New York, 1940), 408–9. See also Miller to Mizell,

Feb. 14, 1890, *Instructions*; Miller to Stripling, Feb. 14, 1890, *Instructions*; Stripling to Miller, April 10, 1890, *Case Files*.

59. Stripling to Miller, April 10, 1890, *Case Files*.

60. *New York Times*, April 17, 1890. According to the *Times*, Mizell's resignation had been "entirely voluntary." Mizell was soon appointed to the lucrative, and perhaps less responsible, position of collector for the Port of Pensacola. *New York Times*, April 22, 1890; Harrison to Miller, April 24, 1890, *Case Files*; *New York Times*, April 24, 1890.

61. *New York Times*, April 17, 1890. There is no evidence to indicate that President Harrison went beyond this published letter to the attorney general with respect to the use of section 5298 of the Revised Statutes and the use of federal troops in Florida. However, at the end of the file in the district attorney's correspondence to the attorney general relating to the Florida election cases is the following undated and unsigned draft:

> Whereas, It has been made known to me, upon satisfactory evidence, that, in the counties of Gadsden and Madison, in the State of Florida, the execution of the process of the United States Courts has been recently resisted, and the United States Marshals attempting to serve said process have been threatened with violence and driven from said counties by mobs and combinations of persons, acting in open hostility to said Courts and officers and to the laws of the United States:
>
> And Whereas, By reason of such unlawful obstructions and combinations of persons it has become impracticable to enforce, by the ordinary course of judicial proceedings, the laws of the United States within said counties:
>
> Now Therefore, By virtue of authority vested in me by the Constitution, and laws of the United States, I, Benjamin Harrison, President of the United States, do command said persons so obstructing the execution of the laws forthwith to disperse and retire peaceably to their abodes.

It is clear that this is a proclamation prior to the calling of federal troops as outlined in section 5298. A similar proclamation was in fact issued by Harrison on July 30, 1892, against strikers in Wyoming and their "opposition of the laws" in that state. (*Public Papers and Addresses of Benjamin Harrison* [Washington, D.C., 1893], 246). Since the draft was neither signed nor dated, it can only be speculated as to who the author of the document might be. The most plausible explanation is that it was written by the district attorney and sent to the attorney general, to be used by the president if he decided it was necessary to send troops to northern Florida. This would explain its location in the correspondence received by the attorney general. In any case, it can be considered further evidence of the seriousness with which all those concerned considered the possibility of using federal troops to enforce the election laws. And while Harrison indicated to Congress his concerns about events in Florida, this document is perhaps significant in light of the fact that at this time Congress had begun considering the so-called "force bill," which the president supported.

62. Miller to Weeks, April 26, 1890, *Instructions*; *New York Times*, April 24, 1890.

63. Weeks to Miller, May 2, 5, 8, 13, and 21, 1890, *Case Files*; Miller to Weeks, May 29, 1890, *Instructions*.

64. Weeks to Miller, June 16, 1890, *Case Files*.

65. Miller to Weeks, July 7, 1890, *Instructions*.

66. Stripling to Miller, July 9, 1890, *Case Files*; Miller to Stripling, Jan. 20, 1890, Feb. 14, 1891, April 17, 1891, *Instructions*; Kercheval to Miner, Feb. 22, 1891, Feb. 24, 1891, *Case Files*; Miller to Bisbee, Nov. 21, 1891, *Instructions*.

67. Weeks to Miller, May 25, 1891, *Case Files*.

68. Miller to District Attorneys, Judges, etc., July 13, 1889, *Instructions*; Chauncey E. Sabin to Miller, June 24, 1890, *Year Files*; Taylor to Miner, June 13, 1890, *Year Files*; Miller to W. D. Wikersham, Aug. 4, 1890, *Instructions*; Parsons to Miller, July & August 1890, *Year Files*; W. C. Craig to Miller, Dec. 9, 1889, *Year Files*.

69. Richard E. Welch, "The Federal Elections Bill of 1890: Postscripts and Prelude," *Journal of American History*, 52 (December 1965): 511. The Lodge bill provided for no new crimes or violations relative to the protection of a voter at any federal election. Rather, it called for the presence of national party officers, from both parties, to be present at such elections, with the hope that this would deter fraud and intimidation by either side. The bill did make the federal circuit courts more involved in the electoral process by giving such courts the power to certify ballot counts and initiate investigations into registration and voting irregularities.

70. Ibid., 522–26. See also DeSantis, *Republicans Face the Southern Question*, chap. 5; and Hirshson, *Bloody Shirt*, chap. 9.

71. Miller to District Attorney, etc., Oct. 31, 1892, *Instructions*.

72. Ibid.

73. Miller to Marshals, undated, *Case Files*; W. B. McDaniel to Miller, Oct. 9, 1892, *Case Files*; Thomas Jones (governor of Alabama) to Miller,

Nov. 8, 1892, Nov. 10, 1892, *Case Files*.

74. E. Allen to Miller, Nov. 8, 1892, *Case Files*; Parsons to Miller, Oct. 26, 1892, *Case Files*; T. R. Borland to Miller, Dec. 20, 1892, *Case Files*.

75. Borland to Miller, Dec. 20, 1892, *Case Files*; James Lyons to R. Olney, Oct. 19, 1893, *Year Files*.

76. 28 *Statutes at Large*, 25. For debate on the bill, see U.S. Senate, *Congressional Record*, 53d Cong., 2d sess., 1894, pp. 698, 925, 1227, 1237, 1313, 1976, and 1999. In the final ballot there were seventeen Senators who did not vote.

7

Bureaucracy, Sectionalism, and the Demise of the "Free Ballot and a Fair Count"

THE FIFTEENTH AMENDMENT'S GUARANTEES of equal voting rights for all citizens did not develop within a strictly constitutional-legal framework in the years following Reconstruction. The enforcement of black voting rights in the South between 1876 and 1893 by the federal government reflected two other important factors, which must be analyzed in order more precisely to understand both the effort at achieving a "free ballot and a fair count" for southern blacks, and the eventual failure of that effort by the beginning of the twentieth century. The first factor was administrative in nature, and was based on the fact that the achievement of political equality by and for the freedman was dependent on the effective enforcement of the Fifteenth Amendment guarantees by the Department of Justice. Constitutional rights became inextricably bound up with bureaucratic organization and efficiency. Thus, it is necessary to look at developments within the Justice Department itself during these years, since such developments had a critical influence on the enforcement of franchise rights in the South.

The second, and related, factor was the policies of Americans and American politicians with respect to the sectional question and the future of the black man and the Republican party in the South, particularly after 1890. As Professor Dewey Grantham concluded, "Republicanism remained a strong force in many southern states in the 1890's, and only after 1900 did a sharp falling off of Republican percentages take place throughout the region." Indeed, only after the removal of active federal protection, the Populist-agrarian upheavals of the 1890s, and the imposition of state constitutional disfranchisement measures did the solid Democratic South take shape. This chapter deals with these two factors and their relationship to both the beginning and the ending of the "free ballot and a fair count" in the South.[1]

Although the concern of the Department of Justice with the enforcement of voting rights in the South during the years 1876 to 1893 was a reflection of the policies of the Republican party during these years, the actual enforcement of the federal election laws also reflected policies and developments within the department itself. To understand the successes and failures of the federal government in protecting franchise rights in the South, it is important to examine the various problems faced by the department in carrying out its general functions as a law-enforcement agency, and the responses to these problems by the department under Attorneys General Devens, MacVeagh, Brewster, Garland, and Miller.

The last quarter of the nineteenth century was a time of significant change and growth in American society. The national government reflected these changes and developments. During these twenty-five years the leadership in Congress, particularly in the Senate, was becoming more organized and institutionalized. In addition, this period witnessed the tremendous growth and expansion of the federal executive bureaucracy. The result of this growth was the beginning of what one historian has characterized as "a permanent bureaucracy with vested interests and powers of its own, a semi-autonomous and self-moving 'fourth branch' of government."[2]

The Department of Justice exemplified this pattern of growth. It had been the tremendous increase in the business and duties of the attorney general during the Civil War years that led to the creation of the department as a full-fledged executive department in 1870. During and after Reconstruction, that increase continued, and attorneys general in the 1870s and subsequently constantly pleaded with Congress for more money, larger staffs, and better facilities. As Attorney General Garland complained in 1888, "With the increased amount of work done during the past four years there has been no corresponding increase of force. I respectfully submit the question of the desirability of a reorganization of the official force of the Department proper, to meet the needs of the increasing business."[3]

The reality of the "increasing business" of the Justice Department can be readily documented. In 1876, the department terminated 3,203 civil suits and 7,441 criminal actions. In 1888, the attorney general reported that during that year the department had terminated 11,499 civil suits and 14,599 criminal prosecutions. By 1896, the number of civil and criminal cases completed during the year had risen to 12,347 and 26,271, respectively. Similar increases can be found in the expenditures by the department for the operation of the entire federal court system. Between 1876 and 1896 these expenditures doubled from $2,830,708 in 1876 to $6,675,239 in 1896. Appropriations for departmental salaries also rose rapidly, although the most important increase was after 1896 when the old fee system for local officials was replaced by Congress with a system of fixed salaries for all department officials. In 1876 the congressional appropriation for department salaries had been $108,820. By 1896 that same appropriation was close to $5 million. Finally, the personnel of the department also expanded tremendously during this period.[4]

As the business and organization of the department developed, the importance of the office of attorney general expanded accordingly. By an act of Congress on January 19, 1886, the attorney general was recognized as fourth in the possible line of succession to the presidency in the event of the death, removal or disability of the president and vice president. The importance, if not always the stature, of the attorney general was also increased through his participation in the party politics of the time. Political considerations and party allegiance were as much factors in the selection of the attorneys general from Devens to Miller as their legal and administrative abilities. All five of these incumbents, especially Brewster and Miller, came to be among the closest advisors and confidants to their presidents. At times, as in response to some government scandal or criminal outrage, each attorney general would be directed by his president to devote his attention entirely to these matters. Given the attorney general's minimal staff and the department's ever-expanding list of responsibilities, it was not surprising that effective oversight of local federal officials and law enforcement suffered during these periods.[5]

Two significant examples of this problem occurred between the years 1881 and 1883, under the attorneys generalship of Wayne MacVeagh and Benjamin Brewster. During his brief tenure as Garfield's attorney general, MacVeagh devoted much of his time and energy in the investigation and prosecution of those involved in the "Star Route" scandals in the Post Office Department, and later, the investigation and trial of Garfield's assassin. MacVeagh's successor, Brewster, likewise spent a good portion of his tenure with these matters.

The Post Office Department scandals had their origins during the Hayes Administration. They involved a ring of western contractors who had succeeded in obtaining from the department padded contracts for the delivery of mail on special routes located throughout the western United States. These routes were marked in Post Office Department ledgers with three asterisks, hence the designation "Star Routes." The discovery of this illegal activity was first made soon after President Garfield took office. Although Garfield was informed of the scandal, he was not made fully aware of its implications politically until he met with his newly appointed attorney general. "Breaking the news to his chief, MacVeagh told Garfield on April 22, [1881] that 'the proceedings may strike men in high places; that they may result in changing a Republican majority in the United States Senate into a Democratic majority; that [they] may affect persons who claim that you are under personal obligation to them for services rendered during the last campaign.'" With the president's complete support and approval, MacVeagh and agents from the Justice and Post Office departments began intensive investigations into the Star Route business. Indictments and prosecutions began at once as numerous instances of lucrative and fraudulent contracts came to light.[6]

The cases were interrupted, however, by the assassination of

President Garfield on July 2, 1881. While waiting in a Washington railroad station, Garfield was shot several times by a "deranged" and frustrated office-seeker, Charles Guiteau. Although Garfield did not die for several months, Guiteau was immediately arrested, and the attorney general and the district attorney of Washington, D.C., began investigation and prosecution of the case.[7]

During the summer of 1881, as Garfield remained critically ill, the attorney general's office was virtually inactive except for the continuing investigations of Guiteau and the prosecution of the Star Route cases. To assist in the prosecution of the Star Route cases, MacVeagh appointed Benjamin H. Brewster, former attorney general of Pennsylvania, and Colonel George C. Bliss of New York as special counsel. "Brewster and Bliss began to master the infinite details of the case, to prepare evidence for the grand jury, and to decide upon their methods of prosecution. Final steps awaited Garfield's death or recovery."[8]

Garfield did not recover, and on September 20, 1881, Chester Arthur took the oath of office as president of the United States. By this time, the Justice Department's failure to convict those most responsible for the Star Route scandals had caused MacVeagh considerable embarrassment. He finally resigned as attorney general on October 24, 1881; soon after, Brewster was appointed to replace him. "The national clamor for the pushing of the [Star Route] trials . . . pointed directly to [Brewster] as MacVeagh's successor. Mr. MacVeagh himself warmly urged the appointment."[9]

During his first months in office, Brewster continued his role in the Star Route proceedings, while the department's business was handled by Solicitor General Samuel Phillips and the chief clerk of the Justice Department, Samuel Milliken. Until the Star Route trials reached their unsuccessful conclusion a year and a half later, the attorney general continued his active involvement in the case. He also maintained interest, and some direction, in the prosecution of Garfield's assassin, until January of 1882, when Guiteau was finally convicted and executed.[10]

The Post Office Department scandals heightened public and governmental awareness of the problem of corruption in the federal bureaucracy, an awareness which culminated in the passage of the Pendleton Civil Service Reform Act of 1883. The concern with ridding the government service of corruption extended as well to the Justice Department. Shortly after taking office, Attorney General Brewster discovered that for years United States marshals and commissioners had been defrauding the government by rendering false accounts. In addition, these officials "were outraging the rights of citizens by arrests on frivolous charges made solely for the sake of fees. . . . Many of these officials, located principally in the South and west of the Mississippi, were powerful in their communities."[11]

To handle this problem the attorney general appointed Brewster Cameron, who like Brewster was from Pennsylvania, to the positions of general agent and examiner general of the Justice Department. Cameron thereby "became charged with the responsibility of directing the investigations into the accounts and conduct of all court officers." Cameron and his subordinate examiners were very active in the South during the years 1881 to 1884. These examiners investigated reports and accusations of corruption and misconduct, and in several instances directed the prosecution of local federal officials. Brewster encouraged the efforts of his examiner general to uncover fraud and "the reprehensible practice of manufacturing business for the sake of their own profits" by such officers, and expressed his intent to "purge the service of the men who committed them."[12]

The attorney general's efforts at ridding the department of corrupt and unscrupulous local federal officials were not universally applauded. In fact, the activities of Cameron and his fellow examiners produced a "storm of wrath" among Republican politicians in Washington. Arthur was pressured to remove Brewster from the cabinet "as a political necessity, as his prosecution of influential Southern Republicans was disrupting the party in those states." The president, however, stuck by his attorney general, and both Brewster and Cameron remained in their respective offices.[13]

The most extensive investigation conducted by Cameron and his examiners in the South was of U.S. Marshal Paul Strobach and several of his deputies in the Middle District of Alabama. Strobach and his deputies were accused of rendering false accounts along with other frauds Strobach perpetrated as "Receiver of Public Monies at Montgomery, Alabama." At various times during the summer of 1883, department examiners and special agents were sent to Alabama to investigate these charges. The case caused a good deal of controversy, especially among Alabama Republicans. According to Department Examiner Joel Bowman:

> The feeling here [in Alabama] is at fever-heat; and I would not be surprised to see bloodshed at any moment. . . . I am very glad that you [Cameron] are not here now, for I do not believe that your life would be safe. . . . The Strobach crowd started the rumor this morning that the President was going to remove the Attorney General on account of this and other prosecutions he had instituted; but no one, except those belonging to the crowd, pay any attention to it.[14]

With the assistance of District Attorney Smith and Judge Samuel Rice, Bowman was successful in his prosecution of Strobach. He was tried and convicted of submitting false accounts to the government. He and his deputies were also accused of, but never tried for, questionable arrests and the issuance of warrants on insubstantial grounds in order to collect additional fees. However, the problem of corruption in Alabama did not end with Strobach's conviction and his removal from office. Soon after the Strobach trials, District Attorney Smith himself was accused of misconduct in office. But through investigation, again by Bowman, it was discovered that the charges against Smith had been instigated by Strobach and his followers "out of revenge" for Smith's part in the former marshal's prosecution and conviction. In June 1884, the district court found Smith not guilty of the misconduct charges.[15]

The Strobach case was but one example of the kinds of problems uncovered by Cameron and his agent. The effect of these disclosures went beyond the confines of the executive branch. The discovery of corruption and fraud among local Justice Department officials, as well as the failure of the department in the prosecution of the Star Route cases, prompted an investigation of the department in 1884 by the House Committee on Appropriations and Expenditures. This was the first such investigation of the Justice Department since its creation as an executive department in 1870, and as such reflected not only a growing concern with corruption in government service generally, but whether or not the Department of Justice was effectively enforcing the laws it was mandated to uphold. Although the enforcement of the election laws was not specifically explored by the committee, many of the witnesses were officials and politicians from the South. The testimony of these persons gives a detailed and often unpleasant picture of the state of the Justice Department field organization at this time. The testimony also lends support to the proposition that the corruption and inefficiency among local officials in the various southern districts was as much a factor in the actual enforcement of the election laws as the willingness or unwillingness of these officials to protect the franchise rights of blacks and Republicans. An example of this raised by the testimony was the activities of Marshal Strobach of Alabama. In preparing his defense and those of his deputies to the charges made against him, Strobach had little time to devote to the prosecution of election law violations in his district after the 1882 canvass. Nor did the district attorney, because of his involvement in the prosecution of Strobach, have much time to devote to election law violations.[16]

The House committee, chaired by Congressman William Springer of Vermont, took several thousand pages of testimony over a period of months on the operation and personnel of the Justice Department. The ability and dedication of the attorney general was defended by Brewster Cameron, who testified that "it is due to the Attorney General . . . that the practice of marshals rendering fraudulent accounts was discovered, exposed, and broken up." Cameron also stated that "the Attorney General has made every personal sacrifice for the good of the public service." On his own behalf, Brewster defended his department's record in the Star Route trials by noting the complexity of the issues and factual situations involved, and the difficulty in securing "solid and non-controverted evidence" upon which successful prosecutions might have resulted.[17]

The final report of the committee was not favorable to the department. The failure in the Star Route trials was emphasized, and the report concluded that "while the evidence against the star route contractors and public officials was strong and conclusive as to their guilt . . . yet no person was convicted or punished, and no civil suits have as yet been instituted to recover the vast sums illegally and fraudulently obtained from the Public Treasury." Although the work of the Justice Department examiners under Brewster Cameron in uncovering fraud and eliminating from the service those convicted of illegal activities was praised, the administration of President Chester Arthur and his attorney general was blamed generally for appointing men who were too often either incompetent or dishonest, or both. However, the result of the Springer committee investigation of the Justice Department was not to bring about any legislative reform, but simply to "provide ammunition for the ensuing political campaign," and to help prevent Arthur from receiving the Republican presidential nomination in 1884.[18]

The investigations by the Appropriations Committee did highlight an important aspect of the Justice Department's field organization: the political nature of local appointments, particularly the offices of district attorney and federal marshal. These positions were generally recognized by presidents and attorneys general alike as patronage to be dispensed among the party faithful. As was true to an even greater extent than with the selection of an attorney general, legal and administrative abilities were often of only secondary importance for the appointment of these local federal positions. The role of political suitability in the appointment of local department officials was particularly critical in the South. Both Republicans and Democrats, especially the former, realized that the maintenance of any viable party organization in that section depended on the proper dispensation of available patronage. And along with the postal, revenue, and customs services, the Justice Department and the federal court system provided a substantial number of available positions.

While the importance of politics was of course evident in the appointments made under Attorneys General Devens, MacVeagh, Brewster, and Miller, the return to power by Cleveland and the Democratic party in 1884 provides the best illustration of this aspect of the operation of the Justice Department. Upon assuming office, Attorney General Garland was besieged by letters, telegrams, and petitions nominating or recommending persons for various department posts. It was assumed that a Democratic attorney general would be amenable to the claims of those office-seekers who were good and loyal supporters of the Democracy.

Garland was especially made aware of the importance of his choices for department officials in the South. According to one Alabama politician, "the necessity for great changes in the incumbency of the offices under the Department of Justice ... is one that is urgent and paramount." Accordingly, the criteria for selection of these new men by the president and Garland was to be "their extraordinary qualifications for the office for which they are candidates ... their great claims upon the Democratic Party ... for faithful and conspicuous service rendered in its trying struggles; and also by the fact that in consequence of these considerations they are popular favorites for the office for which they are candidates." Although there was no immediate purge of incumbent officials, by the end of Garland's administration, all former district attorneys and marshals and their assistants in the South had been replaced by men who were, in Wade Hampton's phrase, "always conservative, staunch & true."[19]

The importance, therefore, of political considerations in the selection of department personnel and officials must be considered in examining the development of the Justice Department as a law-enforcement agency in the late nineteenth century. This is particularly so with respect to the question of voting rights in the South, which itself was a highly political as well as emotional issue. Effective enforcement of constitutional rights and guarantees depended at least as much on the ability, as well as the motivation, of local department officials in the South. And as has been indicated, there turned out to be a fair number of southern district attorneys and marshals who were neither very able nor especially honest public servants.

Beyond the question of politics and the appointment process, there were a number of other problems that affected the functioning of the Justice Department as an efficient bureaucratic organization between 1876 and 1893. These problem areas were often very apparent in the southern districts, and in turn affected attempts at the enforcement of voting rights by department officials in the South. One of the major problems was a lack of money. While the total congressional appropriation for the Justice Department increased during these years, the annual reports of the attorneys general indicate how insufficient such appropriations were considered to be. The attorneys general between 1876 and 1896 were continually faced with shortages of funds with which to run their department. Typical of this was the experience of Attorney General Garland. Soon after he became attorney general, Garland was forced to issue a Circular Letter to all federal marshals indicating that "the appropriations for the several branches of the U.S. Courts for the fiscal year ending June 30, 1885 are in a reduced condition." Garland directed all marshals to confer with their district attorneys and local federal judges as to possible ways of reducing expenditures because "only such expenditures for jurors and witnesses may be incurred as shall be absolutely necessary, as the possibility of their payment will be delayed till the next Congress meets, and possibly till March or July of the year 1886."[20]

Part of this problem was the fact that the fiscal year for congressional appropriations for executive departments ended on June 30. This was often a critical month for southern department officials in terms of election cases. Witnesses, marshals and their deputies, special prosecuting attorneys, and other court officers all had to be paid, and often there was simply not enough funds to do so. The lack of funds to pay witnesses was particularly crucial in election cases, for such witnesses were the basis on which the government's case usually rested. As a result, many cases that might have been successful were either dropped or continued indefinitely. To attempt to remedy this situation, Attorneys General Garland and Miller made greater use of the president's power to authorize additional funds in special instances for the operation of the executive department.

Garland and Miller also appeared to have made a fairly regular practice of submitting to Congress special emergency deficit bills.[21]

Another aspect of the Justice Department's attempts at the enforcement of voting rights was the employment of special deputy marshals for service at congressional elections, but this initiative was often thwarted by the lack of sufficient department funds. Under the revised statutes dealing with federal elections, provisions were made for the appointment and payment of special deputy marshals to protect supervisors of election and voters in cities of over twenty thousand inhabitants. However, as discussed above, under other sections of the election laws, the attorneys general between 1876 and 1893 authorized the appointment of such special deputies in cities of fewer than twenty thousand persons under certain conditions. This procedure was widely used in the South, where there were few cities that could technically qualify for special marshals, but where there were many places where such deputies were much needed. Payment of these officers had to be taken from the regular funds allocated to the marshal's office for his regular operations. Again, these funds were usually insufficient for such regular expenses, let alone for the salaries of special deputies. Thus, in many instances such deputies were forced to "serve without pay, or without hope of reward." Given the hazardous nature of their duties and responsibilities, it is easy to see why the recruitment of such officials was particularly difficult in the South, and when recruitment was accomplished, why the quality of protection and service may not have been of the highest level.[22]

A related problem with which the attorney general was constantly bothered was the record keeping of local federal officials in regard to money matters and keeping track of their business. Although the 1870 act creating the Justice Department had given the attorney general charge of all the accounts of the various local offices and officials, nothing had ever been done by way of systematizing or regulating this control. Department and court officials would generally send in their accounts as they came up, and each district attorney, marshal, and court clerk was free to keep his own accounts in whatever form he might choose.

One of Benjamin Brewster's final acts as attorney general was to institute a "new system" of record keeping for all local department officials. He issued a series of standardized blanks and forms on which all local officials were to keep detailed records of their activities and financial transactions. Forms were provided for requesting additional funds from the attorney general's office. In addition, all marshals were required to keep nine different books, such as account books relating to fees and emoluments and cash on hand, a daily record of all federal cases, and specific record books on admiralty, property, and U.S. commissioner cases. District attorneys were now directed as well to submit regular financial accounts to Washington, which would be subject to department review.[23]

While these new procedures undoubtedly helped organize local accounting and record keeping, they also imposed upon the attorney general and his office the expanded duty of approving even the smallest and most insignificant claims and requests for funds. Between 1884 and 1893 the correspondence of the attorney general's office is replete with replies to vouchers and requests for funds for such items as desk lamps, bookcases, fire escapes for courthouses, and spittoons. Instead of modernizing the department's financial procedures, and presumably leaving the attorney general more time to devote to matters of law and policy, Brewster's "new system" had the opposite effect. After 1884 the system caused the attorney general and his assistants to simply become even further "immersed in the details of departmental administration," as well as having the responsibility of overseeing the financial situation of local units of the department to a greater degree than might have been necessary.[24]

Changes in the structure of American society increased and diversified the responsibilities and business of the Justice Department during the last quarter of the nineteenth century, and this too affected the enforcement of existing federal laws. The growth of industrial monopolies and the passage of the Sherman Anti-Trust Act in 1890 gave the department new responsibilities in the area of business regulation. The development of a national communications network through the invention of the telephone involved the Justice Department in a protracted series of legal battles with respect to the original patent rights on this invention. The development of a transcontinental railroad network also involved the department in a great deal of litigation in attempting to find suitable "pasture for the iron horse." Yet, interestingly enough, the most extensive involvement of the federal governmental bureaucracy and the Justice Department during this time was in neither business and technological developments nor the protection of political and civil rights. The most widespread activity of the national government in the latter part of the century was "the desultory struggle to preserve the public forests."[25]

The Department of Justice, through various congressional enactments over the years, was given the ultimate responsibility for the prosecution of timberland depredations. The illegal removal of timber from federal lands was especially widespread in the South, where such property was in great abundance. Indeed, much of the time and energy of district attorneys and marshals in the South between 1876 and 1893 was taken up with the investigation and prosecution of this kind of activity. In one instance, District Attorney Lewis Parsons and Marshal B. W. Walker of Alabama, along with ten deputies, attempted on their own to prevent the removal of any timber from that state by seizing sawmills, logs, lumber, and timber rafts, and by placing booms across all the rivers flowing out of the state.[26]

During the 1880s, the number of timber cases in the South, as well as the rest of the nation, increased enormously. This increase in Justice Department business was not, however, accompanied by any increase in the successful prosecution of these kinds of cases. Criminal proceedings against timberland trespassers were difficult because of problems in finding witnesses willing to testify against such persons. Civil actions against such trespassers for recompense to the government were equally difficult, particularly against individual trespassers. By 1890, Attorney General Miller indicated, "Indeed, I am not sure but that it would be profitable for the government to abandon all such cases." Miller complained to District Attorney M. C. Elstner of Shreveport, Louisiana, "The expenditures in these cases have not only been disproportionate to the recoveries so far, but are, it seems to me, in excess of any hopes for recovery that the present state of things warrants." The attorney general asked Elstner, as well as other southern district attorneys, if he could suggest any better means of protecting the public forests. "I can almost say that a bold blunder would be better than the present drifting course."[27]

Despite the attorney general's concern, no administrative or legislative changes were made with respect to the problem of timberland depredations. However, during the 1890s the number of timber trespass cases began to decline markedly, largely as a result of the growth of the national conservation movement.[28] Meanwhile, various other kinds of business continued to face southern federal officials and the attorneys general as well. Land problems and land litigation, enforcement of the revenue laws, the handling of pension and various other claims against the national government, and the enforcement of the customs laws are some of the major areas of responsibility that had to be met by local department officials. These duties, along with the enforcement of the election laws, had to be handled with local staffs whose size was already insufficient in many districts in 1870. In a good number of southern districts, a district attorney and marshal, along with several clerks, constituted the permanent federal staff for the district. Instead of increasing the size of regular local staffs, special assistant prosecuting attorneys and special deputy marshals continued to be appointed for special cases. As late as 1892, district attorneys were also unable to hire court stenographers except in certain, and approved, instances. Thus, by the close of the nineteenth century the "local units" of federal law enforcement had hardly changed much since the creation of the department in 1870.[29]

Reform and change within the Department of Justice came, as it had before 1870 in the attorney general's office, on an individual and piecemeal basis. The creation of the department's examiner unit and the new system of record and bookkeeping introduced by Brewster were both comparatively minor attempts at making the Justice Department a more efficient bureaucratic operation. The Pendleton Act of 1883 attempted, among other things, to limit the political activity of federal employees.

Presidents and attorneys general after 1883 issued occasional statements reminding employees that "office holders are the agents of the people—not their masters." In the South, however, political activity by local officials of the Justice Department continued to be the norm rather than the exception.[30]

The single most important reform in the department during these years was the abolition in 1896 of the fee system of payment of federal district attorneys and marshals. Salaries for both categories of officials were now fixed by congressional appropriation. The results of this reform were immediate and apparent. According to then Attorney General Judson Harmon:

> [I]n the districts where abuses of the fee system have flourished without interruption for a generation fewer persons are called from their daily pursuits; private business suffers less interruptions; the tranquility of families and communities is less frequently disturbed by groundless prosecution and the dread of them; the number of persons, who, as informers, professional witnesses, etc., seek to gain a livelihood by methods which often cause and always threaten the prosecution of judicial proceedings is largely diminished; and the general morale of the public service has been raised.[31]

Yet, despite these attempts at reform, the Justice Department in 1896 was in most respects little different from the Justice Department of 1870. The earlier problems of interdepartmental relations, the supervision of the field forces, and the development of an efficient central organization still existed. Corruption and inefficiency continued, especially on the local level. Despite the help of a solicitor general and several assistant attorneys general, the attorney general was required to meet his responsibilities as a presidential and cabinet counselor, chief federal law enforcement officer, and bureaucratic administrator, with resources barely sufficient to handle effectively any one of these responsibilities. And what held true for the attorney general was equally true for his representatives at the local level. Expanding duties and responsibilities within a framework of limited resources could only have a negative impact on the enforcement of existing laws and policies by district attorneys and their marshals and deputies.

In their history of the Justice Department, Cummings and McFarland concluded that "the enforcement of laws is always delicate as well as difficult. Particularly in the field of federal legislation, laws do not find places upon the statute books until the social conditions which they are designed to remedy have become fixed. Even where the justice of legislation is apparent, large groups whose daily lives are entwined with existing conditions constitute an influential opposition. Small groups and large seek to shape law enforcement to their own ends." While the reference is to the enforcement of laws generally, the conclusions are particularly descriptive of the Justice Department's role in the enforcement of voting rights in the South between 1876 and 1893. The enforcement of the federal election statutes, as had been true for the passage of the Fifteenth Amendment and the Enforcement Acts to begin with, was a constant reflection of various "groups" like the Republicans, Democrats, blacks, whites, Independents, and Populists attempting to shape the enforcement of these laws to their own ends. At the same time, such enforcement reflected conditions within the department as well. In this sense, the ultimate failure to prevent the disfranchisement of the freedman was as much an administrative failure as it was a political, social, and moral one. The Justice Department as a law-enforcement agency was not equipped to hold back in the long run the concerted efforts of white Southern Democrats to deny the freedman his civil and political rights.[32]

The failure of the Lodge election bill and the repeal of most of the remaining federal election laws by the early 1890s were symptomatic of growing Republican disinterest with the sectional issue and the protection of the free ballot and fair count. According to Republican leader John C. Spooner, "the interest of the Republicans of the United States in an honest ballot, in maintaining the rights of citizenship, and in holding sacred the pledge of Abraham Lincoln's proclamation to the colored man is dead, or in a slumber too deep for us to arouse it."[33]

Yet, as indicated above, southern Republicanism and black voting continued through the decade of the 1890s. The major impetus for this persistence was the agrarian upheavals of that decade—the so-called "Populist revolt." It is beyond the scope of this work to examine the origins and grievances of southern Populism; it is enough to say that, like the Independents in the early 1880s, the Populists were for the most part agrarian radicals and dissident Democrats. However, the most important link between the Populists and the Independent movement of the 1880s in the South was their common support for the political equality of blacks.[34] Populist leader Tom Watson of Georgia stated this belief when he wrote: "Let it once again appear plain that it is in the interests of a colored man to vote with a white man and he will do it. Let it plainly appear that it is to the interest of the white man that the vote of the Negro supplement his own, and the question of having the ballot freely cast and fairly counted, becomes vital to the white man. He will see that it is done."[35]

In their attempts at achieving electoral success, southern Populists resorted to the Independent tactic of political fusion, whereby Populists and Republicans agreed to support mutually acceptable tickets. However, "fusion was a poor name for the policy, for in no case did either party to an agreement give up its identity or merge with the other. The binding force was plainly expediency, and the only principle Republicans and Populists proclaimed in common was the demand for 'a free ballot and an honest election.'"[36]

Although the Populists were able to achieve some success in the South in the years 1892 to 1896, in the long run their attempt at preventing the solidification of the Democratic South was as ineffective as the Independent movement in the 1880s had been. In terms of black voting rights, the Populist revolt merely postponed, and in some instances hastened, the eventual disfranchisement of black voters in the South, especially after the Populists suffered their major defeat in the election of 1896. As Paul Lewinson concluded, "Everywhere, after the agrarian movement as a national political force had collapsed in 1896, disfranchisement helped to reunite the South."[37]

The vehicle with which white southern Democrats united in the 1890s was the disfranchisement of black voters through the revision of state constitutions and the passage of election statutes designed, in the words of District Attorney Samuel Hawkins of Tennessee, to disfranchise blacks "under the form of law, without the necessity of frauds at the election." Beginning with Mississippi in 1890, southern states adopted a wide variety of legal means aimed at restricting black suffrage, and by 1910 every southern state had such measures. In 1898 the United States Supreme Court, in *Williams v. Mississippi*, gave its judicial acceptance of such methods by upholding the Mississippi Constitution of 1890.[38]

While southern Democrats were thus attacking the last vestiges of southern Republicanism, black political participation, and dissent within their own ranks, northern Republicans were discovering that they were becoming the majority party in America without the benefit of southern votes. In the congressional elections of 1894, Republicans gained a majority of 132 seats, and in twenty-four states not one Democrat was elected and in six other states only one Democratic candidate was successful. "This overwhelming Republican congressional victory . . . was confirmed two years later by what for the Republicans was to be their first decisive presidential victory without benefit of federal protection of Negro voting in the South." The party of Lincoln and Reconstruction was now the party of an industrialized, urbanized America, and after the Depression of the early 1890s, the party of economic prosperity.[39]

The Republican victory in 1896 also marked the submergence, temporarily at least, of what one historian has called the "abolitionist tradition." This tradition included those Americans who before 1860 agitated for the emancipation of the black race in the South, and "once emancipation was achieved, they devoted their attention to achieving complete equality for Negroes in political and civil rights." During the 1870s and 1880s, this tradition underlay the attempts by Republicans and the federal government at securing the guarantees inherent in the Fourteenth and Fifteenth Amendments. Yet, the very nature of American society to which this "reform" tradition spoke was itself rapidly changing. The Republican party was able to adapt to these changes, and as a result became the majority party in the United States until the 1930s. The abolitionists were not so fortunate. "While they showed considerable insight into the problems of the freedman, they only dimly perceived the dimensions of the industrial society into which the freedman had emerged, and in this sense they did indeed fail."[40]

Republican presidents from Hayes to Harrison believed that a solid Democratic South was not inevitable. As a result, these men attempted to foster southern Republicanism and revitalize the southern wing of the Republican party by adopting what one historian characterized as "variations on a theme by Hayes." These variations included the continuation of the Radical Republican policies of direct support of southern conservatives and support for, and coalition with, independent movements in the South, particularly dissident Democratic economic radicals. During their terms of office, Presidents Hayes, Garfield, and Arthur adopted one or another of these strategies; during his eight years in office, Harrison "recapitulated the whole schizophrenic history of southern strategies."[41]

Underlying all three of these variations was at least one common concern, that for the "free ballot and a fair count." For both humanitarian and political reasons, Republican presidents and their attorneys general either accepted or actively supported the role of the federal government in the protection of the voting rights of blacks in the South. The constitutional basis of this protection was the Fifteenth Amendment and the series of election laws passed by Congress in the years 1870 to 1873. Despite several supposedly adverse rulings, the Supreme Court, as well as lower federal courts, in the last quarter of the nineteenth century consistently upheld the power of the federal government to carry out this protection.

The critical issue in the protection of the freedman's vote was, then, the actual enforcement of the election laws by the government. The responsibility for this enforcement rested with the Department of Justice and its network of district attorneys and marshals throughout the South. The evidence presented in this study indicates that after 1877, and up until the repeal of the election laws by Congress in 1893, the department made a genuine attempt at ensuring and protecting franchise rights in the South. Between 1877 and 1893 the Justice Department instituted

1,264 cases in the eleven states of the Confederacy based on the federal election statutes of 1870–73. In five of the eleven states—Arkansas, Florida, Texas, Louisiana, and Virginia—the number of prosecutions brought during this time exceeded the number of prosecutions brought in those states by the Justice Department between 1870 and 1877. It is therefore doubtful that, as Professor Swinney concluded, the federal election laws by 1874 were "virtually dead letters" and that "by 1877 the Negro vote had been largely neutralized and a solid Democratic South assured."[42]

That ultimately this attempt did not prevent the disfranchisement of the mass of black voters in the South should not obscure the fact that the attempt was made. Until recently it has been almost an historical truism that segregation and disfranchisement immediately followed the removal of the last federal troops from the South in 1877, and that the period 1877 to 1900 was the nadir in the history of the black man in the United States. With respect to segregation, C. Vann Woodward has shown that segregation was not inevitable and that the period after 1877 was one of "forgotten alternatives" as to the settlement of race relations in the South. "It was a time of experiment, testing, and uncertainty—quite different from the time of repression and rigid uniformity that was to come toward the end of the century. Alternatives were still open and real choices had to be made." Woodward's conclusions apply equally well to the issue of black voting rights in the South. Woodward himself stated: "As a voter the Negro was both hated and cajoled, both intimidated and courted, but he could never be ignored so long as he voted." Between 1877 and 1893, the federal government, through the Department of Justice, attempted to ensure that blacks could vote, and that there would indeed be a "free ballot and a fair count" in the South for all citizens.[43]

Notes

1. Dewey Grantham, *The Democratic South* (Athens, Ga., 1963), 25. See also George B. Tindall, *The Disruption of the Solid South* (Athens, Ga., 1972), 1–21; and J. Morgan Kousser, *The Shaping of Southern*

Politics: Suffrage Restriction and the Establishment of the One-Party South, 1880–1910 (New Haven, Conn., 1974), chap. 1.

2. For a discussion of the kinds of changes going on in America at this time, see Harold U. Faulkner, *Politics, Reform and Expansion* (New York, 1959); and Robert Wiebe, *The Search for Order 1877–1920* (New York, 1967). On changes in Congress and the federal bureaucracy, see David Rothman, *Politics and Power: The U.S. Senate, 1869–1917* (Cambridge, Mass., 1966); and Loren P. Beth, *The Development of the American Constitution 1877–1917* (New York, 1971), 26. The expansion of the federal bureaucracy is best evidenced by the increase in persons on the civil service payroll, the addition of new executive departments and agencies, and the reorganization of existing departments. Between 1870 and 1901, the number of civilian employees of the federal government rose from 53,000 to 256,000. In 1889, the Department of Agriculture was made a formal executive department and in 1903 the Department of Commerce and Labor was also added to the president's cabinet. In addition, there were created a number of new "detached" regulatory agencies such as the Civil Service Commission and the Interstate Commerce Commission. Leonard White, *The Republican Era* (New York, 1958), 2; Lloyd M. Short, *The Development of National Administrative Organizations in the United States* (Baltimore, 1923), chaps. 11–20.

3. U.S. Congress, *Annual Report* of the Attorney General, 1888, xx.

4. U.S. Congress, *Annual Report* of the Attorney General, 1876, 1888, and 1896.

5. Henry B. Learned, *The President's Cabinet* (New Haven, Conn., 1912), 191–95. See also Arthur Robb, "Charles Devens," in *Biographical Sketches of the Attorneys General* (Washington, D.C., 1946); Harry J. Sievers, *Benjamin Harris, Hoosier President: The White House and After* (Indianapolis, Ind., 1968), and Eugene C. Savidge, *Life of Benjamin Brewster, with Discourses and Addresses* (New York, 1891).

6. John M. Taylor, *Garfield of Ohio* (New York, 1970), 247–49; Theodore C. Smith, *Life and Letters of James Garfield* (New York, 1926), 2:1158; Ellis P. Oberholzer, *A History of the U.S. Since the Civil War* (New York, 1937), 4:116–19.

7. Taylor, *Garfield*, chap. 19; Charles Rosenberg, *The Trial of the Assassin Guiteau* (Chicago, 1968), 79–85.

8. George Frederick Howe, *Chester A. Arthur: A Quarter-Century of Machine Politics* (1935; New York, 1966), 181; Savidge, *Life of Brewster*, 176.

9. Ibid.; Rosenberg, *Trial of Guiteau*, 79–85.

10. Savidge, *Life of Brewster*, 204–5.

11. Ibid.

12. Brewster to E.C. Wade, Feb. 6, 1883, *Letters Sent by the Department of Justice: Instructions to U.S. Attorneys and Marshals*, RG 60, National Archives (Hereafter cited as *Instructions*); Brewster to Andrew J. Evans, May 12, 1882, *Instructions*.

13. Savidge, *Life of Brewster*, 205–8. See also Peter Fish, *The Politics of Federal-Judicial Administration* (Princeton, N.J., 1974), 93.

14. Brewster Cameron to Brewster, May 23, 1883, *Source-Chronological Files*, RG 60, National Archives (hereafter cited as *Source Files*); Bowman to Cameron, June 3, 1883, and July 4, 1883, *Source Files*.

15. Rice to Brewster, July 16, 1883, *Source Files*; Bowman to Brewster, Aug. 1883 (entire box of accounts and statements by Bowman), *Source Files*. For charges of intimidation and arrest by the marshal, see H. H. Herbert to Brewster, July 13, 1883, *Source Files*; J. W. Domnich to Brewster, Feb. 26, 1884, *Source Files*; "Statement of Grand Jury," March 7, 1884, *Source Files*; "Report of Circuit Court Term, May 1884," June 28, 1884, *Source Files*.

16. "Resolution of February 12, 1884," U.S. House, *Congressional Record*, 48th Cong., 1st sess., 1884; "Testimony on Investigations of Expenditures in the Department of Justice," *House Miscellaneous Documents*, 48th Cong. 1st sess., no. 38.

17. Ibid., 876–77.

18. "Report on Investigations of Expenditures in the Department of Justice," *House Reports*, 48th Cong., 1st sess., no. 2165, p. 20. See also the *Minority Report*, 21–22, and Homer Cummings and Carl McFarland, *Federal Justice: Chapters in the History of Justice and the Federal Executive* (New York, 1937), 260.

19. Wade Hampton to Garland, May 7, 1885, *Appointment Files*, RG 60, National Archives (hereafter cited as *Appointment Files*); W. L. Bragg to Garland, March 12, 1885, *Appointment Files*; L. Dalton to Congressman Blanchard, July 9, 1885, *Appointment Files*; "Charges Against A. H. Leonard, etc.," *Appointment Files*, Box 336, generally (1885–89). As discussed in chap. 6 above, when Republicans regained the presidency in 1888, Attorney General Miller was likewise flooded with job applications, and impressed with the importance of filling these positions with good Republicans, particularly in the South.

20. Garland to U.S. Marshals, April 6, 1885, *Instructions*. See also Oberholzer, *History of the U.S.*, 4:352.

21. Brewster to J. M. Hinds, March 24, 1884, *Instructions*; Miller to

Harrison, Nov. 8, 1889, *Year Files,* RG 60, National Archives (Hereafter cited as *Year Files*).

22. Harrison to Marshals, undated, *Case Files,* RG 60, National Archives (Hereafter cited as *Case Files*); John McClure to Miller, June 30, 1890, *Case Files.* For the correspondence relating to the payment of special deputy marshals between 1884 and 1893, see *Case Files* no. 6188, generally.

23. Brewster to District Attorneys, Feb. 8, 1885, *Instructions.* Although not explicitly stated, it seems fairly certain that part of the motivation behind Brewster's action was the investigation and report of the Appropriations Committee and the various revelations of financial misconduct that came of it.

24. Cummings and McFarland, *Federal Justice,* 493.

25. Ibid., chaps. 14–16, and p. 260.

26. Ibid., 260–69; Miller to Parsons, Sept. 30, 1889, *Instructions.*

27. Miller to Elstner, Sept. 30, 1890, *Instructions.* Ten days earlier, Acting Attorney General Samuel Phillips sent a Circular Letter to twenty states, including Alabama, Arkansas, Florida, Louisiana, Mississippi, and Texas, instructing district attorneys in those states to submit full reports on all present and past prosecutions of timber trespass cases in their respective districts. "There seems to be," Phillips stated, "in many districts of the country a carelessness about the management of these suits which the Department has, as yet, been unable to correct." Phillips to Parsons, Sept. 20, 1890, *Instructions.*

28. For the development and significance of the conservation movement, see Samuel P. Hays, *Conservation and the Gospel of Efficiency* (New York, 1959).

29. Cummings and McFarland, *Federal Justice,* 491 and 504–9.

30. Ibid., 499; Miller to Darnell, Sept. 10, 1890, *Instructions;* Miner to J. N. Stripling, Sept. 10, 1890, *Instructions.*

31. U.S. Congress, *Annual Report* of the Attorney General, 1896, 7–10.

32. Cummings and McFarland, *Federal Justice,* 510.

33. Spooner to James Clarkson, quoted in Stanley Hirshson, *Farewell to the Bloody Shirt: Northern Republicans and the Negro, 1877–1893* (Chicago, 1968), 249.

34. The connections between the Populists and the Independents, as well as other southern dissenters in the nineteenth century, are discussed in detail in Carl N. Degler, *The Other South* (New York, 1974), 316–71. See also Grantham, *Democratic South,* 33–41; and Tindall, *Disruption of the Solid South,* 14–18. For discussions of southern

Populism and its origins, see C. Vann Woodward, *Origins of the New South, 1877–1913* (Baton Rouge, La., 1951), chaps. 9 and 10; John D. Hicks, *The Populist Revolt* (Minneapolis, Minn., 1951); and Norman Pollack, *The Populist Response to Industrial America* (Cambridge, Mass., 1962).

35. Tom Watson, "The Negro Question in the South," *Arena*, 6 (October 1892): 540–50. It should be pointed out that in the same article Watson condemned federal interference with elections. However, before the repeal of the federal election laws, southern Populists did accept Justice Department involvement. See, B. W. Walker to Miller, Sept. 10, 1892, *Case Files*; and W. B. McDaniel (secretary of the Peoples Part Executive Committee of Georgia) to Miller, Oct. 8, 1892, *Case Files*.

36. Woodward, *Origins*, 276; Degler, *The Other South*, 332. Degler emphasizes the fact that it "was just this common concern for free and honest elections that threatened the Democrats and the Bourbon South."

37. Paul Lewinson, *Race, Class and Party* (New York, 1932), 79; Grantham, *Democratic South*, 40–41.

38. Hawkins to Miller, June 1, 1891, *Year Files*; *Williams v. Mississippi*, 170 U.S. 215–25 (1898). The most exhaustive and recent study of southern suffrage restriction is Kousser, *Shaping of Southern Politics*. The actual effects of the new southern state constitutions and statutes on black voting has been a matter of some debate. Part of the problem has been the lack of accurate data on the electoral behavior of southern blacks during the 1890s and early part of the twentieth century. The basic theme of this debate was stated by V. O. Key Jr. in 1949 in his monumental work, *Southern Politics in State and Nation* (New York, 1949). According to Key, the formal disfranchisement processes were not responsible for the decline of the southern black electorate after 1890. Rather, these methods "recorded a *fait accompli* brought about, or destined to be brought about, by more fundamental processes." (533) This notion has found acceptance in two recent works on southern black voting. Charles V. Hamilton has placed the motivation behind the disfranchising constitutions on the "strong urge on the part of Southerners . . . to do things in a legal and correct way. It was insufficient . . . to rely on trickery, fraud, and other extra-legal means to keep blacks from the polls. It was better to amend state constitutions and to enact state laws to legalize the condition of black non-voting." *The Bench and the Ballot* (New York, 1974), 20. Similarly, Carl Degler in *The Other South* implicitly accepts the view that formal disfranchisement of black voters in the South came after most black voters had been elim-

inated by other means. However, C. Vann Woodward, in the *Origins of the New South*, suggested caution in applying Key's *"fait accompli"* thesis to all southern states. Kousser's study of suffrage restriction in the South after 1880, *The Shaping of Southern Politics*, picks up on Woodward's suggestion and directly challenges Key's conclusions, and suggests that the Key thesis ought to be "abandoned" (Kousser's work began as a doctoral dissertation done under the direction of Woodward). According to Kousser, significant declines in the percentages of black and Republican votes took place only after formal statutory and constitutional disfranchisement measures by the southern states. And like Grantham in *The Democratic South*, Kousser sees the establishment of the solid one-party Democratic South as being a product of the 1890s when most of this formal disfranchisement activity took place. While Kousser's statistical data is more than convincing, questions about the interpretation of that data might still be raised. For example, while it is true that Republicanism persisted in the 1890s in the South, it was essentially on the state level. In terms of national politics (presidential electoral votes, election of congressmen, etc.), however, southern Republicanism was becoming less of a factor before formal disfranchisement. Thus, in at least one sense, the disfranchisement measures of the 1890s did represent a *fait accompli*—the unimportance of southern Republicanism to the national party fortunes.

39. Carl N. Degler, "American Political Parties and the Rise of the City: An Interpretation," *Journal of American History*, 51 (June 1964): 41–50. See also Paul Glad, *McKinley, Bryan and the People* (New York, 1964).

40. William B. Hixson Jr., *Moorfield Storey and the Abolitionist Tradition* (New York, 1972), 192–201. For a brilliant discussion of the effects of these changes in American society on the thinking on voting rights, see Kousser, *Shaping of Southern Politics*, 250–65.

41. Tindall, *Disruption of the Solid South*, 15 and chap. 1, passim.

42. Everette Swinney, "Enforcing the Fifteenth Amendment," *Journal of Southern History*, 28 (May 1962): 205 and 218.

43. C. Vann Woodward, *The Strange Career of Jim Crow*, 3d ed. (New York, 1975), 33–55.

BIBLIOGRAPHICAL ESSAY

Primary Sources

The basic source material for this study is the *General Records of the Department of Justice,* Record Group 60, in the National Archives (Washington, D.C.). Of particular importance are the letters and reports sent by the various district attorneys and marshals from the South to the attorneys general between the years 1876 and 1893. These are found in the *Source-Chronological Files,* Record Group 60. While parts of these records have been used in past studies on specific aspects of southern history, this study is the first to make intensive use of these valuable records, especially with respect to the development of the Justice Department itself. Letters in the *Source-Chronological Files* are arranged by date and place of origin. After 1884, a new filing system was instituted, and correspondence from southern federal officials are located in the *Case Files* and *Year Files.* Of equal importance are the *Letters Sent by The Department of Justice: Instructions to U.S. Attorneys and Marshals,* Record Group 60, including all correspondence from the attorney general to local officials from August 25, 1876 to March 18, 1893. For information on southern department officials, the nominating petitions and testimonials found in the *Appointment Files* are helpful. Background on some of the more important Supreme Court cases dealing with voting rights can be found in the *Supreme Court Case Files,* Record Group 267.

On the published primary sources, the *Annual Reports of the Attorney General* from 1876 to 1900 contain much information on the growth and development of the department. After 1876 each yearly report contains a section on the enforcement of the election laws. In the *Report* for 1893 there is a complete summary of cases brought under the election statutes and their outcomes during the years 1870–93. Also important are the reports of the various congressional committees investigating elections in the South. The most extensive is the *Report of the U.S. Senate Committee to Inquire into the Alleged Frauds and Violence in the Elections of 1878*, Senate Reports, 45th Cong., 3d sess., No. 855. See also *Report of Committee on Elections in Virginia and Mississippi*, Senate Reports, 48th Cong., 1st sess., Nos. 521 and 579. For information on the problems of fraud and corruption in the Justice Department, see *Report of Investigations of Expenditures in the Department of Justice*, by the Springer Committee, House Miscellaneous Documents, 48th Cong., 1st sess., Document No. 38, part 2. Of some help as well are James A. Finch, ed., *Digest of Official Opinions of the Attorney General, 1881–1906* (Washington, D.C., 1908); and A. J. Bentley, *Digest of Official Opinions of the Attorney General, 1789–1881* (Washington, D.C., 1885). Interestingly, there are no official opinions given by the attorneys general between 1870 and 1893 with respect to any aspect of the election laws and their enforcement. Also consulted is the *Congressional Record*, House and Senate, particularly the debates on the Fifteenth Amendment, the Enforcement Acts, and the repeal of the election statutes in 1893. Also relevant to the operation of the department is Robert M. Cousar, *Digest of the Laws and Decisions Relating to the Appointment, Salary and Compensation of the Officials of the United States Courts* (Washington, D.C., 1895).

Important public pronouncements of the presidents from Hayes to Harrison can be found in James D. Richardson, *A Compilation of the Messages and Papers of the Presidents, 1789–1897* (Washington, D.C., 1897); and U.S. Congress, *Inaugural Addresses of the Presidents of the United States from Washington to Kennedy* (Washington, D.C., 1961). Official political platforms of the Democrats and Republicans can be found in Kirk H. Porter and Donald B. Johnson, eds., *National Party Platforms, 1840–1956* (Urbana, Ill., 1956).

The published papers, diaries, and letters of presidents and important public figures are essential for understanding the political aspects of the "Southern question" and politics in general in the late nineteenth century. See especially George S. Boutwell, *Reminiscences of Sixty Years in Public Service*, 2 vols. (New York, 1902); T. Harry Williams, ed., *Hayes: The Diary of a President, 1875–1881* (New York, 1964); Charles R. Williams, ed., *The Diary and Letters of Rutherford B. Hayes*, 5 vols. (Columbus, Ohio, 1926); Harry J. Brown and Frederick D. Williams, eds., *The Diary of James A. Garfield*, vols. 1–3 (East Lansing, Mich., 1967–76); Burke A. Hinsdale, ed., *The Works of James A. Garfield*, 2 vols. (Boston, 1882); Charles Hedges, ed., *Speeches of Benjamin Harrison* (New York, 1892); James G. Blaine, *Twenty Years in Congress*, 2 vols. (Norwich, Conn., 1886); and Allan Nevins, ed., *Letters of Grover Cleveland, 1850–1908* (Boston, 1933).

As might be expected, the issue of voting rights and the future of the freedman in the South is the subject of many articles and essays in contemporary periodicals. One of the most significant appears in the *North American Review*, 128 (March 1879): 225–83, in which Blaine, Garfield, Wade Hampton, and several other leading American political leaders, from both the North and South, contribute essays addressed to the topic "Ought the Negro be Disenfranchised? Ought He to Have Been Enfranchised?" A similar debate appears in *Forum*, 4–7 (1887–90), especially the essay by one of the most energetic supporters of black voting rights, William E. Chandler, "Our Southern Masters," vol. 5; see also Alfred Colquit, "Is the Negro Vote Suppressed?" vol. 4, 268–78; and E. L. Godkin, "The Republican Party and the Negro," vol. 4, 246–57. A valuable short collection of speeches and articles relating to blacks in the South during these years is Otto H. Olsen, ed., *The Negro Question: From Slavery to Caste, 1863–1910* (New York, 1971). His "Bibliographical Essay" has an exhaustive listing of relevant articles and works from this period. Some of the significant writings of George W. Cable, a journalist who wrote widely on the South, can be found in Arlin Turner, ed., *The Negro Question: A Selection of Writings on Civil Rights in the South* (New York, 1958). Also significant is Herbert Aptheker, ed., *A Documentary History of the Negro People in the United States*, vol. 2 (New York, 1951).

Court decisions involving voting rights can be found in *United States Reports,* 1870 to 1900, for Supreme Court decisions; and *Federal Cases* for all lower federal court decisions. The location of federal laws and statutes for the 1870s can be confusing, as evidenced by the various citations in this study, all of which refer to the laws relating to elections. The explanation for this is that in 1874 Congress authorized a compilation of all existing federal law up until that time, designated as the *Revised Statutes.* Thus, the election laws, the Enforcement Acts, which had been part of the *Statutes at Large* and were cited as such, became part of the *Revised Statutes* after 1873 and included those sections of the election laws repassed by Congress after the *Reese* and *Cruikshank* decisions. In 1893, the one remaining section of the *Revised Statutes* dealing with voting rights which was not repealed became part of the *United States Code*, to which the various Civil Rights Acts of the 1950s and 1960s were added.

Secondary Sources

General histories of the U.S. during the late nineteenth century are plentiful. Dated, but still containing a wealth of information, is Ellis P. Oberholzer, *A History of the United States Since the Civil War*, 5 vols. (New York, 1937). Also relevant is Mathew Josephson, *The Politicos, 1865–1896* (New York, 1938). More recent general studies include: Samuel P. Hays, *The Response to Industrialism, 1885–1914* (Chicago, 1957); John A. Garraty, *The New Commonwealth, 1877–1900* (New York, 1968); H. Wayne Morgan, *From Hayes to McKinley: National Party Politics* (Syracuse, 1969); and Robert Wiebe, *The Search for Order, 1877–1920* (New York, 1967). General constitutional studies of this period are Alfred Kelly and Winfred Harbison, *The American Constitution: Its Origins and Development*, 5th rev. ed. (New York, 1973); Loren Beth, *The Development of the American Constitution, 1877–1917* (New York, 1971); and Charles Warren, *The Supreme Court in United States History*, 2 vols. (Boston, 1922). Charles Fairman's contribution to the *History of the Supreme Court of the United States* series, *Reconstruction and Reunion, 1864–1877* (New

York, 1971), vol. 6, pt. 1, is complete—and massive—only up to 1876.

The only full-length study of the Department of Justice remains Homer Cummings and Carl McFarland, *Federal Justice: Chapters in the History of Justice and the Federal Executive* (New York, 1937). The authors concede that their work deals with only some of the major aspects, or chapters, in the development of the department and that much more work needs to be done. There are a number of studies on the Justice Department, though they are mostly descriptive and not historically analytical. These include: Luther A. Huston, *The Department of Justice* (New York, 1967); Albert Langeluttig, *The Department of Justice of the United States* (Baltimore, 1927); and Luther Huston, Samuel Krislov, et al., *Roles of the Attorney General of the United States* (Washington, D.C., 1968). Two worthwhile studies which trace the growth of the presidential cabinet and the attorney general are Henry B. Learned, *The President's Cabinet* (New Haven, Conn.,1912); and Mary L. Hinsdale, *A History of the President's Cabinet* (Ann Arbor, Mich.,1911). As indicated above in the text, biographical data on Justice Department officials, especially the attorneys general, is scarce. See Robert Sobel, ed., *Biographical Directory of the United States Executive Branch, 1774–1971* (Westport, Conn., 1971); and Arthur Robb, *Biographical Sketches of the Attorneys General* (Washington, D.C., 1946), private copy in Justice Department library. The latter is disappointing inasmuch as it was based on readily available sources such as the *Dictionary of American Biography* and not any special department material. There are biographies of two attorneys general: Eugene C. Savidge, *Life of Benjamin Brewster, with Discourses and Addresses* (New York, 1891); and Farrar Newberry, *A Life of Mr. Garland of Arkansas* (New York, 1908). Both have only a limited amount of material on their subjects as attorneys general. Also, as discussed above, there are few studies of administrative history in the context of late nineteenth century America. The definitive study of administrative history of the period, Leonard White, *The Republican Era* (New York, 1958), makes no mention of the attorney general or the Justice Department. Lloyd M. Short, *The Development of National Administrative Organization in the United States* (Baltimore, 1923) has a chapter on the Justice Department, but focuses on twentieth century developments. See also, Peter G. Fish, *The Politics of Federal Judicial Administration* (Princeton, N.J., 1973); and Felix Frankfurter and James M. Landis, *The Business of the Supreme Court: A Study in the Federal Judiciary System* (New York, 1927). Two recent studies that do focus on the Justice Department and the enforcement of federal laws are Stanley W. Campbell, *The Slave Catchers: Enforcement of the Fugitive Slave Law, 1850–1860* (Chapel Hill, N.C., 1968); and John H. Franklin, "The Enforcement of the Civil Rights Act of 1875," *Prologue*, 6 (Winter 1974): 225–35.

On the politics and passage of the Fourteenth Amendment, see Joseph James, *The Framing of the Fourteenth Amendment* (Urbana, Ill., 1965). On Section 2 of the amendment, which was the first effort on the part of Republicans to deal with the question of voting rights for the freedman, see W. W. Van Alstyne, "The Fourteenth Amendment, The 'Right' to Vote, and the Understanding of the 39th Congress," *Supreme Court Review* (1965): 33–86; F. Zuckerman, "A Consideration of the History and Present Status of Section 2 of the Fourteenth Amendment," *Fordham Law Review*, 30 (1961); and R. Bonfield, "The Right to Vote and Judicial Enforcement of Section Two of the Fourteenth Amendment," *Cornell Law Quarterly*, 44 (1960).

For an excellent general study of voting rights and the electoral process, see Richard Claude, *The Supreme Court and the Electoral Process* (Baltimore, 1970). Also useful is the same author's "Constitutional Voting Rights and Early Supreme Court Doctrine," *Journal of Negro History*, 51 (April 1966): 114–24. An older and much biased (against blacks and women) account of voting rights is Kirk H. Porter, *A History of Suffrage in the United States* (Chicago, 1919). One of the first studies linking Negro suffrage in the South and white politics was Paul Lewinson's *Race, Class & Party* (New York, 1932). As discussed in chap. 1 above, there has been a historiographical debate on the politics and passage of the Fifteenth Amendment. For the Reconstruction background, see two recent essays: Michael Les Benedict, "Preserving the Constitution: The Conservative Basis of Racial Reconstruction," *Journal of American History*, 61 (June

1974): 65–90; and Glenn M. Linden, "A Note on Negro Suffrage and Republican Politics," *Journal of Southern History*, 36 (August 1970): 411–20. The best comprehensive study of the origins and passage of the Fifteenth Amendment is William Gillette, *The Right to Vote: Politics and Passage of the Fifteenth Amendment* (Baltimore, 1965). But see LaWanda and John Cox, "Negro Suffrage and Republican Politics: The Problem of Motivation in Reconstruction Historiography," *Journal of Southern History*, 33 (August 1967). Also worthwhile is the older study by John M. Mathews, *Legislative and Judicial History of the Fifteenth Amendment* (Baltimore, 1909). On the Enforcement Acts, the most extensive study is W. W. Davis, "The Federal Enforcement Acts," in William A. Dunning, *Studies in Southern History and Politics*, no. 9 (New York, 1914). In the same volume, see also W. Roy Smith, "Negro Suffrage in the South," no. 10. There are two studies of the enforcement of the Fifteenth Amendment: Albie Burke, "Federal Regulation of Congressional Elections in Northern Cities, 1871–1894," *Journal of Legal History*, 14 (January 1970): 17–34, deals with only one of the three Enforcement Acts. Everette Swinney argues in his "Enforcing the Fifteenth Amendment, 1870–1877," *Journal of Southern History*, 28 (May 1962): 202–18, that enforcement virtually ended as of 1877. This present work directly challenges Swinney's conclusions. On the development and history of civil rights during these years, see Robert J. Harris, *The Quest for Equality* (Baton Rouge, La., 1960); and Valeria W. Weaver, "The Failure of Civil Rights, 1875–1883, and Its Repercussions," *Journal of Negro History*, 55 (October 1969): 368–82. On the disfranchisement of Southern blacks generally, see William A. Mabry, "The Disfranchisement of the Negro in the South" (Ph.D. diss., Duke University, 1933).

The starting point for any research on Southern history during the latter part of the nineteenth century remains C. Vann Woodward's, *Origins of the New South, 1877–1913* (Baton Rouge, 1951). For a recent and favorable assessment of how Woodward's work has stood up over the past twenty years, see Sheldon Hackney, "Origins of the New South in Retrospect," *Journal of Southern History*, 38 (May 1972): 191–216. For details on the Compromise of 1877, see Woodward's *Reunion and Reaction:*

The Compromise of 1877 and the End of Reconstruction (New York, 1956); and his collection of essays and reviews on Southern history, *American Counterpoint: Slavery and Racism in the North-South Dialogue* (Boston, 1971). In *Origins* Woodward cites the need for studies on the state level of the Redeemer regimes in the South and their effect on the course of black civil and political rights. As a result, a number of excellent monographs have appeared dealing with the Southern states during the period 1877 to 1900. The best of these include: George B. Tindall, *South Carolina Negroes, 1877–1900* (Columbia, S.C., 1952); William J. Cooper Jr., *The Conservative Regime: South Carolina, 1877–1890* (Baltimore, 1968); William I. Hair, *Bourbonism and Agrarian Protest: Louisiana Politics, 1877–1900* (Baton Rouge, La., 1972); Frenise Logan, *The Negro in North Carolina, 1876–1894* (Chapel Hill, N.C., 1964); Lawrence D. Rice, *The Negro in Texas, 1874–1900* (Baton Rouge, La., 1971); Allen Moger, *Virginia: Bourbonism to Byrd, 1870–1925* (Charlottesville, Va., 1968); Malcolm C. McMillan, *Constitutional Development in Alabama, 1798–1901* (Chapel Hill, N.C., 1955); Albert D. Kirwan, *Revolt of the Rednecks: Mississippi Politics, 1876–1925* (Lexington, Ky., 1951); and Olive H. Shadgett, *The Republican Party in Georgia from Reconstruction through 1900* (Athens, Ga., 1964). With the exception of Cooper, all of these support Woodward's views on the nature of the Conservative-Redeemer regimes and their impact on the freedman. Also see Vernon Wharton, *The Negro in Mississippi, 1865–1890* (Chapel Hill, 1947); Robert E. Martin, *Negro Disfranchisement in Virginia* (Washington, D.C., 1938); Margaret L. Wallcott, *The Negro in Maryland Politics, 1870–1912* (Baltimore, 1969); and Joshua W. Caldwell, *Studies in the Constitutional History of Tennessee* (Cincinnati, 1895). Two recent short studies of the New South in the context of twentieth century developments that emphasize the persistence of southern Republicanism after 1877 are George B. Tindall, *The Disruption of the Solid South* (Athens, Ga., 1972); and Dewey Grantham, *The Democratic South* (Athens, Ga., 1973). See also Paul M. Gaston, *The New South Creed: A Study in Southern Mythmaking* (New York, 1970). The most comprehensive—and impressive—study of the disfranchisement of southern blacks is the work by J. Morgan Kousser, *The Shaping of*

Southern Politics: Suffrage Restriction and the Establishment of the One-Party South (New Haven, Conn., 1974). Like Tindall and Grantham, Kousser argues that the Solid South was a product of the 1890s, and not an immediate and inevitable development after 1877. Kousser should be read in conjunction with V. 0. Key Jr., *Southern Politics in State and Nation* (New York, 1949).

The standard history of the black man in America is John H. Franklin, *From Slavery to Freedom: A History of American Negroes* (New York, 1967). See also August Meier and Elliot Rudwick, *From Plantation to Ghetto: An Interpretive History of America Negroes* (New York, 1966). Loren Miller, *The Petitioners* (New York, 1967), tells the story of the Supreme Court and the Negro. Studies that focus on southern blacks during the period 1877 to 1900 are Rayford W. Logan, *The Betrayal of the Negro* (New York, 1967); August Meier, *Negro Thought in America, 1880–1915* (Ann Arbor, Mich. 1963); and, George M. Frederickson, *The Black Image in the White Mind: The Debate on Afro-American Character and Destiny, 1817–1914* (New York, 1971). For the growth of segregation in the South, see C. Vann Woodward, *The Strange Career of Jim Crow*, 3d rev. ed. (New York, 1975). Also relevant is Mary Frances Berry, *Black Resistance, White Law: A History of Constitutional Racism in America* (New York, 1971).

The attitudes and policies of the Republican party during the late nineteenth century with respect to the freedman and the South are analyzed in two complementary studies: Vincent P. DeSantis, *Republicans Face the Southern Question: The New Departure Years, 1877–1897* (Baltimore, 1959); and Stanley Hirshson, *Farewell to the Bloody Shirt: Northern Republicans and the Southern Negro, 1877–1893* (Chicago, 1968). See also Leslie H. Fishel Jr., "The Negro in Northern Politics, 1870–1900," *Mississippi Valley Historical Review*, 42 (December 1955): 466–89; George Sinkler, *Racial Attitudes of American Presidents From Lincoln to Roosevelt* (New York, 1971); Robert D. Marcus, *Grand Old Party: Political Structure in the Gilded Age, 1880–1896* (New York, 1971); and George H. Mayer, *The Republican Party, 1854–1964* (New York, 1964).

Of the many biographies dealing with various political figures during the late nineteenth century, the most useful are: Richard E. Welch Jr., *George Frisbie Hoar and the Half-Breed Republicans* (Cambridge, Mass., 1971); David Donald, *Charles Sumner and the Rights of Man* (New York, 1970); Kenneth E. Davison, *The Presidency of Rutherford B. Hayes* (Westport, Conn., 1972); Theodore C. Smith, *Life and Letters of James Garfield*, 2 vols. (New York, 1926); Horace S. Merrill, *Bourbon Leader: Grover Cleveland and the Democratic Party* (Boston, 1957); Harry J. Sievers, *Benjamin Harrison, Hoosier President: The White House and After* (New York, 1968); Louis B. Harlan, *Booker T. Washington: The Making of a Black Leader, 1856–1901* (New York, 1972). Biographical essays on the justices of the Supreme Court can be found in Fred Israel and Leon Friedman, eds., *The Justices of the United States Supreme Court, 1789–1966: Their Lives and Major Opinions*, 4 vols. (New York, 1969). Of particular value, especially on the *Reese* and *Cruikshank* decisions, is C. Peter MaGrath, *Morrison R. Waite: The Triumph of Character* (New York, 1963). See also Charles Fairman, *Mr. Justice Miller and the Supreme Court, 1862–1890* (Cambridge, Mass., 1939).

On the elections and electoral politics of the 1880s and 1890s, see Harrison C. Thomas, *The Return of the Democratic Party to Power in 1884* (New York, 1919). A more recent analysis of the elections of 1884 and 1896 is Lee Benson, "Research Problems in American Political Historiography," in *Common Frontiers of the Social Sciences*, ed. Mirra Komorovsky (Glencoe, Ill., 1957). See also Carl Degler, "American Political Parties and the Rise of the Cities," *Journal of American History* (June 1964): 41–59; and Paul Glad, *McKinley, Bryan and the People* (Philadelphia, 1962).

INDEX

Adams, Henry, 62
Akerman, Amos, 39
Alabama, 11, 55, 59–61, 113–15, 154–55, 171, 186
Albertson, J. M., 57
Arkansas, 58–59, 155–59
Armistead, W. T., 111
Arthur, Chester A., 83, 86–89, 125, 133, 185, 188, 199
Attorney general: early role of, 25–35; role of, after 1870, 181ff.; *see also* United States Department of Justice *and individuals:* Akerman, Amos; Brewster, Benjamin; Cushing, Caleb; Devens, Charles; Garland, Augustus; Harmon, Judson; Hoar, Ebenezer R.; MacVeagh, Isaac Wayne; Miller, William Henry Harrison; Olney, Richard; Randolph, Edmund; Taft, Alphonso; Williams, George; Wirt, William

Baldwin (district attorney), 58
Ball, William S., 102
Barnes, L. A., 163
Benson, Lee, 142n23
Billings (judge), 115
Bingham, John A., 18n3
Bird, John, 161, 163
Bisbee, Henry, 168
Blaine, James G., 54, 69, 86, 133
Blair, Montgomery, 86
Bliss, George C., 184
Bond, Hugh Lennox, 71, 88, 94–95, 106
Borland, Thomas R., 151–53
Boutwell, George, 5, 7
Bowman, Joel, 186
Boyd, John E., 101–104
Bradley, Joseph P., 126
Brewster, Benjamin, 90–94, 96–97, 101, 103, 114–15, 181, 183–85, 187, 189, 192, 194
Burns, J. R., 58
Butts, Daniel, 40

Caldwell (judge), 156
Cameron, Brewster, 111–12, 116, 185, 187–88
Cameron, James Donald, 169
Cameron, William, 105
Carlisle, John G., 134
Carpenter, E. E., 158–59
Carpetbaggers, 48–49, 54
Chalmers, James R., 107–108

Chandler, Green, 108
Chandler, William E., 90, 96, 108, 139, 171
Chester, I. Morris, 110–11, 123n73
Chisolm, W. W., 52–53
Circuit courts, 11, 38, 60, 99–100, 125, 127, 131; *see also* Bond, Hugh Lennox; Hughes, Robert; Wood, William B.
Civil Rights Act: (1864), 130; (1865), 130; (1866), 11
Civil Rights Congress, 139
Clay, Henry, 48
Cleveland, Grover, 130, 133–35, 138–39, 189
Coke, Richard, 137
Colfax Massacre, 15
Compromise of 1877, 48–50
Conkling, Roscoe, 54
Cook, Charles, 149–50
Cooley v. Board of Wardens, 126
Cox, John, 5–7
Cox, LaWanda, 5–7
Craig, William E., 151
Cruikshank, W. J., 15–16; *see also United States v. Cruikshank*
Cummings, Homer, 196
Cushing, Caleb, 32–34, 36

Daniels, C., 154
Dansby, Thomas, 156
Danville Riots, 132
Darden, Reuben W., 156
Davis, Jefferson, 34
Degler, Carl, 204–205n38
Democratic Party, 5–6, 39–40, 42–43, 48, 51, 56, 61–62, 65, 70, 73, 83, 87, 90, 98, 125, 197–98
Devens, Charles, 50–57, 59, 62–63, 66–67, 72–73, 76–77nn7–8, 84–86, 88, 140n1, 181–82, 189
District attorneys (U.S.), 10–11, 30–32, 50–72, 84, 88–89, 91–100, 104–105, 108–117, 136–39, 140n1, 147–55, 157–63, 165–66, 168, 170, 192–94, 198
District courts: *see* Federal (district) courts
Dockery, D. H., 103
Duskin (district attorney), 114

Earle, William E., 65, 80n52
Eckel, Eugene, 103
Edmunds, George, 74, 169
Election fraud, 8, 10, 55–57, 59–60, 62–63, 66, 68–70, 73, 75, 84, 90, 93–95, 97–99, 101–104, 107, 110–14, 127–28, 132–33, 150–51, 158–59, 162, 198
Election supervisors, 64, 70, 126, 136, 156, 170–71
Electoral Commission, 43
Elstner, M. E., 117, 193–94
Enforcement Acts, 8–9, 11–17, 39–40, 86, 106, 196
Evans, A. J., 112
Ex parte Clarke, 126–27
Ex parte Geissler, 127
Ex parte Siebold, 126–27, 130, 134
Ex parte Yarbrough, 81n68, 107, 125, 127, 129–30, 134

Federal Elections Law (1871), 8
Federal (district) courts, 11, 27, 38, 52, 59, 84–85, 159, 162–63; *see also individual judges:* Billings; Bond, Hugh Lennox; Caldwell; McClure, John C.; Paul; Speer, Emory; Wood, William B.
Federal marshals, 9–11, 27, 29,

35–42, 54–55, 62, 97, 116, 126, 135, 140n1, 147, 165, 170–71, 190–95; *see also individuals:* Keough, Thomas B.; Mizell, John R.; Pitkin; Ramsdell, Charles P.; Strobach, Paul; Turner; Walker, B. W.; Wallace; Wharton
Field, David Dudley, 15
Field, Stephen, 15
Fifteenth Amendment, 1–24, 25, 39, 43, 50, 58, 75, 86, 128–29, 180, 196, 198–99
Filler, Louis, 21, 24
Florida, 59, 88–89, 160–69
Fortune, T. Thomas, 140
Fourteenth Amendment, 2, 8, 12, 18n2, 50, 58, 86, 89, 198
Fraud: *see* Election fraud

Garfield, James A., 49, 54, 83, 86–89, 133, 183–84, 199
Garland, Augustus, 134–35, 138–39, 181–82, 189–91
Garner, William, 12
Georgia, 9, 108–110; ratifies Fifteenth Amendment, 3
Gillette, William, 5–6
Gilmer (murder victim), 52–53
Grant Parish Riots, 15–16, 23n38
Grant, Ulysses S., 3, 41
Grantham, Dewey, 180
Gray, Horace, 131
Greenback parties, 98, 110, 115
Gregg, E. M., 168
Guiteau, Charles, 184
Gutheridge, Edward, 110–13

Haight, Will, 116
Hamilton, Charles V., 204n38
Hampton, Wade, 65, 86

Harlan, John M., 131
Harmon, Judson, 195
Harrison, Benjamin, 125, 146–47, 150–51, 160, 164, 166, 199
Haughn, Charles, 112–13
Hawkins, Samuel W., 157–59, 198
Hayes, Rutherford B., 48–50, 54, 56, 61, 65, 69, 74–75, 76n5, 83, 90, 125, 133, 199
Haywood, H. J., 101–102
Hendricks, Thomas A., 86
Hill, R. A., 52, 78n16
Hoar, Ebenezer R., 50
Hoar, George Frisbie, 145, 171
House Committee on Appropriations and Expenditures, 187–88
Hughes, Robert, 106, 152–54, 171
Hunt, Ward, 14

Independent parties, 90, 96, 100, 103–105, 107–111, 113, 115–17, 131
Intimidation, 5, 8–10, 12, 15, 43, 51, 55–56, 61–64, 73, 113, 125, 127, 131–33, 135–36, 139, 171

Johnson, Reverdy, 15
Judiciary Act, 27–30, 33, 38
Juries, 58, 61, 64, 72, 89, 95, 100, 103, 108, 114, 136–37, 148–53, 155, 158, 162
Justice Department: *see* United States Department of Justice

Kentucky, 12
Keogh, Thomas B., 102–103
Ker, W. W., 94–95
Kercheval, Samuel, 168
Key, V. O., Jr., 204–205n38
Kleburg, Rudolph, 136–39

Knight, Alva A., 59, 89
Kousser, J. Morgan, 204–205n38
Ku Klux Act, 8–9
Ku Klux Klan, 8–9, 12, 109

Lamar, Lucius W. C., 86, 134
Lathrop, Abial, 150–51
Lea, Luke, 51–53, 108
Lee, Samuel, 67
Leonard, A. H., 62, 64, 115–16
Lincoln, Abraham, 196
Lodge, Henry Cabot, 145, 171; see also Lodge bill
Lodge bill, 169–70
Logan v. United States, 131
Louisiana, 15, 42–43, 61–65, 115–17
Lyons, James, 171

MacKey, E. W., 67–68
MacVeagh, Isaac Wayne, 88, 181, 183–84, 189
Madison (Fla.) *Times*, 89
Magrath, C. Peter, 22–23nn31&38
Mahone, William, 105
Marshall, Warren, 94–95
Mathews, J. P., 132–33
Mathews, John Mabry, 3–5
Mayer, Charles E., 55, 57, 60–61, 79n38
McClure, John C., 156
McDufee, J. V., 154
McFarland, Carl, 196
Melton, Samuel, 88, 91–93, 95–96, 98–100, 109, 119n24
Miller, Samuel Freeman, 127–30
Miller, William Henry Harrison, 147, 150, 155, 159–62, 164–71, 177n61, 181, 186, 189–91, 193
Milliken, Samuel, 184
Minor v. Happersett, 128

Mississippi, 9, 51–53, 107–108, 132, 198
Mizell, John R., 161–62, 164–66
Monroe, James, 28
Mott, J. J., 101
Mumford, Robert, 105–106; see also *United States v. Mumford*
Murray, W. W., 157–59

"New Departure," 49–50, 56, 73
New York City, 8
Nicholls, Francis T., 42–43
North American Review, 86
North Carolina, 100–104, 149–50, 157–58
Northrup, Lucius, 65–72, 81n68, 88, 91, 94

Olney, Richard, 171

Packard, Stephen, 43
Parsons, Lewis, 154–55, 193
Patterson, Frank, 88–89
Paul (district judge), 152
Pendergrass (black local politician), 71
Pendleton Civil Service Act, 185, 194
Phillips, Samuel, 12, 22n27, 47n33, 184
Phillips, Wendell, 86
Pierce, Franklin, 32
Pitkin (U.S. marshal), 42
Poll tax, 105
Populist movement, 187
Porter, Kirk R., 5
Post Office Department scandals, 183–84
President, 27, 29, 33
Price, Charles, 149

INDEX

Quay, Matthew S., 169

Radical Reconstruction, 9
Radical Republicans, 7, 18, 49, 199
Ramsdell, Charles P., 40–41
Randolph, Edmund, 27–28, 44
Readjuster Party (Virginia), 104–105, 107, 132, 151
Redeemer movement, 48
Republican Party, 1–3, 5–8, 18, 25, 39–40, 42–43, 48, 51, 54, 56, 61–62, 65, 70, 74, 83, 90, 96, 98, 100, 105, 115, 117, 145–46, 151, 180–81, 190, 197–99; *see also* Radical Republicans
Revised Statutes, 58, 162
Rice, Samuel, 186
Robinson, W. S. O'B., 101, 104
Ruhn, John, 174–75n35
Russell, D. L., 150
Russell, W. Walker, 101

Saunders, Dallas, 92–95
Saunders, W. B., 165
Savage, Charles, 88–89
Segar, Joseph, 40
Sherman Anti-Trust Act, 192
Singleton, W. E., 113
Slaughterhouse cases, 21n24
slavery, 49
Smith, W. H., 114, 186
Snyder, W. P., 99
Solicitor of the Treasury, 32, 36
South Carolina, 9, 61, 65–73, 88, 92–100, 150–51
Speer, Emory, 100, 109–110, 120n44, 122n70, 147
Spooner, John C., 196
Springer, William, 187–88
Stanbery, Henry, 12

Star Route cases, 183–84, 187–88
States' rights, 4, 13, 86
Stephens, Alexander H., 86
Stewart, William Morris, 171
Stickney (district attorney), 59, 84
Stripling, J. N., 160–63, 165–66, 168
Strohbach, Paul, 114, 185–87
Sumner, Charles, 7, 18n3
Swayne, Charles, 162
Swinney, Everette, 39, 200

Taft, Alphonso, 41–44
Taylor, Ezra, 169
Taylor, William H., 152
Teller, Henry M., 70
Tennessee, 157–59, 174n35
Texas, 56, 58, 110–13, 123n73, 135–39
Thirteenth Amendment, 7, 50
Tilden, Samuel J., 42, 51
Timber cases, 193–94
Turner (U.S. marshal), 60
Tweed Ring, 8

United States attorneys: *see* District attorneys
United States Circuit courts: *see* Circuit courts
United States Congress, 2–4, 6–10, 13–17, 27–28, 30–33, 35, 52, 56, 62, 73–75, 86, 106, 125–28, 130–31, 145–47, 181; House of Representatives, 2, 30, 74; Senate, 3, 7, 27, 69, 70, 73, 136
United States Courts: *see* Circuit courts; Federal (district) courts; United States Supreme Court
United States Department of

Justice: creation and organization of, 35–40; expanded scope of responsibilities, 180–96; and voting rights, 1, 10, 11, 14, 17, 18, 25–26, 50ff., 84ff., 180ff.:
—in Alabama, 55, 59–61, 113–15, 154–55, 171, 186;
—in Arkansas, 58–59, 155–57;
—in Florida, 59, 88–89, 160–69;
—in Georgia, 108–110;
—in Louisiana, 42–43, 61–65, 115–17;
—in Mississippi, 51–53, 107–108, 132, 198;
—in North Carolina, 57–58, 100–104, 149–50;
—in South Carolina, 61, 65–73, 88, 92–95, 98–100, 150–51;
—in Tennessee, 157–59;
—in Texas, 56, 58, 110–13, 135–39;
—in Virginia, 59, 104–107, 131–33, 151–53, 171
United States Department of the Treasury, 31–32
United States Supreme Court, 1, 11–24, 25–26, 33, 36, 72, 106–107, 126–31, 139, 170, 199; see also cases.
United States v. Cruikshank, 12, 15–17, 22n31, 154
United States v. Goldman, 21n24, 140n23
United States v. Hall, 11, 12, 23n33
United States v. Mumford, 105–107, 154
United States v. Reese, 12–17, 22n31, 41, 62, 106, 125, 129

Virginia, 59, 104–105, 107, 131–33, 151–53, 171

Waddell, S., 105
Waite, Morrison R., 12–13, 15–16, 22n31
Walker, B. W., 193
Wallace (U.S. marshal), 65–67
Wallace, John T., 102–103
Washington, George, 27–28
Waterman, J. S., 40
Waters, C. C., 155–56
Watson, Tom, 197
Weeks, Edmund C., 166–68
Welch, Richard, 169
Wharton, 62–63
White, Leonard, 26
Wiegand, J., 111–12
Wikersham, M. D., 154–55
Williams v. Mississippi, 198
Williams, George, 12
Wirt, William, 28–31, 34
Wise, John S., 105
Woods, Charles E., 115–16
Woods, William B., 11–12, 125–26
Woodward, C. Vann, 49, 200, 205n38

Yarbrough, Jasper, 109, 127; see also *ex parte Yarbrough*

www.ingramcontent.com/pod-product-compliance
Lightning Source LLC
Chambersburg PA
CBHW051424290426
44109CB00016B/1421